China's Foreign Political and Economic Relations

China's Foreign Political and Economic Relations

An Unconventional Global Power

Sebastian Heilmann and
Dirk H. Schmidt

ROWMAN & LITTLEFIELD
Lanham • Boulder • New York • Toronto • Plymouth, UK

Published by Rowman & Littlefield
4501 Forbes Boulevard, Suite 200, Lanham, Maryland 20706
www.rowman.com

10 Thornbury Road, Plymouth PL6 7PP, United Kingdom

British Library Cataloguing in Publication Information Available

Library of Congress Cataloging-in-Publication Data

Heilmann, Sebastian.
  China's foreign political and economic relations : an unconventional global power / Sebastian Heilmann and Dirk Schmidt.
     pages cm. -- (State and society in East Asia)
  Includes bibliographical references and index.
   ISBN 978-1-4422-1301-2 (cloth : alk. paper) -- ISBN 978-1-4422-1302-9 (pbk. : alk. paper) -- ISBN 978-1-4422-1303-6 (electronic) 1. China--Foreign relations. 2. China--Foreign economic relations. 3. National security--China. I. Schmidt, Dirk, 1968- II. Title.
JZ1730.H45 2014
327.51--dc23
                                                                    2013028269

Printed in the United States of America

Contents

List of Tables, Figures, and Boxes

TABLES

FIGURES

BOXES

List of Acronyms

A2/AD	antiaccess/area denial
ACFTA	ASEAN-China Free Trade Area
AOSIS	Association of Small Island States
APA	Asia-Pacific Committee of German Business
APEC	Asia-Pacific Economic Cooperation
ARATS	Association for Relations across the Taiwan Strait
ARF	ASEAN Regional Forum
ASEAN	Association of Southeast Asian Nations
ASEAN+1	Association of Southeast Asian Nations + China
ASEAN+3	Association of Southeast Asian Nations + China, Japan, and South Korea
ASEM	Asia-Europe Meeting
BAIC	Beijing Automotive Industry Corporation
BASIC	Brazil, South Africa, India, and China
BMU	Federal Ministry of the Environment, Germany
BMZ	Federal Ministry for Economic Cooperation and Development, Germany
BP	British Petroleum
BRIC	Brazil, Russia, India, and China
C4ISR	command, control, communications, computers, intelligence, surveillance, and reconnaissance
CCP	Chinese Communist Party
CCPCC	Chinese Communist Party Central Committee
CCTV	China Central Television
CDM	Clean Development Mechanism

CIC	China Investment Corporation
CMC	Central Military Commission
CNOOC	China National Offshore Oil Corporation
CNY	Chinese yuan (¥)
CSHRS	China Society for Human Rights Studies
CSIS	Center for Strategic and International Studies
DoD	US Department of Defense
DPP	Democratic Progressive Party
DPRK	Democratic People's Republic of Korea
ECB	European Central Bank
ECFA	Economic Cooperation Framework Agreement
EU	European Union
EUR	euro (€)
FDI	foreign direct investment
FOCAC	Forum on China-Africa Cooperation
G20	Group of Twenty
G7	Group of Seven
G8	Group of Eight
GAD	General Armaments Department
GATT	General Agreement on Tariffs and Trade
GDP	gross domestic product
GHG	greenhouse gas
GIZ	German Organization for International Cooperation
GLD	General Logistics Department
GPD	General Political Department
GSD	General Staff Department
ICAO	International Civil Aviation Organization
IFDI	inward foreign direct investment
IISS	International Institute for Strategic Studies (London)
IMF	International Monetary Fund
IPR	intellectual property rights
KMT	Kuomintang (Guomindang)
LDC	least developed country
LSG	leading small group
MFA	Ministry of Foreign Affairs
MIIT	Ministry of Industry and Information Technology
MOOTW	military operations other than war
MRV	measuring, reporting, and verification
NATO	North Atlantic Treaty Organization
NCO	noncommissioned officer
NDRC	National Development and Reform Commission
NPT	Nuclear Nonproliferation Treaty
OFDI	outward foreign direct investment

PAP	People's Armed Police
PBoC	People's Bank of China
PLA	People's Liberation Army
PLAAF	People's Liberation Army Air Force
PLAN	People's Liberation Army Navy
PLASA	People's Liberation Army Second Artillery
PRC	People's Republic of China
RMB	renminbi
ROC	Republic of China
ROK	Republic of Korea
S&ED	Strategic and Economic Dialogue
SAFE	State Administration of Foreign Exchange
SAIC	Shanghai Automotive Industry Corporation
SAR	special administrative region
SASAC	State-Owned Assets Supervision and Administration Commission
SASTIND	State Administration of Science, Technology and Industry for National Defense
SCO	Shanghai Cooperation Organization
SEF	Strait Exchange Foundation
SEPA	State Environmental Protection Administration
SEZ	special economic zone
SIPRI	Stockholm International Peace Research Institute
SME	small and medium-size enterprise
SSBN	nuclear-powered ballistic missile submarine
TEU	twenty-foot equivalent unit
TRA	Taiwan Relations Act
UNCHR	United Nations Commission on Human Rights
UNCTAD	United Nations Conference on Trade and Development
UNFCCC	United Nations Framework Convention on Climate Change
US$	US dollar
WTO	World Trade Organization

Preface

There is no lack of monographs and edited volumes on Chinese foreign relations. Nevertheless, to complement the existing body of literature, we decided to join the fray by making a contribution written from a European perspective.

In this volume we add a new way of understanding the debates about China's global rise. From a European point of view, there is nothing intrinsically wrong with a transition to the multipolar world to which Chinese foreign policy makers obstinately adhere. But American textbooks tend to share an interpretive framework that begins from a US-led international system into which China must be socialized and integrated. At the heart of such analyses, oftentimes obsessed with military capabilities, strategic rivalry, and hegemonic power cycles, lies a paramount concern with defending the predominant global role of the United States in the twenty-first century. The US-led international order that allowed China's rise now insists that China play by the established rules.

As a consequence, many unconventional facets and complex forces behind China's global expansion (e.g., extensive transnational trade and investment interdependencies that invalidate traditional nation-based export-import statistics; China's innovative incremental strategy for internationalizing its currency; and the rapid expansion of Chinese shadow businesses outside government controls in many parts of the world) receive much less attention or trigger sweeping judgments that conceal the competitive and normative challenges resulting from the emerging patterns of Chinese-driven globalization.

Both American and European depictions often characterize China's rise to power in terms derived from the Western historical experience, such as

"Manchester capitalism" (referring to China's domestic economy), "mercantilism" (referring to China's foreign-trade policy), and "neocolonialism" (referring to China's behavior in Africa). These catchwords express moral outrage or political condemnation. Furthermore, they often serve to boost a superficial sense of self-assurance among Western societies in the face of the growing competition from China. Yet sweeping denunciations of China hide many particularly challenging aspects of Chinese expansion by subjecting novel developments and experiences to old and outdated Western patterns of perception.

As a counterweight to such one-sided depictions and interpretations in Western debates, we stress distinctive, nonstandard Chinese approaches, such as the combination of long-term strategic priorities with multilevel policy experimentation and informal business activities, to facilitate China's global expansion. We hold that it is not possible to find appropriate responses to the new challenges that China poses by taking a retrospective or self-absorbed stance.

The authors of this book deliberately avoid embedding their analyses in macrotheories of international relations. We have now entered a phase of international politics in which the earlier assumptions, conceptions, and explanatory models, mostly derived from experiences in the nineteenth and twentieth centuries, are colliding with an environment that is being shaped and driven forward by new patterns of communications, transactions, and norms, as well as by new groupings and networks of actors. Long-established assumptions that in the past were regularly seen as constants, ranging from the reliability of the international monetary system or America's invulnerability as a superpower to the cohesion of the European Union, have become uncertainties in the new global environment of the twenty-first century.

As to the practical purposes of this volume, we provide a basic introduction to the spectrum of China's contemporary foreign relations. The book is based on our personal research over the past twenty years, on a comprehensive analysis of Chinese sources, and on materials on the latest international debates on China's foreign affairs. The text in this concise volume is enriched with the addition of tables, boxes, and figures. It has benefited from studies and suggestions from a host of colleagues. We refer the reader to their works whenever appropriate.

Endnotes (containing only authors' names and the year of publication for each source) point readers to the important literature. Detailed references can be found in the "Sources and Literature" section at the end of the volume. In addition to academic works, this reference section also features a number of Chinese and Western Web portals that provide high-quality information and analyses. These are intended to enable readers to follow up on the developments outlined here and to carry out their own research. We have written the book so that it may be read in its entirety or individual chapters may be read independently. Each chapter also contains cross-references to more detailed information and analyses found in other chapters. This should facilitate use of the book for both study and professional purposes.

We would like to thank all the readers of the draft versions of this manuscript, in particular the classes of undergraduate students who worked with the original text, for their many constructive ideas for improvements. We have attempted to incorporate as many of these suggestions as possible.

We are deeply grateful to Susan McEachern at Rowman & Littlefield, whose sustained interest in this book ensured its completion despite some delays on our part. Nancy Hearst, the librarian of Harvard's Fairbank Center, helped eliminate the worst excesses of our "Teutonic speak," and her copyediting made the text much more readable. Of course, all remaining problems and errors remain our own.

We dedicate this book to Nassim Nicholas Taleb, who teaches us to beware of entrenched cognitive fallacies and confirmatory biases in a political, economic, and technological environment characterized by increased interdependencies and nonlinearities. This caveat is perhaps nowhere more justified than in the study of contemporary China.

Berlin and Trier, October 2013
Sebastian Heilmann and Dirk H. Schmidt
Research Group on the Political Economy of China
www.chinapolitik.de

1

Introduction

What Does China Want?

What does China want? This seemingly simple question lies at the heart of any analysis of China's foreign political and economic relations. It has become even more pressing now that the Chinese government has become one of the most important players in a wide variety of areas, including global monetary policy, trade policy, security policy, and climate-change negotiations. The extension of China's economic and diplomatic influence beyond Asia to other regions of the world, particularly Africa and Latin America, is one reason for the current broad restructuring of international relations. This structural change is manifested in the rapid increase in economic exchanges among emerging and developing countries as well as in the rise to prominence of the Group of Twenty (G20), an international body created to exercise global coordination and crisis management. China's economic expansion and diplomatic initiatives have been instrumental in facilitating these changes. Its achievements in implementing a comprehensive program of national modernization, bolstered through broad-based diplomatic efforts and foreign-trade policies, pose a challenge to the United States, Europe, and Japan, all of which traditionally have dominated world politics and the global economy.

There exist three broad approaches to tackling the above question: the first looks at Chinese intentions as they are displayed in official statements, white papers, or declassified research papers; the second describes Chinese behavior at a given point in an effort to understand its inherent logic; the third goes beyond the daily affairs of Chinese foreign relations and analyzes China's overall (grand) strategy. The remainder of this chapter addresses each of these approaches, with its strengths as well as its inherent shortcomings.

CHINESE VIEWS OF THE WORLD

For some authors the study of Chinese foreign relations should begin with an analysis of official Chinese articulations of its intentions as formulated in the key foreign policy concepts adopted by the Hu-Wen administration (2002–2012)—that is, "peaceful rise" (2003–2004) and "peaceful development" to create a "harmonious world" (since 2005).[1] Speeches by Chinese leaders and official white papers have widely repeated the main elements of these slogans, which Western and Chinese scholars have analyzed extensively.[2]

The International Order

Official Chinese announcements on foreign policy have described the current international order predominantly as conducive to achieving lasting peace and prosperity for all due to the emergence of multipolarity and the democratization of international relations, as well to the rise of the developing and emerging countries. Nevertheless, the following are regularly referred to as forces of inertia and risk: the persistence of power politics and hegemony, the development gap between North and South or between West and East, the attempts by Western nations to impose their own social and value systems on other countries and to promote political upheaval in countries that do not follow the Western model of development, and the ongoing limited military conflicts and nontraditional security threats in areas such as trade and commerce, the Internet, and the environment. Increasingly, Chinese foreign policy makers have adopted an internationalist vocabulary, using terms coined by the West such as "convergence of interests," "community of interests," "win-win" situations, and "shared responsibility."

Despite such rhetorical convergence, the view that competition between nation-states essentially characterizes global politics continues to strongly influence the Chinese perception of international relations. This is why the notion of increasing the People's Republic of China's (PRC) "comprehensive national strength" plays such a key role in Chinese foreign affairs.[3] The Chinese government continues to refer rigorously to the "Five Principles of Peaceful Coexistence," agreed on in the 1950s, and in particular to the principle of negotiating on an equal footing, as guidelines for international relations.

Against this backdrop, Beijing decision makers and policy advisers regard European discussions about the end of the era of the nation-state as a sign of political weakness. The idea of permanently transferring a large amount of national sovereign power to international organizations continues to meet with skepticism in Beijing. Nevertheless, since the 1990s China's claims to sovereignty have been put into perspective: limitations to the PRC's own sovereignty are no longer generally out of the question, provided tangible returns to China's interests make up for any losses. With the consent of the UN Security Council, the Chinese government is also willing to accept intervention in other countries' internal affairs for humanitarian reasons.

In any Chinese assessment of international relations and the international order, the main point of reference is still the United States. This is likely to remain the case in the future as well. After its military operations in Iraq and Afghanistan, the United States is said to have passed the peak of its military and economic power, a claim heard increasingly since the post-2007 global economic and financial crisis.[4] However, most Chinese commentators assume that interactions between a single superpower and several major powers will continue to characterize the international system.

In the opinion of leading Chinese foreign policy makers, the European Union (EU) does not play a major role in terms of being a counterpole, or a model, due to its frequent lack of unity and its inability to take joint action to tackle key international issues and security crises. The EU is taken seriously only in the field of international trade policy—as a heavyweight in the World Trade Organization (WTO), a global counterweight to the United States, and a difficult negotiating partner for China. Given the United States' and European Union's economic shortcomings and political inability to take action in the wake of the global financial and economic crisis, leading Chinese politicians have come to have basic doubts about whether Western political and economic institutions can serve as a model for China's future.[5]

China's Identity as an International Power

With respect to China's status, most Chinese opinions, statements, and publications maintain that the PRC is still "the largest developing country in the world." This is justified by referring to the huge development gaps within China, the country's low gross domestic product (GDP) per capita, and its technological backwardness vis-à-vis the West. In view of China's rise to an international economic power, especially its perceived role as a growth engine that helped pull the world economy out of its global slump after 2009, an increasing number of voices attribute to China specific characteristics of a major power. Chinese foreign policy circles generally agree that the PRC is an ambitious regional power in the Asian region, but it will still need quite some time to catch up with the United States.

China's growing open display of self-confidence is blended, however, with its decades-old "victim narrative"—that is, the notion that China suffered from outside aggression during the "century of humiliation" from 1842 until 1949. This victim narrative, together with constant references to China's glorious past, feed a "sense of entitlement,"[6] a belief that China deserves to retake its rightful place among the global powers. The frequently expressed warnings in the 1990s about hostile forces in the West bent on undermining China come to the fore primarily during acute crisis situations (for example, during the riots in Tibet in the spring of 2008 or when Chinese dissident Liu Xiaobo received the Nobel Peace Prize in December 2010). The prevalent Chinese view of world politics, however, is a sober one that regards anti-Chinese conspiracies as no longer feasible.

Demands for rights to "independently choose one's own social system" and to defend a "diversity of cultures," for both China and all other nation-states, are leitmotifs of Chinese foreign policy rhetoric that are closely related to the "core interests" of Chinese foreign policy, as Chinese leaders repeatedly expounded upon and explained it from 2009 to 2011.[7] Party and state leaders have explicitly defined three groups of "inviolable" and "indestructible" core interests of China's foreign policy:

- Stability of the political system—that is, maintenance of the leading role of the Chinese Communist Party (CCP) and continuation of the independent socialist path of development
- Defense of national sovereignty and security, as well as territorial integrity and national unity
- Safeguarding the prerequisites to achieve China's long-term economic and social development

Relations with Taiwan, regarded as being of key importance to China's territorial integrity and national unity, are also among the PRC's core interests. Rumors in 2010 that the PRC had added the South China Sea to its territorial interests remain unconfirmed.[8]

In upholding these core interests, China's leading politicians regularly reassure the outside world that China will adhere to its "independent foreign policy of peace" and will never seek hegemony or bully others. On the contrary, stressing the benefits of enduring integration into the global economy and world politics for the PRC's continued modernization, government and party documents claim that China will never waver in its commitment to remain open to the outside world.

When analyzing these kinds of foreign policy statements, outside observers face a number of challenges and problems. First, one must pierce through the rhetoric of such statements. For example, China's proposals to leave behind the Cold War mentality and build a more democratic world order are thinly disguised criticisms of the United States. Chinese politicians make accusations of hegemonism when individual nations or national alliances display hegemonic behavior that the government finds unacceptable (such as America's—and its allies'—insistence, without any UN mandate, on the use of force against other countries).

Second, the main problem with official Chinese declarations is the question of trustworthiness. Even if top-ranking policy makers were to reassure the world that the current Chinese foreign policy of peace and cooperation would continue for one hundred or even one thousand years,[9] many in the West would merely regard this as party propaganda or an all-too-obvious Chinese ruse to hide the PRC's true, nonpeaceful intentions.

The third problem is the question of whether there is a homogeneous Chinese view of the international order or of Chinese identity as a global political actor. In fact, many recent studies have shown that Chinese politicians and their foreign policy advisers are engaged in vigorous debates over very fundamental issues regarding the PRC's international positioning and priorities.[10] Those Chinese voices that continue to portray the PRC as a developing country mainly advocate continuation of Deng Xiaoping's foreign policy directive—that is, to promote China's domestic development with great determination but to show restraint with respect to foreign policy and not to strive for a leadership role in international affairs. From this point of view, China has insufficient capacity or resources to take on the role of a "responsible stakeholder" that can shape and maintain the international order in a manner that the United States and Europe would like. In contrast, those Chinese who believe their country is rapidly becoming a superpower favor China's playing an active role in molding the international order and providing the global community with collective goods (in fields such as environmental and climate protection or the nonproliferation of weapons of mass destruction). An even more aggressive foreign policy stance calls for China to openly challenge the global primacy of the United States and to promote alternative ideas regarding the world order that can be derived from the East Asian tradition of nonconfrontational international relations (for instance, the classical Chinese concept of *tianxia*, or a world order characterized by voluntary submission by neighboring states and benevolent leadership by China).[11]

Therefore, the main challenge for the outside world is to differentiate between authoritative, quasi-authoritative, and nonauthoritative statements coming out of China.[12] This is even more necessary with respect to the nationalist anti-Western statements expressed by individual Chinese journalists, scientists, or army officers and eagerly reported by the Western media. We should not take these as signs of a fundamental reorientation of Chinese foreign policy. Anti-Western statements in Chinese publications (such as *Global Times*) that criticize China's foreign policy for being "too soft" toward the United States or with respect to the Taiwan problem are expressions of a more pluralistic society that is attempting to influence public opinion. Since 2007 the global financial and economic crisis has reinforced positions critical of Western power, thereby damaging the credibility of certain Western notions of political and economic order. The steady stream of anti-Western publications also reflects the commercial logic of the Chinese media market in which catchy messages embedded in emotional nationalism draw more attention than nuanced analyses.

CHINESE INTERNATIONAL BEHAVIOR: A NEW ASSERTIVENESS?

Many Western authors agree that China's relations with its neighbors, the United States, and the EU have recently taken a turn for the worse.[13] A number of conflicts and incidents beginning in 2010 (heightening tensions in the territorial conflicts in the South and East China Seas, Chinese diplomatic snubs at regional or international meetings, rising trade disputes with the United States and the EU) have led Western media and scholarly publications to describe China's behavior as "triumphant," "pugilistic," "truculent," "anti-Western," and "belligerent."[14] Scholars and journalists have attributed the reasons for such a hitherto unknown assertiveness to a growing and more independent role of the Chinese military and of hard-liners or leftists from the state security apparatus, the weakening of "liberal, integrationist" forces as a result of the global recession, the pending leadership transition from the fourth to the fifth generation in 2012–2013, instability and social conflicts at home (in Tibet and Xinjiang), and the democratic revolutions in the Arab world, which put the Chinese regime on alert. China's reaction has been to acknowledge that such relations have deteriorated, but while pinning the blame on the outside world, Chinese leaders resolutely reject any notion of a change in Chinese foreign policy.

The main problem with looking at *la crise du jour* is its one-sidedness. Nonconflictual trends and substantive cooperation by China often receive insufficient appreciation. This is true, for example, with regard to the substantial improvement in relations across the Taiwan Strait (see chapter 8) or to Sino-German relations, which both sides have described as better than ever (see chapter 11). It might even be that the permanent stream of news on China and the profusion of Internet blogs dealing with Chinese foreign relations, useful as they are, contribute to an outside sense of permanent crisis with China. The days when Chinese politicians, diplomats, and businessmen could operate under the radar of public scrutiny outside (as well as inside!) China are long gone. In addition, this new focus on China might also blind us to the

Table 1.1.   Important Stages in the Development of the PRC's External Relations

1950	The Sino-Soviet Treaty of Friendship, Alliance, and Mutual Assistance is signed.
1950–1953	The Korean War takes place, involving military confrontation with the United States.
1954, 1958	A military action against Taiwan is unsuccessful.
After 1956	Sino-Soviet tensions grow; cooperation is suspended in 1960.
1959–1962	A territorial conflict/border war takes place with India in the Himalayas.
1964	China first tests an atomic bomb and becomes a nuclear power.
1969	Conflict breaks out along the Sino-Soviet border (Ussuri); fear of war grows in China.
1970–1972	Diplomatic relations are established with numerous Western states, including West Germany (1972).
1971	China replaces Taiwan as a member of the United Nations and becomes a permanent member of the UN Security Council with the right of veto.
1971–1972	China and the United States reach rapprochement, leading to a fundamental reorientation of Chinese foreign policy.
1975	Relations are officially established with the EU.
1979	A policy of opening up to foreign trade is adopted.
1979	Diplomatic relations are established with the United States.
1979	The PRC's "punitive expedition" into Vietnam due to the latter's policy on Cambodia causes heavy losses.
1980	China gains membership in the World Bank and International Monetary Fund (IMF).
1985	A trade agreement is signed with the EU.
1985–1986	Relations with the Soviet Union improve.
1986	China applies for readmittance to the General Agreement on Tariffs and Trade (GATT).
1989	International sanctions against China due to its violent suppression of the urban protest movement result in diplomatic isolation for a short time; the human rights issue becomes a central point of conflict with the West.
1990–1991	The Chinese show a willingness to cooperate on the Gulf War and in Cambodia; high-level international contacts are reestablished.
1991	China becomes a member of Asia-Pacific Economic Cooperation (APEC).
1994	US foreign policy unlinks trade and human rights issues.
1995	China is granted World Trade Organization (WTO) observer status.
March 1996	The Chinese military engages in maneuvers and missile tests in the Taiwan Strait; the United States dispatches two aircraft carriers and supporting craft to the region.
May 1999	The Chinese embassy in Belgrade is destroyed by a North Atlantic Treaty Organization (NATO) air strike during the war in Yugoslavia, resulting in violent anti-American reactions in China.
November 1999	Chinese negotiations on WTO accession are concluded with the United States.
May 2000	Chinese negotiations on WTO accession are concluded with the EU.
April 2001	A Chinese interceptor collides with a US reconnaissance plane; Sino-American relations grow tense.

July 2001	The Sino-Russian Treaty of Friendship and Cooperation is signed.
September 2001	China supports the United States in its bid to fight terrorism and approves military action against the Taliban in Afghanistan.
December 2001	China is admitted to the WTO.
May 2003	The Shanghai Cooperation Organization (SCO) (founded in 2001) establishes a permanent office in Beijing.
2003–2009	The PRC plays a leading role in the Six-Party Talks on the nuclear disarmament of North Korea.
October 2003	China sends its first manned space mission.
September–December 2005	The "path of peaceful development" is established as China's foreign policy doctrine.
January 2007	The PRC conducts a successful antisatellite test (a Chinese missile shoots down one of the country's own weather satellites).
June 2008	Talks, which had broken down in 1999, resume between semiofficial Chinese and Taiwanese liaison organizations.
Beginning in November 2008	China is included in the G20 summits.
January 2009	The Chinese navy participates in antipiracy activity in the Gulf of Aden.
January 2010	The ASEAN–China Free Trade Agreement (ACFTA) comes into force.
June 2010	The PRC and Taiwan sign the Economic Cooperation Framework Agreement.
January–May 2011	Several incidents take place involving ships from China, Vietnam, and the Philippines over disputed territory in the South China Sea.
August 2011– September 2012	China conducts sea trials of its first aircraft carrier (the *Varyag*, renamed the *Liaoning*), stationed in the home port of Qingdao.
September 2011	The foreign policy white paper titled "China's Peaceful Development" is published.
September 2012	Massive anti-Japanese protests in China and boycotts of Japanese goods follow the crisis on the Diaoyu/Senkaku Islands.

recognition that shifting patterns of cooperation and assertiveness have characterized Chinese behavior during the period of reform and opening (for an overview, see table 1.1). As such, the debate on China's new assertiveness in some important respects resembles the debate on the China threat in the mid-1990s. That said, there is no denying that, from the Western perspective, conflicts with China have increased in both number and quality. Therefore, the central question is whether conflicts involving the PRC are isolated incidents, mere ephemeral phenomena, or interconnected dots that form a line pointing toward a shift in the overall direction of Chinese foreign policy. The debate about China's "grand strategy" addresses this question.

DISCUSSIONS ABOUT CHINA'S "GRAND STRATEGY"

We can describe the main features of a national strategy as an "ends-ways-means equation."[15] It is formulated to achieve specific objectives ("ends") in the setting of specific—often changing—circumstances. In order to achieve its goals, several "ways" (concepts, approaches, concrete policies) must be developed. Putting the policies into action requires coming up with the necessary capacities ("means"). To achieve the ends, the ways and means have to be permanently coordinated; otherwise the national strategy is not meaningful. Against this conceptual background, numerous studies on Chinese foreign relations have highlighted the following characteristics of China's national strategy.[16] With regard to ends, a consensus holds that China seeks to (1) protect its sovereignty and territorial integrity, (2) promote economic development and modernization as the major drivers behind its "comprehensive national strength," and (3) earn international respect and maximize, or at least consolidate, China's status as a great power. As the most important way to achieve these objectives, a nonideological, pragmatic, stability-enhancing, and moderate foreign policy stance has been put into action, highlighting international engagement with the outside world, acceptance of international standards, attempts to reassure neighbors of China's peaceful development, and countering by any means possible future constraints on the nation's modernization.[17]

The main bone of contention among scholars is whether this strategy will endure. Some authors call for caution.[18] To begin with, central Chinese objectives point in opposing directions (e.g., the quest for greater international status and an improved image as opposed to defense of national sovereignty and the continued rule of the CCP). Furthermore, the moderate Chinese foreign policy approach is subject to a number of variables that, at least to some extent, are outside China's control (e.g., developments across the Taiwan Strait; internal developments in the United States, Japan, and North and South Korea) and therefore will create a considerable degree of uncertainty for years to come. Another group of scholars sees the role of capacities (the "means" in the definition of national strategy) as the most important element deciding China's future foreign relations.[19] Referring to historical precedents (the rise of the German Reich prior to World War I or of Japan, leading to the war in the Pacific in the 1940s), they argue that with China on the path to becoming the world's biggest economy, the United States and China are locked in a rivalry for Asian and global dominance. Authors who claim that China is embedded in the maintenance of the status quo dismiss this pessimistic outlook. On the one hand, according to their logic, the influence of international rules and institutions and the web of interdependence between China and the rest of the world (especially the United States) put pressure on China to cling to the status quo.[20] In addition, after more than thirty years of opening to the outside world, there are now so many stakeholders and vested interests in the current strategy within China (Chinese companies as part of transnational production networks, parts of the Chinese bureaucracy) that disengagement would be too costly to pursue.[21]

Again, the debate on China's longer-term strategy has several problems and shortcomings. This begins with the fact that official Chinese conceptions of how to designate the future international order are still unclear. The concepts of a "harmonious world" and "peaceful development," touted as a "major theoretical and practical contribution," fail to go beyond the announcement of vague diplomatic notions of "peace," "development," and "cooperation" as aims to pursue in a future world order. The overarching concept of "peaceful development" in foreign policy is an attempt by the Chinese leadership under Hu Jintao to harmonize competing identities (as a regional power, developing country, and superpower) and rival goals (for instance, defense of national interests and concern about the PRC's international image) by resorting to ideological language already tested successfully on domestic policy. So far, Chinese debates demonstrate a widely shared interest in the gradual adaptation and transformation of the international order rather than its destruction or national isolation.

The second caveat is the question of whether China has a strategy at all. More recent studies by influential Chinese foreign policy researchers have pointed to the increasing difficulty that China's leaders face in their bid to design and implement a consistent foreign policy strategy based on the growing variety of conflicting perceptions of (and interests in) foreign policy and trade within China itself.[22] Perhaps even the scholarly attention to China's strategy is misplaced. With a view to the constantly changing international circumstances and the permanent need for crisis management, intentions by the Chinese government to pursue a well-defined grand strategy may result in nothing more than "the realities of the immediate overtak[ing] the aspirations for the long term, the urgent sweep[ing] aside the important, and the tactical overpower[ing] the strategic."[23] This assumption is shared by experts with in-depth experience in administrative affairs who note that *ex-ante* roadmaps and manifestos appear fine in theory but most of the time are not helpful in coming to terms with unanticipated challenges.[24]

This book aims to tackle these complex issues and to give due consideration to the above arguments. We have formulated a preliminary answer to the question, What does China want? (see box 1.1).

In practice, Chinese diplomacy consists of a series of tactical approaches (see box 1.2) that are rooted in traditional strategic thinking. Chinese

BOX 1.1. BASIC ASSUMPTIONS AND
KEY OBJECTIVES OF CHINESE FOREIGN POLICY

Basic assumptions in Chinese foreign policy:

- The historic "Middle Kingdom" deserves to occupy a central position in international relations.
- International relations are primarily determined by power politics and competition between nation-states.
- As a nation-state, China has not yet reached the zenith of its power. Therefore, only tactical concessions should be made in matters of national sovereignty and territorial integrity.
- International "enemy forces" are attempting to hold China down as it strives to achieve more power and influence.
- Multilateral ties are a double-edged sword: limitations on national sovereignty are admissible only if balanced by corresponding benefits (such as a say in the creation of internationally acceptable rules, access to markets, or enhancement of the country's status in international organizations).

Key objectives of Chinese foreign policy:

- Maintaining national sovereignty and security
- Combating any move that might challenge China's territorial integrity (such as calls for the independence of Taiwan, Tibet, or Xinjiang)
- Ensuring international conditions that are favorable for economic modernization (especially access to natural resources)
- Increasing China's "comprehensive national strength"
- Striving to achieve a positive international image as a major power displaying a sense of responsibility and a willingness to cooperate with other nations
- Preventing international isolation or a permanent hardening of attitudes toward China

diplomats are considered masters in using carefully planned negotiation tactics, which their Western counterparts often realize too late or not at all.[25]

In the remainder of this book, we attempt to present the reader with carefully verified information and sound appraisals concerning China's global role. The purpose is to encourage readers to form independent, well-informed opinions on controversial aspects of Chinese foreign relations.

Our goal is to help our readers to acquire a sound understanding of the prerequisites for China's role in world politics and the global economy, as

**BOX 1.2. STANDARD TACTICAL
APPROACHES TO FOREIGN POLICY IN CHINA**

- Conducting detailed analysis of any lack of preparation or knowledge or any other personal or policy differences expressed by the other parties in order to make use of this information to further the Chinese position
- Taking the moral "high ground" in negotiations with Western nations by referring to their past colonial policies in China (historical "humiliation")
- Mobilizing support from the developing countries in situations where China faces difficulties in international forums
- Cultivating relationships with foreign friends who understand China, with the help of frequent invitations and other special treatment, thereby sidelining critics of China
- Inviting a large contingent of foreign advisers to China in order to achieve maximum benefits as a result of competition among financiers
- Participating in international negotiations and agreements, even though China still lacks the institutional capacity to implement them, and making subsequent requests for international support in order to build up the necessary capacity

well as to grasp the effects of such a role in these two areas. To this end, we explain changes in foreign policy in relation to both global and domestic Chinese processes. We pay particular attention to power shifts, changes in perception, and learning processes in foreign-relations and foreign-trade policy that continue to have an influence beyond short-term events and that characterize China's position in the world. In particular, we explore the basic patterns in foreign policy decision making in a selection of key problem areas (security, foreign trade, the environment, and human rights), as well as in a number of bilateral relations to which Chinese foreign policy attaches particular importance.

This book has the ambitious aim of providing an integrative representation and analysis of current foreign policy and foreign-trade issues. In addition to featuring a comprehensive chapter on China in the world economy, it also looks into the importance and interaction of trade and investment flows, topics covered in detail in each chapter on bilateral relations. Furthermore, China's role in the world cannot be properly understood without systematically linking the political and economic factors. We feel it is misleading to treat foreign policy (traditionally regarded as a field in political science) and foreign trade (traditionally a field in economics) as separate areas for the sake of academic analysis, as doing so fails to reflect the actual situation.

Unlike the first eleven chapters of this volume, which employ decidedly analytical and sober approaches, the final chapter, "Empire and Guerrilla," is intended to stimulate discussion. We take clear positions in this concluding chapter, pointing out a number of new challenges to society, state institutions, and the business sector that have arisen as a result of China's global expansion but thus far have received insufficient attention.

NOTES

1. Heath 2012.
2. For Chinese leaders' speeches and white papers, see Dai Bingguo 2010; Hu Jintao 2005a, 2009, 2011; Zhonghua Renmin Gongheguo Guowuyuan Xinwen Bangongshi 2005, 2011b. For Western and Chinese scholars, see Chase 2011; Lai and Lye 2007; Medeiros 2009; Murphy 2008; Zheng and Tok 2007.
3. Lampton 2008.
4. Wu Xinbo 2010, 2012; Yan and Qi 2012.
5. Thornton 2008.
6. Medeiros 2009.
7. Dai Bingguo 2010; Hu Jintao 2009; Zhonghua Renmin Gongheguo Guowuyuan Xinwen Bangongshi 2011b.
8. Swaine 2011.
9. Dai Bingguo 2012.
10. Irvine 2010; Shambaugh 2011; Zhu Liqun 2010.
11. Carlson 2011.
12. Swaine 2012c.
13. Bader 2012; Shambaugh 2013b.
14. Brown and Loh 2011; Christensen 2011; Swaine 2010; Wei Da 2010.
15. Finkelstein 2011, 1.
16. Medeiros 2009; Sutter 2012.
17. Gill 2007; Lampton 2008; Medeiros 2009; Saunders 2006.
18. Sutter 2012.
19. Friedberg 2011; Kaplan 2011; Mearsheimer 2001, 2006.
20. Ikenberry 2013.
21. Kennedy 2012.
22. Wang Jisi 2011; Wu Xinbo 2013; Zhu Liqun 2010.
23. Finkelstein 2011.
24. Bader 2012.
25. Solomon 1999.

2

Foreign Policy Decision Making

International and domestic factors that have undergone great changes since the 1990s shape the making of foreign policy in the People's Republic of China (PRC). The influence of international standards, rules, debates, and agendas affecting the PRC has increased significantly, shaping and limiting the courses of action open to Chinese foreign policy making. However, centralized decision making has been limited by actors within China itself.

Foreign-trade initiatives, for instance, often originate at local levels (i.e., cities, provinces, or the associated state-owned enterprises) or in transnational companies and production networks, thereby putting the central government in the position of having to respond and "catch up" with locally driven changes and initiatives.[1] At the same time, the decentralization of foreign relations has also opened up new possibilities. The Chinese central government now authorizes and even encourages certain provinces to foster neighborly relations and economic exchanges with bordering countries (Guangdong with Southeast Asia, Fujian with Taiwan, Yunnan with Myanmar and Laos, Guangxi with Vietnam, and the northeastern cities of Dalian and Shenyang with Japan and Korea, for instance).[2] Conversely, local coastal governments have been actively pressuring the central government apparatus to grant them special rights to pursue economic interests abroad. For example, for years the Hainan provincial government has lobbied ministries and the State Council to open the Paracel Islands to tourism, leading to fierce criticism from Vietnam and the Philippines.[3]

New communication and information technologies are increasing the influence of societal groups on foreign policy decision-making processes.[4] A good example is the widespread nationalistic statements in online forums and their subsequent effects on policy toward Japan.[5] In contrast, public opinion thus far has had a very limited influence on the shaping of Chinese government policy toward Taiwan.[6]

During the last decade, Chinese companies have been expanding beyond China's borders (see chapter 5). This has led to tens of thousands of Chinese citizens taking up posts abroad and created yet another kind of social pressure. Chinese workers abroad are becoming increasingly caught up in domestic conflicts in the countries to which they have been sent (e.g., Libya, Nigeria, and Sudan), often falling victim to internal strife, civil war, kidnapping, or personal violence. The Internet provides a platform to exert considerable pressure on the government to guarantee the safety of Chinese citizens abroad and to intervene if lives are in danger.

These recent developments coincide with generational, institutional, and ideological innovations that have reshaped foreign policy consensus building and decision making.[7] Foreign policy decision making today is considerably less burdened by ideology and hierarchical, autocratic structures and much less personality driven than it was under the leadership of either Mao Zedong or Deng Xiaoping. Reflecting changes in the domestic policy process, protracted consultations and consensus building among bureaucratic bodies, government-linked experts, and top leaders often characterize foreign policy making.[8] When it comes to complicated regulatory matters, accommodation and consensus building within the bureaucracy, rather than top-down political leadership, are of decisive importance.

In times of perceived crisis, however, whenever tensions arise in strategic areas of foreign policy (e.g., in China's relations with other major powers or with Taiwan), decision making is highly centralized and dominated by individual leaders or a small circle of advisers. Even though decision-making processes are more transparent today than they were in the past, there is still a considerable degree of intentional secrecy on the part of the Chinese leadership. High-level and otherwise well-informed academic policy advisers are frequently left in the dark about which actors actually steer foreign policy, particularly with respect to delicate matters such as the PRC's relationship with the two Koreas (see chapter 9).

Figure 2.1 presents a summary of the most important actors in the foreign policy decision-making process and their interactions.[9]

The formal decision-making structure continues to be hierarchical, with party bodies generally assuming a greater role than government institutions (unless they are essentially identical). At the very top of the decision-making structure is the Standing Committee of the Politburo of the Chinese Communist Party (CCP), which deals with strategic foreign policy matters and makes decisions during periods of international crisis. Within the Standing Committee, the general secretary of the CCP Central Committee (Hu Jintao, 2002–2012; Xi Jinping, 2012–present) plays a prominent role,

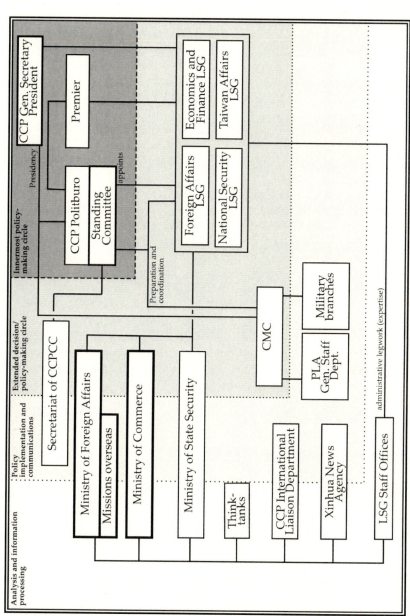

Figure 2.1. Actors involved in the making of Chinese foreign policy.

holding the state positions of both president of the PRC and chairman of the Central Military Commission of the PRC.

Foreign policy coordination takes place in what are known as the leading small groups (LSGs), which link several policy domains and operate on a supraministerial level under the Politburo. Of these special groups, the Foreign Affairs LSG, the Taiwan Affairs LSG, the National Security LSG, and the Economics and Finance LSG have the most influence on foreign policy. The general secretary of the CCP often heads them directly. Decision makers from relevant state, party, and military bodies sit on these groups since their cooperation is necessary to coordinate and implement policy. In addition to the permanent LSGs, there may also be ad hoc LSGs, such as that set up to deal with the tense situation in the South China Sea in late 2010 (see chapter 3).[10]

The advisory and working staffs of the LSGs prepare decisions on behalf of the Politburo or its Standing Committee, based on preparatory work carried out by specialist departments in the Ministry of Foreign Affairs (MFA), Ministry of Commerce, Ministry of State Security, and the Central Military Commission. General coordination of policy adjustments and cross-disciplinary tasks related to the work of the ministries of commerce, foreign affairs, and finance, as well as the Central Bank, is entrusted to the Economics and Finance LSG, and it is the task of the National Security LSG to coordinate responses in cases of domestic or foreign crises.

Although often overlooked in the West, two other bodies play a significant role in foreign policy issues: the International Liaison Department of the CCP Central Committee (particularly with regard to North Korea) and the United Front Work Department of the CCP Central Committee (with a bureau to deal solely with the Taiwan issue). The leaders of each of these bodies also sit on the respective leading small groups. Despite the lack of any formal responsibility for foreign affairs work, the General Office of the CCP Central Committee does play a role, as evidenced by the director of the General Office's accompanying General Secretary Hu Jintao on almost all his trips abroad.[11]

On the government side, there is generally a state councilor—below the premier and the vice premiers in the state hierarchy but above the ministers—who is permanently responsible for coordination of foreign policy. The state councilor for foreign affairs, who often has decades of diplomatic experience either from serving previously in the MFA or as part of the leadership of the International Liaison Department of the Central Committee, is also director of the Staff Office of the Foreign Affairs LSG. This office acts as a filter mechanism for foreign policy suggestions and initiatives passed on to the party leadership.

The MFA plays a relatively minor role as compared with its counterparts in other countries. Its overseas missions (embassies and consulates) are involved in fact-finding, analysis, and the preparatory stages of decision-making processes, as well as, with the help of bilateral and multilateral diplomacy, implementing foreign policy guidelines. However, its role is limited in terms of coordinating foreign policy because it is only one among several ministerial-level agencies under the State Council. It even faces difficulties in surmounting resistance by local governments because provincial governors hold the same cadre rank as the foreign minister. In its mission to improve the PRC's image abroad, the MFA often comes up against foreign economic interests. A national work conference on foreign relations held in 2006 explicitly criticized the uncoordinated and selfish behavior of Chinese companies abroad, as their actions could have a negative effect on China's reputation and credibility on the world stage.[12] The MFA has also been accused in Internet forums (and even by other state and military bodies) of betraying Chinese interests due to its conciliatory and prudent positions, which have come about as a result of the negative diplomatic effects of excessively vigorous foreign-trade and security-policy initiatives.

The Ministry of Commerce, responsible for all foreign-trade and investment-related issues (including those related to the World Trade Organization) often competes with the MFA in certain aspects of China's relations with its foreign counterparts. As economic questions are granted overriding importance in Chinese foreign policy, the influence of other groups of actors who play increasingly prominent roles in the foreign policy decision-making process is growing. One group of such key players includes the members of the National Development and Reform Commission (NDRC), who, together with the relevant ministries, establish long-term goals and programs and also help make decisions in many foreign policy areas, covering anything from Chinese businesses "going global" to supplies of energy and raw materials and even climate-change negotiations.

China's central bank—the People's Bank of China (PBoC)—has also played an increasingly important role in Chinese foreign relations over the last decade due to its policy of stockpiling huge foreign-currency reserves. It has received pointed criticism from abroad for its foreign exchange policy, and it increasingly has to coordinate its own activities with the central banks of other countries (see chapter 5).

For its part, the State-Owned Assets Supervision and Administration Commission (SASAC) is beginning to face problems from regional governments and large state enterprises that attempt to circumvent centralized foreign direct investment (FDI) supervision and regulations by the national government (see chapter 5). However, we should not overrate the activities of Chinese state-owned enterprises abroad in terms of their political intentions or orientations.[13] On the one hand, large Chinese companies (especially the national oil companies) carry out extensive lobbying for their own expansion at both the domestic and the international levels (particularly on the commodities market). On the other hand, much of this influence is due to the fact that many heads of the state-owned enterprises also hold high positions in the CCP, as members of the Central Committee or even as ranking vice ministers in the cadre hierarchy.[14] These "party-member managers" inevitably focus their interests on obtaining preferential treatment for their particular sector or company rather than on actively shaping foreign or security policy outside their own sphere of activity.

Two credit institutions currently offer special funding for foreign investments (export credit and investment financing) and occupy a pivotal position in helping Chinese companies expand and achieve a global presence: the politically well-connected and rapidly growing China Development Bank and the Export-Import Bank, a less prominent political player and lender. These banks support Chinese firms wishing to expand into foreign markets by providing very generous lending, which includes everything from subsidizing exports (in a nontransparent system) to openly participating in foreign infrastructure programs and buying shares in commodity companies. According to a study by the *Financial Times*, in 2009–2010 Chinese banks provided more long-term loans, in the amount of US$110 billion, to developing countries than the World Bank during the same period due to the increasing (and highly risky medium- and long-term) financing costs of large-scale projects and major investments.

The Ministry of State Security's exact role in foreign and foreign-trade policy is, by its nature, opaque. According to information available, it not only carries out the usual intelligence operations in political and military relations with other countries but is also behind large-scale foreign-trade espionage, meaning it plays a key role in the acquisition of the latest civil and military technology.

The Western media often play up and dramatize foreign policy activity and intervention by military players on the Central Military Commission (which in peacetime also holds supreme command of the army) and in the Ministry of National Defense (primarily responsible for military diplomacy and the military attachés stationed in overseas missions, thus, much less important on an operational level than the defense ministries in other countries), the four general departments (staff, political, logistics, and armaments), and the service arms (navy, air force, and second artillery) of the People's Liberation Army (PLA).

However, experts on the Chinese military generally agree that the highest-ranking officers in the army primarily serve the interests of their own sectors (such as budget maximization and financing for new weapons systems intended for certain groups in the armed forces) and do not represent an independent military interest in foreign policy decision making that is distinct from and in opposition to the civilian leadership (see chapter 4).[15] Despite numerous objections from the military, the authority of the civilian party leadership in foreign policy, even when it comes to dealing with Taiwan, has never been called into question.[16]

As a result of the ongoing professionalization of the armed forces, under post–Deng Xiaoping leaders there has been a growing bifurcation of civil and military elites, with no high-ranking officer in the army holding a seat on the Politburo Standing Committee since 1997. The resultant bureaucratic and communications division between the civil and military hierarchies has become an obstacle when it comes to speedy yet appropriate crisis management during tense national-security scenarios (such as the collision of a US spy plane with a Chinese military aircraft near Hainan Island in 2001 or the bombing of the Chinese embassy in Belgrade during North Atlantic Treaty Organization's (NATO) air campaign in Yugoslavia in 1999).

In addition, horizontal coordination of decisions between the state and the army at the top level has largely been transferred to the LSGs, and the role of the PLA is relatively ineffective at the top level and is almost nonexistent at lower levels.[17] This has led to a long list of foreign policy inconsistencies. On one occasion, the MFA pledged to send Chinese troops to help UN missions, but it did so without checking with the PLA leadership as to the actual availability of a sufficient number of men. In another incident, the MFA granted permission for a US aircraft carrier to dock in Hong Kong, a symbolic gesture that the PLA leadership then successfully blocked.[18]

The proliferation of agencies involved in the foreign policy decision-making process defies any notion of a Leninist-type straightforward, top-down structure. As an in-depth analysis by the International Crisis Group demonstrates, with regard to the South China Sea, nine ministerial-level bodies, in addition to the PLA navy and the provincial governments, are involved, and thus there is little or no effective coordination authority and no high-level cohesive policy.[19]

These interorganizational conflicts of interest and information blackouts, on the one hand, and the interdependence of the domestic and foreign policy decision-making processes, on the other, have far-reaching consequences for China's behavior in international negotiations. As even Chinese analysts frankly admit, the Chinese administration is finding it increasingly difficult to enforce international agreements that affect the interests of various powerful domestic players. As a result, Chinese delegations sent to take part in multilateral negotiations are often very large, as their members represent the range of bureaucratic interests involved in that particular policy, although they generally have very limited mandates.[20] In many cases, the resulting internal blockades and paralysis in negotiations lead to frustrations in the foreign countries and can only be resolved by energetic intervention from individual leaders.[21] Foreign negotiators receive conflicting signals from the different Chinese players, depending on whether these people have vested political or bureaucratic interests. Furthermore it is often difficult to discern who has the final word in negotiations and who is ultimately responsible for implementation of those international commitments that the PRC has officially accepted. For this reason alone, it is absolutely essential to have sound knowledge about the political and bureaucratic power constellations that currently exist in China.

NOTES

1. Zweig and Chen 2007.
2. Cabestan 2009; Jakobson and Knox 2010.
3. International Crisis Group 2012.
4. Hao Yufan 2013.
5. Hong Junhao 2005.
6. Cabestan 2009.
7. Cabestan 2009; Hao and Su 2005; Jakobson and Knox 2010; Lai Hongyi 2010; Lampton 2001; Sutter 2012.
8. Liao Xuanli 2006.
9. Cabestan 2009; Jakobson and Knox 2010; Lai Hongyi 2010; Lu Ning 1997, 2001.
10. International Crisis Group 2012.
11. Glaser 2013.
12. Glaser 2007.
13. Yu Jie 2012.
14. Li Cheng 2011.
15. Cabestan 2009; Finkelstein and Gunness 2007; Lu Ning 2001; Scobell and Wortzel 2005; Swaine 2012a, 2012b.
16. Blasko 2012.
17. Swaine 2012a, 2012b.
18. Cabestan 2009.
19. International Crisis Group 2012.
20. Pearson 2010.
21. Bader 2012.

3

Reorientations in China's Foreign Policy

Official Chinese accounts of the development of the country's foreign policy indicate a fundamental continuity in what the government calls its "independent foreign policy of peace" since the beginning of the 1979 structural reforms and liberalization. This long-term continuity becomes apparent if we look closely at China's progressive integration into transnational trade and capital flows and note the obvious decrease in the number of military security issues (i.e., perceived threats) and the People's Republic of China's (PRC) acute sensitivity to any questions regarding its national sovereignty and territorial integrity.

A great number of reforms and shifts in emphasis under both Jiang Zemin (1989–2002) and Hu Jintao (2002–2012) go beyond the scope of some of the assumptions, goals, and instruments that previously shaped China's foreign policy. A series of far-reaching events generated these changes. Although China was only partially affected by the direct effects of the Asian financial crisis of 1997–1999, it was still the greatest economic shock to which China had been exposed since the beginning of the reform period.[1] The Chinese government helped to resolve the crisis by not devaluing its currency, which would have exacerbated the situation. This step, obviously also in its own interest, helped the PRC gain a reputation as a responsible superpower, a reputation it has been at pains to retain ever since.

However, the Asian financial crisis had another important consequence. The Chinese leadership confronted limitations to its national economic sovereignty, despite its strict capital controls. Beijing reacted by taking the bull by the horns. By joining the World Trade Organization (WTO), the PRC abandoned conventional Chinese notions of sovereignty that had affected foreign-trade issues in order to become integrated into transnational markets governed by the set rules and discipline of the international organization. The government believed that the positive effects of economic globalization on Chinese exports and structural reforms outweighed the risks to national economic security.

The First and Second Gulf Wars and America's fight against terrorism also played a pivotal role in the area of Chinese security policy (see chapter 4). On the one hand, America's swift victories against Iraq in 1991 and 2003 made the PRC very aware of its own military shortcomings, a situation that led China to make concerted efforts to modernize the People's Liberation Army (PLA). On the other hand, the Chinese leadership also quickly learned from US mistakes in Afghanistan and Iraq and made efforts to turn the resulting damage to the United States' reputation to China's own advantage. China's gradual broadening of initiatives to raise its profile in regional and global multilateral organizations and its attempts thereafter to use "soft power" (see below) should be seen as a response to American unilateralism and the US focus on the classic "hard-power" policies of the George W. Bush administration.

Additionally, since the late 1990s China has actively built up relations with regions largely neglected by the West. The rediscovery of Africa, Latin America (see below), and Central Asia in Chinese foreign policy should be seen in the following context.[2] The basic motive for stepping up bilateral and multilateral relations in these regions is to safeguard Chinese interests against nontraditional security threats (such as acts of terrorism in Central Asia), in the ongoing diplomatic contest with Taiwan, and, most importantly, in terms of foreign-trade priorities (e.g., ensuring supplies of raw materials and energy and opening up new markets for Chinese products). The following chapters describe some of these changes in Chinese foreign policy in more detail.

CHINA'S NEW MULTILATERALISM

Until well into the 1990s, China primarily focused on bilateralism and was highly suspicious of involvement in multilateral groups due to their potential to limit the PRC's freedom of action.[3] Since then, however, the Chinese government has been much more prepared to engage in multilateral cooperation.[4] According to data from the Chinese Academy of Social Sciences, by the middle of the first decade of the twenty-first century China had joined about three hundred intergovernmental and more than twenty-six hundred nongovernmental international organizations.[5] This new multilateralism takes many different forms and is important on both the regional and global fronts, as well as in the problematic areas of economic and security policy.

On the global dimension, we can point to China's role within the United Nations and the WTO and as a member of the Group of Twenty (G20) as a result of the 2008 financial crisis. As a UN member, China evolved from a rebel outcast that did its best to oppose the system into a strong UN supporter. The PRC sees international cooperation as a way to underpin China's entitlement to equal participation in world politics. The Chinese leadership considers the United Nations to be a central pillar in developing a multipolar world and keeping US domination in international politics in check.[6] So far, however, China has generally avoided openly confronting the United States within the United Nations. In 1997–1998 and 2003, for example, it left fellow Security Council members Russia and France to criticize the US-planned military operations against Iraq. China also continues to be skeptical of UN sanctions against states such as Iran, Myanmar, and Zimbabwe, which are important raw material suppliers; at the same time it attempts to make sure that it is not isolated in its stand against the United States or against the West in general. For this reason, when it comes to sanctions, China has always sought solidarity with Russia in the Security Council.

The Chinese leadership recognizes that it can no longer establish national security unilaterally based only on military and economic power. Thus, it has shown a greater willingness to participate in security-related multilateral cooperation, for instance, by signing nuclear nonproliferation treaties and agreeing to the comprehensive test ban on atomic weapons.[7]

Since the beginning of the 1990s, the PRC has also played a substantial role in UN peacekeeping missions, sending a total of 17,400 troops on nineteen separate peacekeeping missions between 1990 and the end of 2010 (according to its 2010 white paper on national defense). In September 2012, 1,922 Chinese soldiers, police officers, and other security forces participated in twelve UN missions—a considerably larger contingent than those provided by the other permanent members of the Security Council. According to data provided by the UN Department of Peacekeeping Operations, as of September 2012 the national contingents consisted of the following: from France, 990; from Russia, 88; from the United Kingdom, 276; and from the United States, 146.

Such involvement reflects a change in Chinese views on peacekeeping missions. For a long time China regarded these missions as incompatible with its demand for unconditional respect of its territorial integrity and state sovereignty. Today, however, the PRC is prepared to support intervention, provided such operations have the backing of a UN Security Council resolution and the affected country's advance permission. Here we can clearly see a pragmatic realignment of Beijing's interests with respect to support for intervention beyond its borders (fostering the image of China as a responsible superpower, stabilization of the surrounding region, and so forth).[8]

China has also made particularly far-reaching concessions with regard to adapting its foreign-trade regulations to align more with the guidelines of the world trade regime (also see chapter 5). For this, the government has passed substantial reforms to its foreign-trade system and commercial law and has lowered customs tariffs across the board. In comparison with other emerging economies, such as India and Brazil, observers consider China a highly open economy.[9] Furthermore, the PRC contributes both actively and constructively to the WTO.[10] Nevertheless, noncompliance with WTO obligations has led to some particularly contentious issues between China, on the one hand, and the United States and the European Union (EU), on the other. Both the Americans and the Europeans have complained about China's slow pace in opening up its service sector and its breaches of intellectual property rights (IPR) and industrial property rights, as evidenced by the vast numbers of counterfeit brands and products coming from China, as well by the numerous nontariff trade barriers set by the Chinese, such as technical and sanitary standards and nontransparent administrative procedures, creating difficulties for foreign companies.[11]

This partly inadequate implementation of WTO agreements arises mainly from the conflict of interests between the Chinese central government and local government authorities. WTO rules represent a real threat to those players at the local levels who profit from special decentralized arrangements regarding foreign trade and circumvention practices or who take advantage of ways to exploit the current situation for their own gain, as in the case of product and brand piracy. If openness to foreign trade leads to an increase in social upheaval and employment problems in China, many Chinese officials will see offering at least covert resistance to any lowering of domestic barriers to foreign trade as not only economically necessary but also politically legitimate. If in doubt, Chinese government agencies are much more likely to contravene WTO rules than to accept any kind of domestic social or political unrest. Basically, the question revolves around the extent to which China's political elite can allow pressures from international competition to endanger or reform existing political and economic structures in the PRC—the political and economic authority of Chinese officials and the related economic players is at stake. For this reason, in the near future we are more likely to see an increase, rather than a reduction, in Chinese trade disputes with Western states.

China's role in the G20—the world's twenty most important industrial and emerging nations—is a measure of just how willing it is to play an active role in responsible global economic governance. This body, which has existed since 1999, was initially established as a coordinating forum for finance ministers and governors of central banks. But in 2008 it began to attract wide attention when it staged a summit of heads of state in Washington in response to the global financial and economic crisis.

Beijing currently views participation in the G20 forum rather ambivalently.[12] On the one hand, China has welcomed the fact that the G20 has gained in significance at the expense of the Group of Eight (G8), which it considered nothing more than a group of rich nations intent on consolidating their hold on the international system. The G20, in contrast, according to China, represents a forum particularly suited to finding solutions to pressing global economic problems facing the emerging countries and one in which China can stand alongside Brazil, Russia, India, and South Africa. Chinese leaders have decided to play a larger role in shaping international mechanisms through the G20, becoming a "rule maker" rather than a "rule taker" when it comes to such things as regulating financial markets, stabilizing the international monetary system, and preventing protectionist practices.

On the other hand, it is impossible to overlook China's very limited involvement in the G20. As far back as the first three G20 summit meetings, in Washington (November 2008), London (April 2009), and Pittsburgh (September 2009), the Chinese government held the industrial nations of the West fully responsible for the outbreak of the economic crisis, denouncing them for deregulating their financial markets and encouraging speculative bubbles and debt-fueled consumption due to shortsighted interest-rate policies and lax financial supervision. China's key contribution to solving the global financial crisis was its vast national economic stimulus program, which was intended also to help stimulate demand in other economies as well.[13]

The Chinese government watered down the idea of taking shared responsibility in order to limit global disparities in trade and current account deficits, first mentioned at the G20 summit in Pittsburgh, at subsequent G20 meetings, and to this day the idea still remains a point of contention between the United States and China. As pressures on the G20 to tackle the acute issues brought on by the crisis declined, the G20 members found that they actually had a much smaller range of shared interests than originally thought. Thus, the Chinese government is not solely responsible for the fact that the international macroeconomic coordination and international regulations that the G20 intended to impose on the various financial markets have come to a halt.

The PRC has been particularly dynamic with respect to its multilateral policy in a regional context as a member of the Association of Southeast Asian Nations (ASEAN), the Asia-Pacific Economic Cooperation (APEC), and the Shanghai Cooperation Organization (SCO).[14]

China took an important step toward reducing its diplomatic isolation in 1991 when it joined APEC. As a member of this body, it has been able to take advantage of transpacific trade liberalization, but it has also used the fact that in terms of development it still lags behind other nations as an excuse for delaying a complete opening of its market. In 2001, China changed course even with respect to APEC. Up to that point, Beijing had vehemently opposed politicization of the group, but since then it has used the organization as a forum for posing questions regarding counterterrorism and defense against other new security concerns.

Aside from stepping up its bilateral relations with all of the Southeast Asian countries, China has become increasingly involved in ASEAN since the start of the 1990s, and in rapid succession it established a number of bilateral and multilateral discussion forums. To name but a few, China has been a member of the ASEAN Regional Forum (ARF, the security-policy arm of ASEAN) since 1994, an ASEAN dialogue partner since 1996, and a member of ASEAN+1 (China) and ASEAN+3 (China, Japan, and South Korea) since 1997; it has also been instrumental in arranging the East Asia Summit since it was first set up in 2005 (this body originally consisted of the ASEAN+3 along with India, Australia, and New Zealand; in the meantime, Russia and the United States have also joined). Both ASEAN and China share an underlying belief that institutional cooperation should follow a loose approach that focuses more on establishing specific processes than on obtaining specific results and that envisages nonbinding consultation without interference in any other country's domestic affairs.

Two particular Chinese undertakings within the ASEAN framework have attracted attention on a regional and international level. The first was the economic initiative China took in 2000 to set up the ASEAN-China Free Trade Area (ACFTA), which, coming into force in January 2010, envisages a progressive reduction in trade tariffs among participating nations.[15] This first free trade agreement, since followed by several others, is actually the world's biggest if one takes into account the populations affected, their joint gross domestic product, and the trade flows.[16] The most striking detail regarding this agreement is the increase in trade between China and the ASEAN member states, which rose from US$41.6 billion to US$361.2 billion between 2001 and 2011 (see figure 3.1), making ASEAN China's fourth most important trading partner after the EU, the United States, and Japan. Furthermore, based on data provided by the ASEAN Secretariat, China's share of ASEAN foreign trade was 11 percent in 2010, making it ASEAN's number one trading partner ahead of the EU27, Japan, and the United States.

These statistics are absolute figures that apply to ASEAN as a whole. Of course, the great majority of Chinese trade with ASEAN members is with the group's most important founding members: Singapore, Malaysia, Thailand, and Indonesia. Among the newer members of the association, only Vietnam can be described as playing a significant role with respect to trade with China. Since the mid-1990s, China has been pushing its way to the forefront of transnational Asian production networks, which have recently

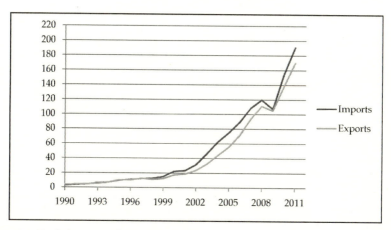

Figure 3.1. Trade between China and ASEAN member states, 1990–2011 (in US$ billions).
Sources: IMF Direction of Trade Statistics; Zhonghua Renmin Gongheguo Guojia Tongjiju 2012; Ministry of Commerce of the PRC.

displayed a high division of labor and specialization across national borders.[17] Initial worries among the ASEAN states that China's relations with the association would divert an increasing amount of trade to the detriment of the smaller nations have not been borne out (in fact, trade has grown both between the members of ASEAN and between ASEAN and China). Nevertheless, a number of tensions in trade relations are visible. Indonesian metal producers complain of markets being flooded with Chinese products, Thai farmers face growing imports of agricultural products from China, and well-established electronics and information technology firms in places such as Malaysia regard China's growing influence as a potential threat. Although trade between China and ASEAN member states has grown rapidly, foreign direct investment (FDI) between the two sides is still unbalanced. A number of ASEAN members, particularly Singapore, have invested heavily in China for years. However, between 2008 and 2010 China was the source of only 5.5 percent of FDI to ASEAN (in comparison, the EU invested 21 percent and Japan and the United States 10 percent each). Chinese companies apparently regard ASEAN members as good trade partners when it comes to imports and exports, but they do not see the region as a lucrative place to invest.

A second significant issue involving relations between China and ASEAN members centers on the South China Sea territorial disputes based on a series of historical, geographical, and legal arguments (see figure 3.2).[18] This area, contested due to its abundant fish stocks and oil and gas reserves, was repeatedly the scene of Chinese petty military hostilities with the Philippines and Vietnam until the 1990s.[19] But at the end of 2002, the Chinese

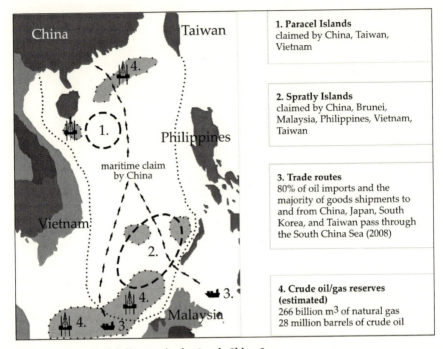

Figure 3.2. Territorial disputes in the South China Sea.
Source: US Department of Defense 2010; GlobalSecurity.org.

government expressed a willingness to draw up a declaration on a code of conduct with ASEAN member states with the intention of reaching a peaceful settlement.

During the ensuing period, however, China did not abandon any of its claims to sovereignty over the regions in the South China Sea. Despite the contestants' different legal positions, however, Chinese foreign policy followed the very pragmatic approach of suggesting joint exploration of the maritime region for material deposits. At a meeting between Chinese and ASEAN ministers held in Bali in July 2011, the foreign ministers of the various nations agreed on a new framework (the Guidelines on the Implementation of the Declaration on the Conduct of Parties in the South China Sea) and discussed specific steps to implement long-lasting and cooperative measures to settle the territorial disputes.

As for the Central Asian states and Russia, the PRC has increasingly relied on multilateral mechanisms to ensure peace in the area. In conjunction with Russia, Kazakhstan, Kyrgyzstan, Tajikistan, and Uzbekistan, China founded the SCO in 2001, with the primary intention of combating regional terrorism, separatism, and religious extremism (the so-called Three Evils). In addition, SCO members have also pledged to settle their respective border disputes by contractually agreeing on the course of their frontiers, to undertake confidence-building measures (such as reciprocal reductions in troop numbers along their borders), and to perform joint troop maneuvers. Since 2003, with the inclusion of economic topics on its agenda, the SCO has become a more comprehensive regional organization.[20]

Complex reasons underlie China's closer cooperation with ASEAN and the SCO.[21] At first glance, it was a matter of dismantling historically perceived threats and building cooperation and mutual trust on questions of security policy. But economic considerations quickly found their way onto the parties' respective agendas. Southeast Asia has become increasingly important to China in terms of trade and investment. The provinces of Southwest China, much less economically developed than the rest of the country, are to be linked more closely with the neighboring Southeast Asian nations with the help of cross-border infrastructure measures (such as road building and railroads) in order to create new opportunities for growth. In addition, Central Asia (particularly Kazakhstan) serves as an important supplier of raw materials—predominantly oil and gas—to China. Cross-border infrastructure building in Central Asia should be seen within the context of the economic development of western China, particularly Xinjiang autonomous region. This region is also the main focus of antiterrorist activities, which are part of the SCO mission as well: the Chinese government wants to shield Xinjiang from Islamist forces based in neighboring countries. Ultimately, all of these initiatives aim to counterbalance the role of the United States in the region, in response to US encroachments on China's outer borders as part of its global fight against terrorism.

China's multilateral ventures into Asia, however, are subject to tight restrictions.[22] Despite Beijing's diplomatic "charm offensive," increasing economic interdependence, and efforts to reduce the conflicts in the South China Sea, distrust of China has not diminished in large parts of the region, and in recent times it has actually grown.[23] This apprehension is particularly apparent in the flare-up of tensions since 2009 in the South China Sea.[24] In May 2009, China presented to the UN Commission on the Limits of the Continental Shelf its first official map illustrating its claims across almost the entire South China Sea (showing the so-called nine-dashed line). Tensions heightened further in 2010 when rumors spread that control over the South China Sea had become one of China's core interests. In response, the United States declared protecting the sea routes in the region a matter of its own national interest.[25] Time and again, Vietnamese and Philippine fishermen have reported incidents with Chinese ships in the disputed areas, and in 2009 Chinese craft aggressively threatened an American ship taking sonar readings of the seafloor. It is too early to know with certainty whether these incidents represent a new Chinese assertiveness, implying a fundamental change in Chinese strategy, or can be better understood as driven by a multitude of government agencies pursuing their own agendas without central government coordination.[26] It is certain that the tensions in the South China Sea have considerably damaged China's reputation in the region. Several neighboring Southeast Asian states (the Philippines, Singapore, and Thailand) have intensified bilateral military cooperation with the United States, and Vietnam has offered the Americans increased diplomatic and military cooperation and announced it will expand arms cooperation with Russia.

How should we assess China's newfound multilateralism, and how should we gauge the opportunities for involving China in more international decision making? The PRC already complies with and shapes a number of international regulations, particularly in terms of trade and technical standards, and it has made great progress in becoming involved in questions of international security. It has also recently shown growing flexibility, even in areas where it previously had adopted an uncompromising position, citing national sovereignty issues in its defense (e.g., territorial disputes or the dispatch of UN peacekeeping troops). China's initiatives in both the global and regional multilateral contexts aim to dispel fears regarding its ascent and to convey an image of a responsible superpower that believes in maintaining the status quo.

However, even Chinese authors have pointed out how selective the Chinese government has been when it comes to taking on new regional and global responsibilities.[27] Rather than any recognition of the intrinsic value of multilateralism, more or less skillfully masked cost/benefit considerations continue to determine China's conduct in multilateral organizations.[28] The Chinese government believes that it should use any form of multilateral cooperation as a means to further its own national interests and international position, not as a driving force to foster political-learning processes or institutional alignments within China. In short, multilateral cooperation is nothing more than a Chinese foreign policy instrument; it is certainly not one of the PRC's actual goals.

As a rule, official Chinese statements deal with the notion and functions of multilateralism in a contradictory manner. The term "multilateralism" often serves as a synonym for the multipolarization or democratization of international relations, making it a code word for China's objective of limiting America's global and regional influence. Therefore, in the short and medium term, with respect to Chinese foreign policy, the goals with the highest priority or greatest symbolic meaning—such as maintaining domestic stability and retaining the Chinese Communist Party's (CCP) grip on power, safeguarding territorial integrity (Taiwan and Tibet), and ensuring economic development—will prevail over any desire to be seen as a responsible, cooperative superpower.

REDISCOVERING THE DEVELOPING
AND EMERGING COUNTRIES

In terms of development and current status, China's relations with the developing countries in Latin America and Africa reveal several striking parallels. During the first three decades after its establishment, the PRC's ideology-tinted Third World policies—which basically consisted of the fight against imperialism, hegemonism, and colonialism and derived from its precarious position in the power triangle with the United States and the Soviet Union—heavily influenced Chinese relations.[29]

In official rhetoric, ideological principles continue to play a role to this day: emphasizing the Five Principles of Peaceful Coexistence, relating to the colonial experience China has in common with African nations, and supporting mutually advantageous South-South cooperation among the developing countries.[30] China makes great efforts to present its goals, principles, and methods as viable alternatives to American and European policies toward Africa and Latin America, but specific diplomatic and economic interests—even when looked at from a Chinese perspective—quite clearly shape its current relations with the countries on these two continents.[31]

For one thing, Africa and Latin America remain the stage on which China and Taiwan are still waging a complex diplomatic contest. As early as 1971, the African states played a key role in ensuring that the PRC would replace the Republic of China (ROC) as a member of the United Nations. Since the mid-1990s, the PRC has succeeded in luring important African partners (e.g., South Africa, Liberia, Chad, and Senegal) away from Taiwan; whereas twenty-two African countries formerly had relations with Taiwan, now only four do (Burkina Faso, Gambia, São Tomé and Príncipe, and Swaziland). Out of the twenty-three countries that still retain diplomatic relations with Taiwan, twelve are in Latin America. Even though China and Taiwan engaged in bitter diplomatic contests in the past, efforts to lure diplomatic partners away from one another have let up significantly since 2008 (see chapter 8).

We can trace one political reason for China's increased involvement in Africa in the 1990s back to Beijing's diplomatic isolation as a result of its violent repression of the urban protest movement in 1989. China has attempted to capitalize on the fact that US and European criticism frequently targets a number of African nations for their lack of democracy and disregard for human rights, and the PRC has offered itself as a partner to counterbalance the influence of the Western democracies by proclaiming every country's sovereign right to choose its own path of development. Primarily due to intensified relations with the African states, Chinese diplomacy repeatedly, since the turn of the century, managed to fend off UN resolutions by Western nations critical of China's human rights situation.[32]

More recently, the PRC has used support from African and Latin American members of the WTO to safeguard its foreign-trade interests. Beijing's trade diplomats draw attention to the fact that the Latin American states, unlike the Western states, recognize China as a market economy.

Undoubtedly, economic interests have been the source of China's increased interest in Africa and Latin America. The Asian financial crisis of 1997–1999 revealed just how vulnerable the Chinese economy could be to external shocks and that the risks of foreign-trade dependencies—particularly in terms of raw materials sourcing, which is so important to economic growth—need to be spread out as much as possible. As a result, the PRC, a net importer of crude oil since 1993, has been courting the developing and emerging countries in Africa and Latin America, both as raw materials suppliers and as sales markets. In addition to a long list of other foreign policy initiatives, an accelerated realignment of Chinese development strategy since 2001 has led to the promotion of more capital-intensive industries and investment in infrastructure. For example, Jiang Zemin and Hu Jintao both visited Latin America, in 2001 and 2004 respectively. China's diplomatic "Africa year" in 2006 gave the continent a much greater role in China's foreign policy after the first summit meeting of the Forum on China-Africa Cooperation (FOCAC) was held in Beijing, with participation by all forty-eight African states with diplomatic links to China.[33]

Chinese trade with Latin America and Africa has grown steadily against the backdrop of expanding political and diplomatic relations. Trade links with Latin America grew from US$15 billion in 2001 to US$241.4 billion in 2011; during the same period trade with Africa rose from US$10 billion to US$166.3 billion (see figures 3.3 and 3.4). Within a short period, China overtook France, the United Kingdom, and the United States as Africa's most important trade partner. But despite recent growth rates of 30 percent in trade with Latin America, China is still only that continent's third-largest trading partner (it is number one in Brazil and Chile), and its Latin American trade is only about one-quarter of Latin America's trade with the United States.

In 2011, Latin American and African trade accounted for the relatively modest shares of 6.6 percent and 4.5 percent, respectively, of China's foreign trade. Additionally, this trade tends to be limited to only a few countries: in Africa, to countries rich in natural resources, such as Angola, the Republic of Congo, Equatorial Guinea, Sudan, South Africa, and Egypt; in Latin America, to Brazil, Chile, Mexico, Venezuela, Argentina, and Peru.

Up to the present, Chinese trade with Latin America and Africa has been quite balanced, with exports and imports at about the same levels. However, this is not the case in terms of types of products: oil, gas, minerals, and metals make up the bulk of Chinese imports, whereas the Chinese generally deliver finished products, machinery, and transportation equipment.

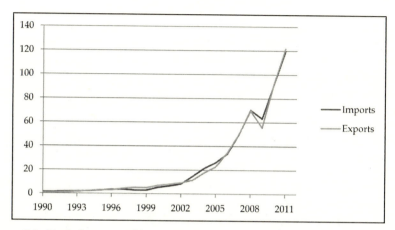

Figure 3.3. Trade between China and Latin America, 1990–2011 (in US$ billions).
Sources: IMF; Ministry of Commerce of the PRC.

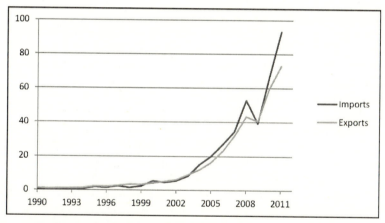

Figure 3.4. Trade between China and Africa, 1990–2011 (in US$ billions).
Sources: IMF; Ministry of Commerce of the PRC.

Comparative cost advantages can explain these differences, which largely correspond to Western trade patterns in these regions.

Over the last few years, Chinese direct investments in Africa and Latin America have also grown substantially. According to Chinese sources, at the end of 2011 Chinese direct investments in Africa totaled a cumulative US$16.2 billion (in 2003 the comparable figure was US$450 million), and in Latin America they totaled a stock of US$55.2 billion (in 2003 the comparable figure was US$4.6 billion). They were also firmly concentrated in those countries that were also important trading partners. However, these direct investments represented a very small share of the total volume of China's foreign investment, and Chinese investments in either Africa or Latin America still lag far behind those of the United States (cumulative 2011 US investments amounted in Latin America to US$831 billion and in Africa to US$57 billion).[34] Loans have been much more important in the case of Latin America. Chinese state banks (in particular, the China Development Bank) since 2005 reportedly have lent Latin America US$75 billion, and in 2010 alone they lent more than the World Bank, the Inter-American Development Bank, and the US Ex-Im Bank combined.[35]

China's growing relations with Africa and Latin America did not immediately attract attention in the West. But over the past few years, they have started to provoke deep mistrust and to trigger harsh Western criticism. In development-policy circles, the PRC has been accused of pursuing "neomercantilist policies," "petrodiplomacy," and even "neocolonialism," thereby forcing Africa into a "raw materials trap."[36] With regard to Latin America, Washington views with concern China's close diplomatic relations with left-wing populist governments, some of which, such as Venezuela, are also openly critical of the United States.[37]

A main source of criticism is China's attitude toward nations that the West regards as pariah states, such as Sudan and Zimbabwe, which Beijing has supported with logistical aid, weaponry, and diplomatic backing.[38] When granting loans to African or Latin American nations, China does not make its decisions based on the political conditionality criteria (i.e., respect for human rights, institutional reform aimed at promoting democracy, good governance, or fighting corruption) set by Western nations and multilateral institutions for allocating development aid. Furthermore, China has engaged in prestigious projects and built grand buildings in some of the nondemocratic African states (e.g., parliamentary buildings in Mozambique and Gabon and soccer stadiums in Tanzania, Mali, and Djibouti). Yet when it comes to infrastructure projects, the Chinese rarely employ local workers or use domestic suppliers, and when they do, they tend not to pass on any technical expertise or knowledge derived from practical experience. In addition, the West accuses China of flooding its target markets with cheap Chinese consumer goods (particularly textiles and toys), thereby forcing out local producers.

In recent years a significant number of expert studies on China's foreign policy in Latin America and Africa have attempted to scrutinize such criticisms.[39] However, evaluations of these research papers have yielded mixed results.

Findings regarding China's "petrodiplomacy" have been inconclusive. Admittedly, the PRC has managed to reduce somewhat its earlier one-sided dependence on oil imports from the Middle East due to its targeted shift toward African and Latin American markets, bringing about a more balanced mix of suppliers (see figure 3.5). But China imports only 18 percent of its total oil supplies from Africa, whereas the respective shares in the United States and the EU are 25 percent and 31 percent (see figure 3.6).

From a Chinese point of view, there are really no viable alternatives to African oil reserves, either in smaller countries (like Gabon and Equatorial Guinea) or in politically unstable states (such as Sudan and Nigeria), for most other known reserves are already firmly in the hands of Western multinationals (British Petroleum [BP], ExxonMobil, Royal Dutch Shell, and TotalFinaElf) or oil companies in the emerging economies (e.g., Petronas).

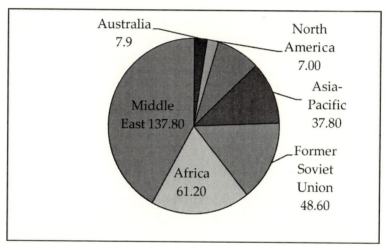

Figure 3.5. China's sources of crude oil imports, 2011 (in millions of metric tons).
Source: British Petroleum (BP) Statistical Review of World Energy 2012.

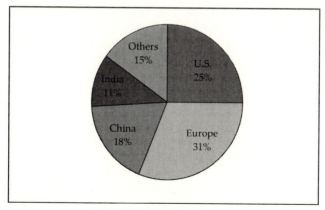

Figure 3.6. Countries to which African oil is exported, 2011.
Source: BP Statistical Review of World Energy 2012.

However, the stakes that Chinese state oil companies have acquired in African or Latin American fields (so-called equity oil) are not useful in serving China's raw materials needs directly. Admittedly, Chinese state investors are able to accept considerably greater risks (due to the extremely advantageous financing conditions offered by state-run banks), but Chinese activity in the African oil sector still mainly takes the form of a few joint ventures with other companies. In fact, most of the extracted oil is not shipped to the PRC; rather, it is sold on the world market, where it attracts higher prices.

Moreover, it would be wrong to regard the largest Chinese oil companies simply as an extension of the Chinese government. They evade supervision by state regulators in many business fields, compete heavily among themselves for market shares, and have no primary political aims.[40]

Even though the largest Chinese state-run companies in the energy and raw materials sectors and the state development banks dominate headlines in the West, they constitute only a limited proportion of the complex network of players involved in Chinese business in Africa and Latin America. The majority of active state-run companies are associated with provincial or city governments and have only become players in their own right after entering into partnerships with other players on a subnational level.[41]

As for the claim that China is exhibiting "neomercantilism" in its relations with Africa, in many cases we see that the Chinese government is simply following the well-known Japanese practice of complex countertrading that has been evident over the last several decades. The Chinese grant loans to African states such as Angola or Congo, which in turn are dependent on orders for Chinese machinery, or financial resources are given to African countries to finance infrastructure projects, which are then offset against oil and raw materials exports to China.[42]

Chinese private entrepreneurs are beginning to take over from the more visible large state-run companies. Unlike the latter, their hands are not tied by political mandates, and their activities are not subject to state supervision.[43] It is estimated that more than 5.5 million Chinese citizens are currently working outside China; of these, approximately 1 million are in Africa (around 50,000 in Sudan and Nigeria, respectively, and 40,000 in Zambia and Angola, respectively). The great majority of these expatriates are employees of Chinese companies who are sent to Africa to work on specific projects (it is not uncommon for them to remain after their contracts expire). In addition, a large number of Chinese traders (of anything from consumer goods to scrap metal), restaurant managers, and other adventurous entrepreneurs have decided to seek their fortunes and to expand their businesses in the much less strictly regulated African setting rather than at home, where the authorities supervise them closely and competition is fierce.[44] According to journalists' reports, the Chinese diaspora in some regions of Africa is so large that locals talk of an "invasion": more Chinese have moved to Africa during the last ten years than Europeans did during the last four centuries.

Outside observers frequently tend to overlook the sheer range of different players from China in Africa and Latin America. The media generally report on China's unquenchable thirst for oil, gas, ore, and minerals, but they oversimplify a much more complex situation: Chinese investment in Africa and Latin America is remarkably varied, ranging from huge fish farms off the coast of Namibia and extensive soybean cultivation in Brazil to cattle farming in Argentina and participation in South Africa's financial sector. In 2006, Chinese state enterprises (supported by diplomatic initiatives and loan schemes from the Chinese government) began to set up special economic zones (SEZs) in a number of African countries (they are already operational in Mauritius, Zambia, Angola, and Nigeria). Target countries expect Chinese companies to focus their investment activities in these SEZs while at the same time transferring organizational and technological expertise to local partners. The results of such initiatives have been extremely mixed: many of the announced zones are still in the preparatory or initial phases, despite having existed for five years.[45] In zones that are up and running, there is no uniformity in terms of the type of involvement by Chinese state-run companies: some run the project simply as a foreign arm of the company, with little involvement by the local workforce; others include African workers and make sure that expertise is passed on (knowledge transfer).

In many respects, the negative aspects of Chinese involvement in African and Latin American projects quite accurately reflects widespread Chinese business practices back home: disregard for legislation, corruption, the use of low-quality materials for large building projects, exploitation of raw materials, destruction of the environment (even in protected areas), and illegal operation of small mines without the necessary safety standards, resulting in a large number of serious industrial accidents as well as industrial conflicts due to unpaid wages.

But the admittedly often horrifying social and ecological downsides of Chinese investment in Africa and Latin America should not overshadow the positive aspects of China's involvement.[46] China has contributed to improving infrastructure in several African states, building hospitals, schools, roads, canals, dams, ports, and electric and cell phone networks. Many African states have praised Beijing's health diplomacy—China sent medical teams to forty-seven African countries and provided training programs to combat tropical maladies and HIV—as a positive contribution to preventing the spread of disease.[47]

It is significant that due to the Chinese demand for raw materials and trade advances, many African countries have been able to reenter the global economy after years of economic marginalization. The doubling of the average level of per capita income between 1997 and 2008 in countries south of the Sahara would not have been possible without the expansion of trade and investment from China. But Chinese investment has not reduced income and asset inequalities and susceptibility to local government corruption; in fact, on many counts these have actually grown worse.

It is also highly unlikely that the dynamism we have recently seen in Sino-African and Sino–Latin American relations will continue along the same path in the future or that, as some have speculated, a "South-South axis" will usher in a new phase in globalization and lead to "the South" being decoupled from demand in the most advanced industrial nations in "the North."

These future scenarios do not sufficiently take into account the already highly visible elements of conflict in China's relations with the two regions. Chinese citizens are increasingly becoming caught up in domestic strife (e.g., in Sudan, Nigeria, and Libya) and in some cases are being actively targeted. This has led to calls within China to protect PRC citizens abroad and, if necessary, to evacuate them, with the help of the navy or the air force, from areas of serious conflict, challenging Beijing's strict noninterventionist policy when it comes to the domestic affairs of other countries. Chinese businesspeople and diplomats also complain about widespread local problems in Africa, such as poorly qualified staff, low morale among workers, corruption, and bureaucratic hurdles.

In several of the democratic states in Africa and Latin America, the negative consequences of trade relations with China (loss of local jobs, exports of raw materials, environmental issues, corruption, and so forth) have already become electoral issues. For example, Brazil and Argentina have passed laws aimed at reducing the sale of land to foreigners and other regulations that indirectly affect Chinese investors who seek to purchase agricultural land so as to export agricultural products back to China. In addition, the WTO has received numerous complaints from Latin American countries regarding Chinese price dumping, and in 2010 and 2011 Brazil was one of the most vociferous opponents of China's monetary policy (see chapter 5).

In short, China's outward sympathy for Brazil, India, and South Africa, expressed in its sophisticated rhetoric on solidarity with the developing and emerging countries, is unable to mask the existing conflicts that are likely to increase over time.

"SOFT POWER" AS A NEW INSTRUMENT

The term "soft power" describes a nation's ability to promote its own strategic visions and interests, not through force (military power) or material incentives (economic power), but rather through the desirability of its ideas or the power of its national cultural, economic, social, or political systems.[48] The concept has also been applied to China's global presence: numerous publications have analyzed the country's distinctive understanding of soft power as part of its foreign policy strategy.[49]

A number of critical events since the mid-1990s have resulted in a broader Chinese diplomacy than that of the past. Demonstrations of military muscle in the South China Sea and aggressive demands on other Southeast Asian states to reduce their military cooperation with the United States were not only unsuccessful but actually fed the traditional mistrust of China. In contrast, the Chinese government has noted that the country's cooperative behavior during the Asian crisis of 1997–1998 resulted in a high level of approval and recognition, whereas US indifference and the role of the International Monetary Fund (IMF) received heavy criticism. (Observers have particularly recognized the stabilizing effect on the crisis of the Chinese refusal to devalue the yuan, despite substantial risk to China's export economy.)

Since then, the government has gone to great pains to turn about the worldwide mistrust of China by taking a softer approach. China now portrays itself as a reliable, cooperative, and friendly player in international relations—whereas the United States has increasingly lost face due to its military operations abroad and economic crises at home. Japan has also shed much of its former status and influence due to its prolonged economic stagnation.[50]

One concrete goal of this global "charm offensive" by the Chinese government is to win over ethnic Chinese living in other countries (known as "overseas Chinese").[51] The government hopes to persuade these foreign citizens to help boost China's reputation abroad by promoting Chinese culture and society in their host countries.

These goals reveal an instrumental understanding of the use of soft power. According to the Chinese logic, a country's appeal and influence are more than a matter of the outside world's recognizing a country's admirable and exemplary social and cultural achievements; Beijing regards these qualities as a result of a long-term active state project to create a positive international image.[52] The PRC hopes to correct misconceptions about China abroad and misunderstandings about China's intentions and behavior with the help of the global appeal of traditional Chinese culture (which Chinese politicians sell as being "not just Chinese, but global"), the success of its economic modernization program, and references to China's special national and cultural characteristics.

In order to improve its image abroad, particularly in the developing and emerging countries, Chinese diplomats have initiated a series of high-level international conferences in the PRC and have sent high-ranking delegations on extended trips abroad, especially to those countries that Western governments often shun. In addition, as a complement—or even an alternative—to existing global forums, China has organized numerous informal summits that include participation by international or regional opinion makers. One example is the Boao Forum for Asia, a regular, high-ranking regional forum very similar to the Davos World Economic Forum, which takes place in Hainan province.

Whereas states in the West (as well as Taiwan) have been cutting back on such programs, China is spending increasing sums on its external cultural policies. The Confucius Institutes (of which there were 387 in 108 countries and regions as of July 2012) host elaborate cultural events abroad in order to promote Chinese language and culture. The Chinese government has hired professional public relations and lobbying agencies to improve China's international image and reputation, and young volunteers (similar to American Peace Corps volunteers), doctors, and teachers are being sent abroad. The country has opened local universities up to foreigners, often with very generous scholarship programs for students from neighboring states. Over time, China has transformed from a net receiver of foreign aid into a donor, and it now also provides help abroad during major disasters.

According to many Chinese diplomats and political advisers, the differences between hard and soft power are fundamentally questionable. The promotion of soft power from the Chinese viewpoint corresponds to the logic of international competition over "comprehensive national strength." States, especially many Western countries, have always used cultural allure as a political instrument. The United States, some accuse, has hoped to bring about a "peaceful evolution" and cultural colonization ever since the days of the Cold War—particularly in countries that do not share Western/American values and ideas of government—with the aid of its culture and movie industry as well as its comprehensive programs of privatization and liberalization.

Against the backdrop of a politicized understanding of cultural exchange, documents issued by the Chinese government have made clear that the global popularization of Chinese culture is an integral part of its "overseas propaganda initiative." State-owned media companies (in particular Radio China International, China Central Television [CCTV], and Xinhua [New China] News Agency) play an important role in promoting China's soft power. The globally present Chinese media, supported by huge investments from the government, compete directly with global enterprises like CNN and Al Jazeera. Even though they remain in the background in operational terms, the Central Propaganda Department of the CCP very much determines their programming.

On certain fronts, China's soft-power strategy seems to be working: international opinion polls over the last decade have shown that China's popularity has increased in many countries in Africa, Latin America, and

Southeast Asia, at least on a temporary basis (of course, such polls depend on current events), and China is gaining increasing respect in terms of its economic development. This is even the case in countries with once strained relations with China, such as Vietnam and Russia, or nations that maintain close ties with the United States, such as Australia. China's popularity is also evident in the huge rise in the number of people studying Chinese language around the world, the number of foreign students in China (290,000 in 2011), and the improved social situation of overseas Chinese in Southeast Asia who can be open about their ethnic background. China's improved global standing is also apparent in the lively international discussions on the Chinese development model (known as the "Beijing consensus"), which has found a great deal of support in the developing and emerging countries as an alternative to Western models of development.[53]

However, there are still many basic limits to the use of Chinese soft power.[54] Despite admiration for China's culture and successful economic modernization, neither China's governance model nor its social system exerts a great global influence. For this reason, surveys on perceptions of China in the United States, Canada, Japan, and Western Europe are generally much more negative than those conducted elsewhere. In contrast to China, the United States is much more attractive to the outside world due to its pluralistic culture and advanced innovations, its music and movie industries, its educational and scientific institutions, and the global dominance of the English language.

China's image abroad is likely to remain volatile and conflicted as a result of the conspicuously dark side of China's modernization policies (pollution, social inequality, political repression, corruption, food and pharmaceutical scandals, and so forth). Chinese domestic policies will always have an effect on views of the PRC abroad, much more so than either its economic progress or its diplomatic initiatives.[55] The widespread international criticism of China's handling of the civil unrest in Tibet in the spring of 2008 and reprisals against government critics in 2010–2011 clearly reveals the boundaries of the government's charm offensive. Active soft-power strategies can only mask the fundamental differences of China's values and political order in relation to other nations and societies temporarily. These differences will come to the fore time and time again, possibly even with increased intensity, depending on the cause.

NOTES

1. Moore and Yang 2001.
2. Eisenman, Heginbotham, and Mitchell 2007.

3. Christensen 1996; Kim 1994; G. Segal 1995.
4. Sohn 2011; Zhang Yunling 2010; Zhao Suisheng 2011.
5. H. Wang and Rosenau 2009.
6. Kim 1999.
7. Gill 2007; Medeiros and Fravel 2003.
8. Davis 2011; Foot and Walter 2011; Gill 2007; Taylor 2008.
9. Branstetter and Lardy 2008; Lardy 2006.
10. Chan 2006; R. Lawrence 2008.
11. US Trade Representative 2011.
12. Foot and Walter 2011; Walter 2011; H. Wang and Rosenau 2009.
13. Heilmann and Schmidt 2010.
14. Sohn 2011; Zhang Yunling 2010; Zhao Suisheng 2011.
15. Devadason 2010.
16. Song and Yuan 2012; Zeng Ka 2010.
17. Devadason 2010.
18. Ba 2011; Emmers 2010; Goh 2011; Rosenberg 2010.
19. Valencia 1997.
20. Yuan Jing-dong 2010.
21. Gill 2007; Lampton 2008; Sohn 2011; Zhao Suisheng 2011.
22. Sutter 2012.
23. Kurlantzick 2007.
24. Buszynski 2012; de Lisle 2012; Fravel 2011; Goh 2011; Tonnesson 2010.
25. Swaine 2011.
26. International Crisis Group 2012.
27. Zhang and Tang 2005.
28. Foot 1998; Sutter 2012.
29. Alden 2007; Alden, Large, and Soares de Oliveira 2008; Sutter 2012.
30. Xinhuashe 2006; Zhonghua Renmin Gongheguo Guowuyuan Xinwen Bangongshi 2008.
31. Alden and Large 2011; He Wenping 2007; Li Anshan 2007.
32. Li Anshan 2007.
33. Gill, Huang, and Morrison 2007; Hofmann et al. 2007; Michel and Beuret 2009.
34. Jackson 2012.
35. Gallagher, Irwin, and Koleski 2012.
36. Eisenman and Kurlantzick 2006; Kleine-Ahlbrandt and Small 2008.
37. Dumbaugh and Sullivan 2005.
38. For more information on Sudan, see J. S. Morrison 2008.
39. Alden, Large, and Soares de Oliveira 2008; Brautigam 2009; Eisenman 2007; Ferchen 2011; Gonzalez-Vicente 2011; Michel and Beuret 2009.
40. Houser 2008; Kong Bo 2006; J. Lee 2012; Lieberthal and Herberg 2006; Payette and Mascotto 2012.
41. Alden 2007.
42. Brautigam 2009.
43. Alden and Large 2011; Gill and Reilly 2007; Gu Jing 2009.
44. Ma Mung 2008; Y. J. Park 2009.
45. Brautigam, Farole, and Tang 2010.

46. Alden 2007; Alden, Large, and Soares de Oliveira 2008; Brautigam 2009; de Grauwe, Houssa, and Piccillo 2012; Eisenman 2012; Ferchen 2011; Taylor 2009.
47. Thompson 2005.
48. Nye 2004, 2010; Nye and Wang 2009.
49. Breslin 2011; Ding Sheng 2008, 2010; Gill and Huang 2006; Lampton 2008; Li Mingjiang 2009a, 2009b; H. Wang and Lu 2008.
50. Zhang Wanfa 2007.
51. Kurlantzick 2007.
52. Breslin 2011.
53. Kurlantzick 2007; Ramo 2004.
54. Nye 2010; Nye and Wang 2009; Zhao Suisheng 2009.
55. Breslin 2011.

4

China's Security Policy

China's security policy is a core reason why the country's rise has met with so much mistrust abroad, especially in the United States. This chapter focuses on the role of the People's Liberation Army (PLA), Chinese threat perceptions and security-policy doctrines, China's military modernization program, and discussions of China as a military threat. Chapters 8 to 11, which cover regional and bilateral relations, will explain specific examples of tensions and conflicts in greater detail.

THE PLA AS A FOREIGN POLICY ACTOR

The role of the PLA in China's foreign relations is often subject to wild speculations and sweeping generalizations that do not stand up to empirical facts. This section attempts to address some of these misconceptions by highlighting that the PLA is not a "normal" actor; nor is it an independent or homogenous one.

The PLA—Not a "Normal" Actor

Unlike Western militaries, the PLA is not a nonpartisan national army. Rather, it is the last line of defense for China's one-party rule.[1] The close party-army relations rest on several pillars:

- *History:* After the Red Army's establishment in 1927, during the Chinese Civil War (1927–1937, 1945–1949) and the Anti-Japanese War

(1937–1945), and until the founding of the People's Republic of China (PRC) in 1949, the Chinese Communist Party (CCP) and army were hardly distinguishable and enjoyed a symbiotic relationship. In several cases of deep internal turmoil (the 1966–1976 Cultural Revolution, the 1989 Tiananmen demonstrations), the party called the PLA in to quell protests and to restore order.

- *The Chinese constitution, the National Defense Law, and the party constitution*: All these enshrine the basic principle that the PLA is under the "absolute leadership" of the party.
- *Military doctrine*: Consequently, the PLA's loyalty to the CCP has always been an important aspect of military doctrine. The first of the "new historic missions" that President Hu Jintao introduced to the PLA after assuming leadership of the Central Military Commission (CMC) in 2004 (see below) stressed once again the PLA's role "to provide an important guarantee of strength for the party to consolidate its ruling position."
- *Organizational setup*: The CCP penetrates the army apparatus by several means: at the top of the hierarchy there is the parallel party and state CMC (see below); party committees with extensive decision-making powers exist at every level in the command chain, from the company level upward; many noncommissioned officers (NCOs) and virtually all career officers (at least all officers above the rank of senior colonel) are CCP members; in all PLA units, functional organizations, and headquarters, political commissars supervise political reliability, party organization, and personnel affairs and share joint leadership with the military commanders.

The relation between state and party organs is critical to an understanding of the PLA's role in foreign policy (see chapter 2). National-level institutions charged with domestic security (the Ministries of State Security, Public Security, and National Defense) formally report to the State Council. But command authority over the PLA lies with the CMC. On paper there are two CMCs, one of the state (answering to the Standing Committee of the National People's Congress) and one of the Chinese Communist Party (answering to the party Politburo). But since both bodies have the same members, they operate as a unitary body under CCP leadership.

As the military's highest decision-making organ, the CMC sets and coordinates implementation of military and security policies and decides the size, course, and composition of the PLA. The CMC also makes and approves the decision to procure major weapons systems. It comprises one chairman, several vice chairmen, and currently eleven ordinary members, who, since 2004, represent all the service branches and the four General Departments. The Central Committee appoints all CMC members. Since

1989, the office of the CMC chairman has been in the hands of the incumbent general secretary of the CCP (Jiang Zemin, 1989–2004; Hu Jintao, 2004–2012; Xi Jinping, 2012–present); a second civilian is often a vice chairman being groomed to become the next CCP general secretary and thus CMC chairman (e.g., Xi Jinping in 2010–2012) or the new CCP general secretary if the outgoing general secretary clings to his CMC job for a transitional period (e.g., Jiang Zemin in 2002–2004).

The Ministry of National Defense is occasionally mistaken for the highest authority on military affairs; actually, it is a rather small ministry under the State Council headed by a senior military officer and tasked with foreign military liaising and civil-military relations. It is important to note that the Ministry of National Defense is outside the operational chain of command of the CMC, the four General Departments, and the services.[2] The minister's power depends on his standing in the CMC (during most of the last fifteen to twenty years, the minister was only an ordinary member of the CMC, not a vice chairman) and on his personal relationships with other senior leaders.

The PLA—Not an Independent Actor

In the first decades of the PRC, civilian and military elites were more intertwined than they are today. Most of the early CCP leaders were involved to some extent in the revolution and thus had close personal relationships with the armed wing of the party, and many uniformed officers had political responsibilities or had been promoted to their ranks due to their political reliability. However, since in the mid-1980s and especially after the mid-1990s, the party has pressured the PLA to become more professional—with less indoctrination and politicization and growing stress on accountability, technical and functional expertise, and corporate know-how. The resultant external orientation, decreased involvement in domestic politics, and withdrawal from business activities under Jiang Zemin and Hu Jintao led to more institutional autonomy for the PLA but increased jurisdictional/governmental oversight over the PLA (especially with regard to the budgetary process). Two other trends that reshaped army-party relations accompanied and reinforced this process: First, with the passing or retirement of the revolutionary generation, the informal civilian-military links were loosened. Second, the career paths of civilian and military elites diverged dramatically. Today they are educated in separate institutions, employed in different functional systems, and promoted mainly on the basis of technical skills and professional performance. Thus the armed forces and civilian leaders have little opportunity to interact or to cooperate until they advance to higher positions. This bifurcation of civil-military relations means that the civilian and military leaderships may develop different,

and perhaps contradictory, views on foreign policy and international security, whereby the PLA may have a distinctive esprit de corps whereas the
civilian elites lack an understanding of military affairs.[3] A broad body of
literature stresses that the increased professionalism of the PLA has made
routine civilian oversight more difficult, rendering the need for improved
coordination and communications (especially in crisis situations) between
government and military bodies all the more urgent (see below).[4] However,
this bifurcation has not led to the PLA becoming an independent actor in
Chinese politics with increased influence over Chinese foreign relations for
the following reasons:

- The bureaucratic disconnect between civilian and military leadership
  exists at the operational but not the strategic level.[5]
- Despite all the resources that have gone into its modernization, PLA
  officers have not gained additional political influence, as indicated
  by their representation on key party decision-making bodies (the Politburo and its Standing Committee, the Central Committee). Since
  1997 there has been no military officer on the Standing Committee
  of the Politburo, and among the full members of the Politburo, there
  have been only two generals (the two CMC military vice chairmen);
  since the Fourteenth Party Congress, PLA representation on the Central
  Committee has been constant, at around 20 percent.
- Contrary to popular belief, the PLA is not directly in charge of weapons programs. The production of domestic military weapons and
  equipment is in the hands of a civilian defense industry, which is
  coordinated and supervised by the (civilian) State Administration of
  Science, Technology and Industry for National Defense (SASTIND)
  under the auspices of the Ministry of Industry and Information Technology (MIIT).
- Caution is warranted regarding the role of the PLA in elite politics.
  Reports on factional struggles involving PLA officers, rarely based on
  facts, rely on poorly researched speculation from Hong Kong, Taiwan,
  or Falungong-affiliated media.[6]

In sum, there is no denying that the professionalization of the PLA has led
to a bifurcation of army-party relations. But we should not mistake this for
PLA independence. Quite the contrary, on many occasions (usually around
Army Day on August 1) the party has made clear that it rejects the so-called
three erroneous ideas—"depoliticization," "de-party-ification," and "na-
tionalization"—code words for the PLA to become a national army.[7] For
the PLA to become a truly independent actor, the Ministry of National Defense (led by a civilian) would have to be strengthened vis-à-vis the role of
the CMC; this would require bringing the army under the State Council and

breaking up party-army fusion as embodied in the CMC by, for example, restricting CMC membership to military officers.[8] None of this is currently in the offing.

The PLA—Not a Homogenous Actor

The PLA consists of the ground forces, the People's Liberation Army Navy (PLAN), the People's Liberation Army Air Force (PLAAF), the Second Artillery (PLASA), and their respective reserve units. The PLAN, PLAAF, and PLASA each have their own commanders and separate national-level headquarters in Beijing. The ground forces have no separate service headquarters. Geographically, the PRC is divided into seven military regions (Shenyang, Beijing, Lanzhou, Ji'nan, Nanjing, Guangzhou, and Chengdu). Under the CMC there are the four General Departments—the General Staff Department (GSD), the General Political Department (GPD), the General Logistics Department (GLD), and the General Armaments Department (GAD)—tasked with execution of CMC policies and directives. The GSD, led by the chief of staff, is responsible for (among other things) military operations, intelligence gathering, electronic warfare, communications and informationization, mobilization, education, and foreign affairs. The GPD is in charge of party supervision over the army (including the political commissar system), propaganda, discipline, and legal and personnel affairs. The provision of military supplies, infrastructure, health services, transportation, and financial matters (e.g., the remuneration of soldiers) rests with the GLD. The GAD was set up in 1998 as part of a large, comprehensive reform process during which the state-owned Chinese weapons industry was restructured and put under civilian control. The GAD manages the acquisition and maintenance of military weaponry and ammunition (including nuclear weapons) and supports facilities for weapons research, development, and testing, as well as China's nuclear test base and its civilian space program. As a whole, the four General Departments serve as national-level army headquarters with direct links to the military regions.[9]

As such an enormously large military, the PLA cannot be regarded as one monolithic entity; nor can it pursue a one-dimensional set of interests or speak with a unitary voice. It thus should come as no surprise that there are numerous examples of inter-PLA bureaucratic rivalries:

- The PLAAF, PLAN, and the PLASA have long resented the overrepresentation of the ground forces, whose officers dominate command of the General Departments and the military regions.
- Traditionally, the PLAAF and the PLASA have competed for control over China's nuclear weapons and over combined operations.

According to Western sources it is still unclear which of the two is responsible for air and missile operations.[10]

- The PLAN has gained disproportionally from China's modernization program. This is due at least in part to a powerful "naval lobby complex" consisting of the naval defense industry, academics, civilian authorities in charge of maritime issues, retired officers, and press commentators who successfully describe the PLAN as the "guardian of national sovereignty."[11]
- Even within the PLAN, different communities (e.g., submarine versus surface fleets; North Sea versus East Sea versus South Sea fleets) are lobbying for a bigger share of the pie and capabilities commensurate with their needs.
- The best case to illuminate the blurred lines between civilian and military projects is China's space program, with its plethora of involved actors: the GAD oversees the space program (research and development, manufacturing, and space-launching services); the State Council is involved with the "863 program," which offers extrabudgetary funding; and the Ministry of Science and Technology, MIIT, defense industry, Academy of Sciences, and civil universities each have their own interests. Obviously, instead of effective, streamlined, and integrated, organization, operational planning, and acquisitions are fragmented, and civilian oversight is only loosely coordinated.[12]

THREAT PERCEPTIONS AND MILITARY DOCTRINE

Threat Perceptions

The biennial white papers on national defense published since 1998 by the State Council Government Information Office (Zhonghua Renmin Gongheguo Guowuyuan Xinwen Bangongshi) outline the international challenges, risks, and threats that influence modern Chinese foreign and security policy (the last paper at the time of this writing appeared in 2010). The Western literature has analyzed these issues in great detail.[13] Although certain ideological concepts have remained the standard repertoire of foreign policy for decades (e.g., identifying the principal and secondary contradictions and criticizing hegemonism and alliances between the major powers), specific evaluations of China's current security situation have undergone significant changes.

Up to the end of the 1980s, the greatest fear in China was that a land war would break out or that there would be a nuclear attack by the Soviet Union or the United States, but this threat no longer exists today. Current Chinese analyses focus instead on identifying the general interactions between internal and external risks and traditional and nontraditional threats, which are regarded as the main challenges facing the nation. There are parallels to corresponding analyses of threats by Western nations, particularly with regard to nontraditional security challenges (i.e., terrorism, economic instability, climate change, nuclear proliferation, information security, natural disasters, infectious diseases, and transnational organized crime).

In addition to these common problems, a series of uniquely Chinese issues also influences the perception of risk to the future of the country—mainly, the often cited threats to national security and unity arising from separatist movements (as in Taiwan and Tibet) and from terrorism or religious extremism (in Xinjiang). The analyses also clearly express the Chinese fear that other nations may try to block China's rise to power, either alone or as part of an alliance, although this only refers to states whose "comprehensive national strength" is comparable to that of the PRC and with which China has experienced historical, ideological, or territorial conflicts, such as the United States, Japan, and India. China considers America its main economic and military rival, particularly with regard to the Taiwan problem. Since 2010 the so-called US pivot to Asia under President Barack Obama has met with much Chinese criticism, as Beijing interprets the improved relations between the United States and Indonesia, Malaysia, the Philippines, India, and others as encirclement and part of a US strategy to contain China's rise. In addition, Chinese leaders assert that the "US return to Asia" has emboldened China's neighbors to make more aggressive claims in territorial conflicts in the South and East China Seas.[14]

The white paper titled "China's National Defense in 2010" expresses concern over political forces abroad spreading mistrust of China (due in part to misunderstandings and in part to animosity), meddling in China's domestic affairs, and attempting to restrict China's room for maneuver. The PRC feels vulnerable because of its dependence on volatile market forces (commodities and financial markets) and the unpredictability of certain regional hot spots, such as the Korean Peninsula.

Military Doctrine

Chinese military doctrine is a peculiar blend of ancient Chinese thinking, Mao Zedong Thought as revealed in the lessons of the Chinese revolution, and the strategic guidelines put forward by the Chinese civilian military leadership (Deng Xiaoping, Jiang Zemin, and Hu Jintao in their capacities as chairmen of the CMC), often reflecting the war-fighting experiences of foreign powers. This section sketches each of these constituent elements to give an overview of the most prominent features of present-day Chinese military doctrine.[15] The section on the modernization of the PLA provides details about the more operational service-specific doctrines.

Ancient Chinese Thinking

Since the turn of the twenty-first century, classical Chinese military thinking, especially the teachings of Sun Zi, has experienced a political and military renaissance. The most important aspects that have become part of current Chinese military thinking are (1) taking advantage of an enemy's weaknesses (to evade where he is strong, strike where he is weak, not attack places that are fortified, and not defend places that are difficult to hold), and (2) using deception as a strategic and tactical means. The idea is to gain a favorable position by rendering the other party uncertain about one's intentions and capabilities. Such a deceptive strategy can be applied at the tactical, operational, and strategic levels and also with regard to foreign relations. Thus, Beijing often deliberately shrouds important elements of national-security decision making and strategic intentions in secrecy. In addition, China does not release much information about its possession of specific weapons, the organization and location of major units, the records of its main military exercises, or the exact breakdown of its defense budget spending (see below). Only recently has the PLA tried to increase transparency in order to improve its image by, in addition to publishing the official defense white papers, engaging in joint military exercises with foreign armies (most often in the Shanghai Cooperation Organization [SCO] context), implementing confidence-building measures, or holding regularized defense dialogues with other countries. Nonetheless, outside analysts still consider transparency inadequate.[16]

Mao Zedong Thought

The lessons of the Chinese revolution prior to 1949, as set out in Mao Zedong's concept of "people's war," were dominant in Chinese military thinking up to the end of the 1970s. According to this concept, a technologically superior invading enemy was to be lured into the Chinese landmass in order to bring the enemy to his knees by prolonged attrition and guerrilla warfare, with the help of China's enormous population instead of conventional forces with advanced weapons. This continental, defensive, man-centered doctrine reflected tensions with the United States (in the 1950s) and the Soviet Union (from the mid-1960s on), as well as Mao's belief that China had to prepare for an "early, major, and comprehensive war" that would be fought all over the globe with the use of nuclear weapons.

Following Mao's death and due to the impact of China's shortcomings in its border war with Vietnam in 1979, Deng Xiaoping changed the doctrine to "people's war under modern conditions," which held that Chinese defense should begin at China's borders, rather than in the hinterlands, and should rely more on mechanized, better-equipped forces and less on human factors. With the improvement in China's security situation after the mid-1980s, Deng played down the risks of an all-out major nuclear war; in 1985 he called on the Chinese military to prepare for "local [limited] wars" to be fought on China's periphery for limited (i.e., ethnic, religious, or political) objectives using nonnuclear weapons.

A series of wars successfully led by the United States (the First and Second Gulf Wars, the NATO campaign in the Balkans, and the conflict in Afghanistan) demonstrated to the PLA that it faced a "revolution in military affairs." The spectacular display of modern warfare, especially joint services operations (involving tanks, armored personnel carriers, infantry, and artillery) and combined arms (the interplay of ground and air services), the accuracy and impressive lethality of single weapons systems (e.g., long-range precision strikes by ballistic and cruise missiles, stealth aircraft, precision-guided munitions, antimissile and antiaircraft defense, and so forth), and the role of modern information technology for command, control, and intelligence made obvious the technological and doctrinal gaps between the most advanced militaries and the PLA. It was against this backdrop that from 1993 to 2002, Jiang Zemin, as chairman of the CMC, refined the doctrine, first to "local wars under high-technology conditions" and then (since 2002) to "local wars under informationized conditions." Local wars under high-technology conditions refers to armed conflicts that are restricted in their geographical scope, time frame, and objectives but are fought simultaneously in all battle dimensions (ground, air, sea, and space) around the clock under all weather conditions. They are also characterized by a reliance on sophisticated weapons, a high degree of mobility, joint logistics, and the towering role of command, control, communications, computers, intelligence, surveillance, and reconnaissance (C4ISR). The doctrine of local wars under informationized conditions, which the PLA has regularly debated in the biennial white papers since 2004, further refines the doctrine of local wars under high-technology conditions to stress informationization. Informationization basically involves digitalization and networking, meaning that all relevant military activities (planning, operations, surveillance, and communications) have to be digitized and integrated into a high-technology information infrastructure.[17] Mechanization and informationization are to be pursued in tandem, with the former to be concluded by 2020 and the latter by 2050.

Jiang Zemin's successor as CMC chairman, Hu Jintao (2004–2012), put his mark on military thinking by coming up with a list of "new historic missions" for the PLA to accomplish: to serve as an important source of strength for consolidating the party's ruling position, to provide a strong security guarantee during the important period of strategic opportunity for national development, to serve as forceful strategic support for safeguarding national interests, and to play an important role in upholding world peace and promoting common development.[18] Whereas the first and second missions more or less represent the classic tasks of upholding CCP rule and protecting core interests, the third mission represents defense of China's fledgling global interests—namely, protection of Chinese nationals abroad, of overseas investments, of Chinese assets in cyberspace and outer space, and of the sea lines of communication (the Indian Ocean and the Straits of Hormuz, Malacca, Sunda, and Lombok) through which China's imports of resources have to pass.[19]

In sum, some aspects of Chinese military doctrine set it apart from other militaries. This is especially true for the Maoist concept of "active defense," which applies to all services and serves as the highest-level strategic guidance for all PLA activities.[20] According to official statements, active defense means that the PRC, in pursuit of a defensive strategy, has no intention of starting any war to achieve its strategic goals. At the same time, however, offensive measures may be employed operationally and tactically in order to prevent or defuse crises or to stem any conflict over China's national sovereignty by launching surprise attacks against key enemy positions, bringing down intelligence, command and control systems, interrupting enemy logistics, and destroying the enemy's fighting spirit by ensuring a high number of casualties at the start of fighting.

Also going back to Mao Zedong is the notion of "asymmetric warfare." After the collapse of the Soviet Union, and thus after the end of the strategic triangle, it became clear that the United States would be China's main strategic rival in the Asia-Pacific. Chinese leaders knew that the PRC would not stand a chance against the United States in a head-on arms race. Hence, China invested vast resources to leapfrog development (to make technological leaps by relying on existing technology available on the international market) and quickly gain niche capabilities, that is, weapons and strategies for asymmetric warfare. The PLA's primary aim in this scenario is to exploit the vulnerability and weaknesses of enemy forces and to establish niche capabilities in the areas where it is the strongest. The best-known and most debated component of asymmetric warfare is what the Chinese call "counterinterventionism," or what the United States refers to as "antiaccess/area denial" (A2/AD). These are efforts to discourage adversaries in a conflict involving core interests from entering a given theater or to restrict freedom of action within an existing theater by threatening to inflict unacceptable harm.[21] Of course, the central focus of counterinterventionism is the United States, which is to be prevented at all costs from complying with its bilateral or regional mutual defense agreements—particularly with Taiwan or its Southeast Asian allies—should a major armed conflict erupt. Never again shall the United States be able to thwart Chinese ambitions for a military solution in the Taiwan Strait as it did in 1996 when it dispatched two aircraft carrier groups to the vicinity of Taiwan. To this end, the PLAN, PLAAF, and

PLASA are expected to match US weaknesses with their own strengths (for more details on the necessary capabilities, see below).

The decades-old Maoist concept of people's war is most prominently adapted to present-day use in the form of cyber warfare as a means of asymmetrical warfare. Civilians with advanced information technology skills from all sectors of Chinese society shall be mobilized and drafted into reserve and militia units to wage cyber attacks alongside the official army against foreign computer networks in the event of a major international conflict. These measures are meant to be accompanied by the so-called three warfares: psychological, media, and legally justifiable warfare techniques, such as influencing popular opinion, widely distributing film and photographic material, and using international legal standards as justification for military action.

Viewed in general terms, recent Chinese military doctrine shows a considerable potential to carry out offensive military operations. However, Beijing deliberately keeps the motives, nature, and goals of possible military strikes secret. Thus far, the PLA's military strategy does not involve projecting its military might in a global context. It generally focuses efforts on possible regional conflict areas, thereby safeguarding Chinese sovereignty or territorial integrity (first and foremost with regard to Taiwan) and protecting strategic shipping routes.

MODERNIZATION OF THE PLA

Bringing the PRC's armed forces up to date was not a priority in the PRC's "four modernizations" program until the early 1990s. From today's perspective, it is remarkable that PLA leaders put up with the low priority of defense modernization for so long without offering much opposition to the civilian leadership. Since the 1990s, however, the military leadership has managed to secure considerable funding increases for its forces. We can identify five drivers behind the modernization program: the 1989 Tiananmen demonstrations, the demise of communism in Eastern Europe, the 1991 collapse of the Soviet Union, the 1991 Gulf War, and the 1996 Taiwan Strait crisis, all of which either called into question regime survival and/or demonstrated the technological, doctrinal, and organizational backwardness of the PLA.

As a result, over the last two decades state funding for the army has seen double-digit growth rates. For years, however, the exact size of the Chinese defense budget has been the subject of great speculation. Western governments and think tanks (see table 4.1) are in agreement that estimates of actual Chinese defense expenditures are far higher than the official figures suggest. For example, the official 2011 defense budget, according to the

Chinese government, was US$91.5 billion. The highest Western estimates, however, provide figures as high as US$180 billion. As table 4.1 shows, independent sources (for instance, the Stockholm International Peace Research Institute [SIPRI]) suggest that actual Chinese defense spending may be 40 to 50 percent higher than Beijing officially acknowledges.

The Chinese government either explains these high growth rates in the military budget as primarily a result of the huge number of military personnel (including militias and reserve forces) or claims that the figures are actually relatively low in relation to the country's gross domestic product (GDP), as compared to comparable figures for other nations (in China, the military budget is less than 2 percent of GDP; in the United States, it is more than 4 percent). These growth rates may also reflect China's strategic insecurity as well as the increasing number of nontraditional security missions abroad.

The reasons for such uncertainty regarding China's actual military expenditures are the numerous means of funding that exist in addition to the official defense budget.[22] For example, the strategic rocket forces (including the space program) have their own budget, and the Chinese State Council buys weaponry purchased abroad directly. Funding for military research-and-development projects or the maintenance of paramilitary units comes from the budgets of other departments or provincial governments, and

Table 4.1.   China's Military Expenditures: Official Figures and Unofficial Estimates

Year	Official PRC Figures (¥ Billions)	Change from Previous Year (%)	SIPRI (¥ Billions)	SIPRI (US$ Billions)	US DoD (US$ Billions)
1992	37	14.4	68.9	21.9	n/a
1994	55	29.3	86.9	19.4	n/a
1998	93	15	150	25.9	n/a
2002	171	17.6	262	45.9	45–65
2003	185	9.6	288	49.8	50–70
2004	220	15.3	331	55.2	n/a
2005	245	12.6	379	62.1	–90
2006	284	14.7	452	72.9	70–105
2007	351	17.8	546	84.1	97–139
2008	418	17.6	638	92.7	105–50
2009	473	15.3	752	110.1	> 150
2010	532	7.5	820	121.0	> 160
2011	601	12.6	923	129.3	120–80
2012	670	11.2	n/a	n/a	n/a

Note: ¥ = Chinese yuan.
Sources: Ministry of Finance of the PRC; SIPRI Military Expenditure Database; US Department of Defense, *Military Power of the PRC* (beginning from 2002); *White Papers on China's National Defense* (beginning from 1998).

the budget for the People's Armed Police (PAP) is also not included in the defense budget. This is nothing out of the ordinary, however—the costs for American nuclear forces, for example, come out of the budget of the US Department of Energy, not the Department of Defense, as one might expect. In addition, the Chinese government has had to compensate the PLA for its 1998 retreat from business activities; the costs of modernization of the PLAN and PLAAF are technology, and therefore capital, intensive, as are the maintenance and training costs; and indeed a high degree of spending goes to the higher remuneration and better social services for the armed forces (e.g., PLA officers are now often better paid than employees in state-owned enterprises). There is no doubt that the PLA, with the help of the double-digit growth of the economy over the last thirty years, now has much more cash at its disposal than ever before, but as leading PLA expert Dennis Blasko has made clear, this funding is still relatively modest when compared to the PLA's overall size or with that of other militaries.[23]

The financial resources that flow into the military are mainly used to fund an extensive modernization program, which, according to official reports, has the primary aim of completing mechanization of the army by 2020 and informatization of the army by 2050, including the adaptation of doctrine; the streamlining of force structure; the improving of human resources in terms of recruitment and promotion; the upgrading of equipment, weapon systems, and logistics; the reform of military training and exercises; the development of indigenous innovation in the defense industry; and the procurement of homemade weapon items.[24] This modernization program is broad and deep, affecting all combat arms in every dimension.[25]

The general trend in modernization has been to emphasize quality over quantity. Thus, four major rounds of personnel reductions (1985, 1997, 2003, and 2005) cut the size of the PLA by 1 million, 500,000, 200,000, and 130,000, respectively, bringing its overall size down from more than 4 million to the current 2.3 million.[26] Also, war-fighting systems have been significantly reduced in number and replaced in part with modern equipment. As prescribed by military doctrine, the focus is on investments in A2/AD niche capabilities and the development of a cutting-edge C4ISR infrastructure (Chinese military writings often refer to this as the "system of systems") for real-time battlefield awareness (communications among one's own troops and detection and tracking of enemy forces). So-called force multipliers (i.e., advanced tactical mobility, personnel training, and joint logistics) have also been the subject of improvements. Particular focus is placed on modernizing the defense industry and on military research and development. More than four hundred thousand scientists and technicians are currently working directly on military research projects, and the PLA also maintains about three hundred research institutions and ten universities. The thinking behind this is that modern (particularly space-based) command, control, communications, reconnaissance, and surveillance capacities should primarily be homegrown rather than purchased from other countries. By buying modern weapons, developing indigenous innovation and technology, and obtaining know-how through illegal channels, such as industrial espionage and intelligence operations, China has been able to cut costs and leapfrog rather than having to develop every component on its own. With regard to education and recruitment of troops, the PLA has endeavored to downsize and modernize the military academy structure, revamp curricula, improve research at military academies, recruit more officers from civilian colleges, and set up a program to better qualify the NCO corps and support and logistics personnel. Another focus of modernization has been to overcome deficiencies in training. For much of its history, the PLA trained mainly in summer and spring, during daylight and good weather conditions.[27] Today's training in all services is much more realistic (artillery live-fire exercises, multiservice exercises, and night and minimum-altitude flights also during bad weather) with more use of simulations and computer war games. In addition, training now includes joint maneuvers abroad (especially in the SCO context) and large-scale drills (involving brigades rather than divisions), and it is more contingency based (submarine and antisubmarine exercises, amphibious landing attacks).[28] Air force pilots are now said to practice about two hundred hours per year, approaching Western standards, as compared to the previous practice time limit of only about twenty-four hours.[29]

Apart from these general trends, specific features of modernization relate to the PLA service branches.

PLA Ground Forces

The ground forces, which have profited the least from the modernization program, accordingly have received the least international attention.[30] But due to their prominent role during the Chinese revolution, World War II, and the Korean War (1950–1953), the ground forces have dominated the PLA. Their main mission is still to guarantee domestic stability by providing backup for the PAP antiriot units and to defend China's borders. As a result, some of the best PLA troops are stationed near Beijing or close to the Sino-Korean border. However, to some extent, the role of the ground forces has now changed. They are no longer static, inward looking, or exclusively defense oriented, as they were until the late 1980s. Today the tasks of the ground forces, including counterterrorism and antiseparatist missions, are more outward looking, with the intention of improving offensive, long-reach capabilities.[31] In UN peacekeeping operations, the ground forces take part with engineers, logisticians, and medical personnel rather than with other combat units.

In the course of the modernization program, the ground forces shed the largest number of troops; their size now totals about 1.25 to 1.5 million soldiers. Traditional large infantry units unsuited for combined warfare have been turned into smaller, mechanized units, with particular emphasis on special-purpose units and airborne troops. Thus the number of group armies has been reduced from twenty-four to eighteen, and infantry divisions have been trimmed from ninety to twenty-six, whereas the brigade level was increased from seven to about thirty.[32] These smaller force units are supposed to be more versatile so as to be more readily moved across military regions to operate wherever necessary along the borders, or in cases of natural disasters, anywhere in the country. According to the logic of improved mechanization, the ground forces have received more modern battle tanks, artillery with increased firepower and accuracy, armored personnel carriers for joint arms warfare (interplay of tanks and infantry), and more sophisticated air defense systems with improved radar, command-and-control devices, and advanced surface-to-air missiles of various ranges.

PLA Navy

Probably the best-researched part of China's modernization program is the development of the PLAN, probably because it has been the main beneficiary of all services.[33]

The PLAN's traditional task was near-coast defense—that is, keeping the enemy away from China's coast and protecting the nation's sovereignty in the "near seas" (the Yellow Sea and the East China and South China Seas).[34] Today the PLAN is assigned three main missions:[35] (1) It must prepare for a Taiwan contingency in which it might be involved in a sea blockade or an amphibious invasion of the island, and it must play an important role in China's A2/AD strategy vis-à-vis the United States, namely, in preventing the United States from coming to Taiwan's support with its naval assets. Therefore, the PLAN has aptly been dubbed an "antinavy."[36] (2) According to the new historic missions, the PLAN must perform an increasingly nontraditional role: protecting resource supplies that go through several pirate-infested and/or internationally disputed waters (the Straits of Lombok, Malacca, and Sunda). China's participation in the UN-led Gulf of Aden antipiracy operations since 2008 can be viewed in this context. (3) With increasing numbers of Chinese citizens living and working in unstable regions around the world, there has been mounting national pressure to use the PLAN to assist expatriates in times of turmoil in their host countries.[37] This was prominently the case in 2011 in Libya when China dispatched a frigate to the Mediterranean to escort a civilian ship with evacuated Chinese nationals on board. Other missions also in the context of so-called military operations other than war (MOOTW) come in the form of humanitarian assistance, disaster relief operations, and naval diplomacy (e.g., port calls outside Asia by Chinese hospital ships to provide medical assistance).[38] Thus, the PLAN has been given new responsibilities and assigned to new fields, and it has profited from the fact that it is a versatile branch that can perform multiple roles—from providing a sea-based strategic deterrent to merely "showing the flag" abroad. However, one thing not called for by even the most hawkish PLAN planners is creation of a "global Far Oceans blue-water navy," as the United States has today or the Soviet Union had before 1991, because of the costs and political liabilities.

The modernization has included all of the PLAN's 255,000-strong five service arms (submarine, surface, naval aviation, coastal defense, and marine corps), but with discernible focal points. These begin with attempted improvements in space-based systems for navigation, sensing, and communications, especially for China's submarine fleet. Submarines are considered indispensable as antiship missile delivery platforms, and massive efforts have been made to commission new models (either imported from Russia or indigenously developed) that are quieter, harder to detect, faster, and able to remain submerged for longer periods.[39] China now has about sixty submarines, the majority of which are diesel-powered attack submarines, and less than a handful of nuclear-powered ballistic missile submarines (SSBN) that can carry nuclear intercontinental missiles. Since the mid-1990s the PLA has also modernized its arsenal of surface vessels (destroyers, frigates, and missile patrol boats), in part with stealth capabilities and amphibious landing platforms. The commission of China's first aircraft carrier (the *Liaoning*) in September 2012, bought from Ukraine in 1998 and refitted at Chinese shipyards, attracted much attention abroad. We should not overrate this move, however. The carrier is smaller than its US counterparts, it has fewer aircraft on board, and due to technical restrictions, it cannot launch heavier aircraft.[40] Since years of ongoing training as well as several aircraft carrier strike groups are required so that at least one carrier is always operational at sea, for the time being the *Liaoning* is of only limited military use. Instead, it confers prestige (China was the last of the five permanent UN Security Council members to have such a carrier), and it will probably be used primarily for training purposes so that the PLAN can master the technological challenges to produce one or two newer, more capable indigenous carriers in the future.[41]

All in all, with regard to the number of new vessels commissioned since the 1990s, China now lags behind only the United States and Russia, and with about 220 surface vessels and submarines, the PLAN now boasts the largest navy in Asia.

PLA Air Force

Hardly less impressive than the modernization of the PLAN has been the modernization of the PLAAF.[42] First, the PLAAF has air defense responsibility for all of China, in particular for the Beijing area.[43] For a long time the PLAAF was considered a supporting force for the ground forces. Only after the impressive performance of the US Air Force in the 1991 Gulf War was the PLAAF upgraded from a mere support force to a strategic one, from defense only (i.e., defense against air strikes) to both offense and defense missions (with equal importance in strikes against enemy forces). The PLAAF is assigned a special role in a Taiwan scenario whereby it is to gain air superiority so as to assist PLAN and ground force units. Like the PLAN, the PLAAF is now also tasked with search-and-rescue and disaster relief operations.

As part of its modernization program, the PLAAF's manpower was cut by 25 percent to about 300,000 or 330,000, and its fighter force was reduced by half. Modernization efforts focused on better paratrooper capabilities, air defense systems (both are under the PLAAF rather than the ground forces), airborne early warning and control aircraft, and state-of-the-art radar systems with air-to-air guided missiles as well as precision-guided ammunition, instead of older unguided gravity bombs. Until several years ago, the PLAAF either relied on Russian imports or produced Soviet-licensed technology. Now, through extensive reverse engineering of Russian aircraft, China is increasing its share of domestically produced fighter aircraft, and it has even been able to test two separate prototypes of stealth fighters, thus far a technology mastered only by the United States. To highlight the PLAAF's advances, it is illustrative to compare its capabilities over the years.[44] In 2000 the PLAN and the PLAAF possessed thirty-two hundred fighter aircraft. Of these, only seventy-five were "fourth generation," and twenty-one were "third generation." The remainder was based on outdated standards of Soviet origin from the 1950s. By contrast, in 2010 the PLAAF operated sixteen hundred fighter aircraft, of which less than about one-quarter were "fourth generation."

PLA Second Artillery

With regard to the modernization of missiles, it is important to differentiate between conventional and nuclear forces.[45] Before the 1990s the PLASA's main mission was confined to nuclear deterrence. Thus, its goal was "assured retaliation"—that is, to ensure the survivability of its small nuclear missile force in case of attack so as to be able to use it (or its remaining parts) for retaliation.[46] In principle, this deterrent stance has not changed. China abides by its "no first-use" policy (vowing not to use nuclear weapons unless attacked first with nuclear weapons by another country) and on several occasions has declared that it rejects any nuclear arms race with other nations.

China's conventional missile force was only recently discovered to be an important strategic asset.[47] In general, conventional ballistic missiles and land-attack cruise missiles are increasingly regarded as a possible cornerstone to gain control over a contested maritime area. Again, this has much to do with the A2/AD vis-à-vis the United States: by fielding a massive conventional missile force with the potential to strike US assets at sea or US bases in the western Pacific, Beijing will reduce the prospect of US intervention in conflicts on China's periphery. The one thousand to twelve hundred short-range ballistic missiles that the PRC has stationed within the reach of Taiwan not only have an operational value but also were conceived by Chinese military planners to be cost-effective weapons of intimidation and deterrence against Taiwanese independence.

Given these strategic considerations, the modernization of China's conventional missile arsenal prizes precision-strike capabilities with higher accuracy, an expanded infrastructure, and more sophisticated warheads with greater destructiveness.[48] China also aims to diversify its missiles depending on their respective purposes. It has a large arsenal of ground-launched, ship-launched, and submarine-based ballistic and cruise missiles to hit short-range, medium-range, and intercontinental targets. Its nuclear missile forces are being updated to improve its second-strike capabilities by deploying better delivery systems (road-mobile, solid-fuel missiles instead of the older silo-based, liquid-fuel missiles) with more accurate and effective warheads and to make the existing inventory more "survivable" (by hardening, hiding, or dispersing the launch sites). According to the *Bulletin of the Atomic Scientists* and the Union of Concerned Scientists, China today has about 140 to 150 land-based nuclear missiles, of which about 70 can reach US territory and 40 can reach the continental United States.[49] Since each Chinese missile most probably can carry only one warhead, the total number of Chinese warheads (including sea-based warheads) is estimated to be about 240, roughly the same number as in the United Kingdom but far fewer than the United States (8,000) and Russia (10,000) have at their disposal.[50]

Space, Cyber, and Electronic Warfare

Although they do not form a distinct branch like the ground forces, the PLAN, the PLAAF, and the PLASA, space, cyber, and electronic warfare are dealt with extensively due to their potential role in China's concept of "asymmetric warfare."[51] After PLA planners analyzed US war performance since the 1990s, they concluded that US superiority was rooted in precision-strike capabilities and joint operations based on advanced information collection, processing, and transmission by integrated computer networks and space-based assets. To win a high-tech war, it is vital to deny enemy information, disrupt enemy communications, and gain informational dominance or superiority.[52] With the United States most vulnerable in its C4ISR installations, Chinese military analysts believe China could paralyze the United States and achieve a quick victory at low cost simply by hitting the "brains" and "nerve centers" of US military systems via antispace operations, electronic warfare, and computer network operations.[53] Gaining such mastery calls for striking first, including preemptive and surprise attacks against enemy C4ISR installations at the beginning of operations. Computer network attacks are attractive not only because they involve lower costs and are technologically less challenging, covert, and highly destructive operations but because they also convey a high degree of deterrence. They can be used as an A2/AD device to deter an opponent from entering into armed conflict with China simply by signaling that China is capable of inflicting unacceptable costs.[54]

As a result, China has invested heavily in its space program, which is also a symbol of its competition for comprehensive national strength. The program has a two-pronged approach: on the one hand, it will provide a means to protect China's space assets; on the other, it will enable the PRC to attack an adversary's space assets by blinding or jamming satellite sensors and disrupting GPS signals (so-called soft kill attacks) or to take down enemy satellites with kinetic kill vehicles (so-called hard kill attacks).[55] For the purpose of reconnaissance, providing high-resolution images day and night, independent of weather conditions, China has launched more than thirty advanced remote-sensing satellites. In addition, data-relay satellites for communications between satellites and between satellites and the ground, as well as navigation and positioning satellites, have been put into service. Due to the rapid extension of its manned space program since 2000, China has been able to establish an infrastructure for space-launching facilities and vehicles, as well as ground equipment and support items that can also be used for military purposes.

An integral part of Chinese cyber warfare in times of peace consists of computer reconnaissance (i.e., infiltrating foreign computer systems to identify vulnerabilities and to access critical information, all the while without disrupting the systems). In combat situations, computer network operations will not only target enemy military facilities (command-and-control centers, radar sites, air defense installations, antiship missile systems, and so forth) but also hit civilian networks, financial centers, utilities, logistic hubs, and transportation facilities.

IS CHINA A MILITARY THREAT?

A large body of literature on China's foreign relations has focused on the question of whether China should be considered a military threat, discussing the issue from various perspectives. Some scholars proceed from the systematic theories of great power rivalry to predict a looming military confrontation with China.[56] Others analyze the potential for military conflict by focusing on the military balance of power within Asia or among the main contestants (China versus the United States, Taiwan, Japan, and so forth).[57] Still others attempt to determine potential triggers or concrete contingencies for an armed conflict.[58] In addition, a voluminous literature on Chinese decision making in crisis situations includes studies using a strategic culture approach or quantitative analyses to identify patterns of Chinese use of force.[59] These studies overlap with other analyses of Chinese behavior in territorial disputes.[60]

These studies have in common their aim to identify variables in order to come to grips with whether or not China poses a threat, and if it does, how great and to whom. This section presents the most important of these variables. They mirror intentions, capabilities, and actual behavior as presented above. It is striking that discussion of a possible "China threat" is a particular concern among US authors; discourse on China as a strategic challenge is almost nonexistent in Europe because European countries do not have strategic interests in the region.

From a Chinese point of view, any allegation of a Chinese threat is unreasonable and unjustified. Furthermore, most Chinese analysts and decision makers consider the China threat theory a sinister plot from abroad (especially the United States) to contain China's rise. When looking at official Chinese statements, outside observers are overwhelmed by Beijing's "peace-loving rhetoric," such as its concepts of "peaceful rise, peaceful coexistence, peaceful development, and a harmonious world." At the Eighteenth Party Congress in November 2012, outgoing CCP general secretary Hu Jintao stressed in his congress report that building a strong national defense and powerful armed forces is commensurate with China's international standing and only intended to meet the needs of China's security and development interests. According to Hu, China's national defense is defensive in nature, and its armed forces have always been a staunch force upholding world peace.[61] Hu Jintao's party congress report thus echoes the 2011 peaceful development white paper, which states that the purpose of China's military modernization is to safeguard sovereignty, security, territorial integrity, and the interests of national development and that the PRC's defense expenditures are appropriate and moderate. Therefore, China does not pose a threat to other countries and adheres to the principle of not attacking others unless it is attacked first. Peaceful development, according to the white paper, is necessitated by history, a strategic choice that follows Chinese cultural tradition and reflects the deeply ingrained Chinese peace-loving character.[62]

Chinese Intentions and Capabilities

Analysts of Chinese military modernization have identified the following strengths against China's past record and in comparison with other countries:

1. China has considerably improved its niche capabilities to wage asymmetric warfare. It has strengthened its information warfare capabilities so as to be able to cause harm to the C4ISR infrastructure in the United States and to impede or complicate American military operations. The PLAN now commands a capable conventional submarine force, and its new naval base on Hainan Island may enable it to project force into the South China Sea. The PLASA has at its disposal one of the world's largest and most sophisticated arsenals of short- and medium-range ballistic and cruise missiles.

2. China's defense industry has made impressive improvements in its capacity to mass-produce indigenous fourth-generation fighter aircraft and modern warships. Although still not regarded as matching US standards, it probably already eclipses Russia's defense industry.

3. This trend is set to continue with China's integration into the global economy, which will allow the country easy access to cutting-edge technologies (information and computer technology; civil aircraft research-and-development and production capacities).

4. The PLA already constitutes a threat to Taiwan, which, judging by its doctrine, modernization priorities, troop structure, and tactical exercises, is the focus of all scenarios that the army has been trained to tackle thus far. The balance of military power has shifted visibly in favor of the PLA. This is due to the concentration of troop units and the number of short-range missiles (currently around twelve hundred) stationed along the coast facing Taiwan, but it is also the result of obstacles to modernization in Taiwan.

Notwithstanding these improvements and newly established strengths, the PLA also faces a number of ongoing shortcomings and weaknesses:

1. The PLA profited from the rapidly rising defense budget, but its resources pale when compared with those in the United States, which in 2012 had military expenditures of almost US$703 billion (for the official defense budget and spending on the war on terror), accounting for about 45 percent of global arms spending compared to China's paltry 5.5 percent.

2. Chinese modernization does not take place in a vacuum.[63] With its unmatched resources, the United States is able to neutralize Chinese niche capabilities (e.g., with national and regional missile defense or

antisubmarine warfare). In addition, its allies are also modernizing their armed forces, also to counter Chinese assets.

3. Despite progress in indigenous weapons development and production, the Chinese armed forces (especially the PLAAF) still depend heavily on imports of weapons and components (e.g., modern aero engines, avionics, and flight control systems). Because access to Western imports is blocked due to the weapons embargo still in place, China has had to turn to Russia, which appears more reluctant than in the past to provide modern technology because of strategic considerations and fears of nurturing a future competitor in global armament markets.[64]

4. The record of Chinese military modernization of key war-fighting systems remains at best checkered. Less than one-third of its tanks, half of its infantry fighting vehicles, and less than one-quarter of its artillery systems are modern (i.e., developed and deployed within the last fifteen years), and ground forces are supported by a very limited number of transport and attack helicopters.[65] In the PLAAF only some three hundred out of seventeen hundred fighter aircraft are modern, aerial refueling and strategic airlift capabilities are inadequate, and a heavy long-range bomber fleet is still lacking. Due to insufficient transport aircraft, larger troop movements still have to rely on rail transportation, as was evident during the Sichuan earthquake in 2008.[66] Only 25 percent of the PLA's vessel inventory is modern, and even its modern submarines are considered relatively noisy and inert.[67] The PLAN, in contrast to the Japanese Maritime Self-Defense Forces, is generally out for only brief cruises or exercises and has no experience with larger formations in distant waters.[68] The PLASA has no expertise in synchronizing mass launchings of missiles or coordinating missile attacks with simultaneous PLAAF operations.

5. In general, new, modern types of weapons sit next to weapons that are decades old, creating huge problems for logistics and maintenance as well as for training.[69]

6. "Jointness," the integration of weapons systems and the service branches under a unified command, still remains more a theoretical concept and an aspiration than a reality.[70]

7. This is also true for information gathering and processing, which still face considerable obstacles.[71] (Bad) information is a "controlled commodity," technical information is only disseminated on a "need-to-know" basis, and even within the military system, in many organizational subsystems (e.g., command, operations, logistics, intelligence, and so forth) information passes only up and down the hierarchy rather than horizontally.[72]

8. The human factor also plays an important role at the operational and tactical levels.[73] Traditional Chinese conservatism in thought and

behavior, a preference for the status quo, and the tendency of individuals to shy away from autonomous, risky decisions and to pass them up to higher levels in the hierarchy all run counter to modern war-fighting requirements for ad hoc, swift, and responsible decision making under shifting circumstances.

9. Finally, the PLA has a stunning lack of war-fighting experience. Its last combat situation was with Vietnam over disputed islands in 1988, its last land combat was with Vietnam in 1979, its last major air combat occurred during the 1958 Jinmen crisis, and no joint operations have taken place since the 1954–1955 joint operations in the Taiwan Strait. This is all the more problematic for the PLA since in peacetime its military structure is based on the seven military regions, whereas integrated command structures transcend the service branch boundaries only in wartime. What is worse, although party control over the army at every level promotes stability and loyalty, during wartime or periods of crisis, this might turn out to be a liability.[74]

Apart from these general remarks on Chinese capabilities and intentions, there is special concern about the threatening aspects of Chinese cyber warfare and the PRC's nuclear forces, both of which are discussed below.

China: A Cyber Threat?

Several reports in the United States have expressed concern about Chinese cyber-warfare capabilities.[75] Some media have even discussed a potential "second Pearl Harbor" or another "9/11" in the United States. Chinese officials retort that China does not sponsor hacking, that its cyber strategy is only defensive in nature, and that China itself has been a victim of cyber attacks.

Indeed, a couple of worrying trends can be identified:

1. There are clear indications in Chinese doctrinal articles and military exercises that computer network operations are considered part of an "informational confrontation." This means that striking the enemy's information networks and infrastructure (if necessary, preemptively) is fundamental to Chinese strategic thinking.[76] Organizationally, the PLA under the GSD has set up units for integrated network electronic warfare.

2. That China has the necessary hardware and software seems beyond doubt, given its state-of-the-art commercial information technology industry, generous funding for academic civilian and military research, and access to dual-use Western cutting-edge technology.

3. There have been countless hacking incidents over the last several years (e.g., several against US government institutions, against CNN after it covered the 2008 riots in Tibet, and against the Nobel Prize website after the Nobel Peace Prize was awarded to Liu Xiaobo in 2010). Especially during diplomatic crises over territorial disputes, so-called patriotic hacker groups have attacked websites of foreign governments, banks, companies, or universities. Since these attacks sometimes require a level of coordination and resources that only a state can provide, outside observers speculate that the Chinese government has at least tolerated, if not supported, these hackers, perhaps as way to provide valves for nationalist, dissatisfied citizens.[77]

4. In addition, many credible press releases report that the Chinese military regions are recruiting hackers from the huge pool of more than 500 million Internet users in China and that information technology specialists from research institutions, universities, and private companies have been integrated into the 8-million-strong regular militia, with the clear task of penetrating foreign networks.

5. Realistically, the true motivation of Chinese hackers is not to destroy foreign government information technology infrastructure systems but to steal intellectual property from private companies abroad.[78]

However, we should not overdramatize the challenge from Chinese cyber warfare:

1. Thomas Rid convincingly argues that the media hype cyber warfare and that an actual cyber war has never taken place in the past and will not take place in the future.[79] Rid maintains that cyber attacks do not qualify as warfare because they are neither lethal, instrumental, nor political. Therefore, one should more aptly think of them as acts of sabotage, espionage, and subversion. The cyber attacks that have occurred (e.g., Russia against Georgia and Estonia) did not bring the target countries to their knees or result in permanent damage.

2. The central question focuses on the loyalty of the Chinese hackers. There is no evidence that they are under actual government control. It is often impossible to fathom who is behind the attacks, whether the government is actively involved, merely passively allows the hackers to continue, or is simply unable or uninterested in checking them effectively. Given the PLA's esprit de corps and the party's obsession with keeping things under control, it is highly doubtful that the PLA would rely on outside hackers during a conflict or allow them leeway to pick targets and act on their own.

3. Contrary to popular belief, China does not pursue one coherent, centrally coordinated cyber-security policy. Responsibility for cyber

security is fragmented and shared among several entities: the Ministry of Public Security, the CCP Central Office Confidential Bureau, the State Secrets Bureau, and the GSD's Third and Fourth Departments. In addition, numerous universities, government agencies, and commercial high-tech companies are also involved.[80]

4. International research has vindicated China's official claim of its own vulnerability to hackers. Cases in which both the hackers and the victims are Chinese constitute a growing problem within the PRC. Of the top one hundred viruses infecting computers in 2011, in every case China was the number one affected country, with nearly all of the viruses also originating in China.[81] China suffered five hundred thousand attacks in 2011, only 15 percent of which came from the United States.[82]

5. Again, much talk about Chinese cyber warfare is about aspirations, not actual capabilities. As Desmond Ball has shown, even though China attempts to create the image that it can inflict damage, its capabilities are most probably significantly weaker than those of the United States.[83]

China: A Nuclear Threat?

The modernization of Chinese strategic nuclear missile forces has resulted in the question of whether China poses a nuclear threat.[84] Academic research has put forward the following arguments to substantiate the proposition that it does:

1. China is the only one of the five initial nuclear weapons states that is increasing its arsenal of nuclear-tipped missiles. It is reluctant to be drawn into nuclear arms control processes and instead calls on Russia and the United States to first massively reduce their own arsenals.

2. China's nuclear capabilities are improving not only in numbers but also in quality as more modern types of missiles enter its arsenals (especially submarine-launched ballistic missiles).

3. With only China and Russia able to attack US territory with ballistic missiles, Washington has greeted the discourse within China about whether to discard the no-first-use policy with alarm.[85]

4. In its modernization drive China has practiced a "unique duality."[86] It has avowed a no-first-use policy for its nuclear missiles. At the same time, it considers its conventional missiles to have potential for preemptive attacks. That some of its delivery systems can be tipped with conventional and nuclear warheads and its missile bases are home to both conventional and nuclear missiles confounds this ambiguity. The situation therefore has real potential to escalate due

to possible miscalculations, misunderstandings, or miscommunications in crisis situations.[87]

Yet again, some contrary factors should also be taken into account. For the time being, China seems satisfied with a small but effective deterrent. Speculation about hidden or secret masses of additional Chinese weapons of mass destruction remains unsubstantiated. Obviously, the PRC is not engaging in a "rush to parity" with the United States or Russia by acquiring thousands of nuclear warheads. No Western expert expects China to increase the number of its warheads to more than three or four hundred. China has learned the lesson of the failure of the Soviet Union and does not want to become entangled in a nuclear arms race with the United States, preferring instead to concentrate on niche capacities and asymmetric warfare.

Chinese Behavior in Crisis Situations and Territorial Conflicts (Use of Force)

One of the widespread assumptions in Western media is that conservative, nationalist hawks within the PLA drive Chinese foreign policy in a more "pugilistic," "aggressive," or "belligerent" direction (especially with respect to territorial disputes).[88] In addition, the reasoning goes that in times of crisis (e.g., during the 1995–1996 PLA missile tests in the Taiwan Strait, the US-China tensions after the NATO bombing of the Belgrade embassy 1999, or the 2001 incident in which a Chinese interceptor collided with a US EP-3 spy plane within China's exclusive economic zone), the PLA either acts on its own or pushes the civilian administration to take a hard-line stance.

Research by leading scholars, however, has made clear the need for caution.[89] The precise role of the PLA in each of these crises remains elusive and is deliberately kept secret. Instead of making sweeping generalizations, observers should be much more context sensitive. The causes, severity, and outcome of a given crisis, as well as the role and degree of involvement of the PLA, hinge on whether the crisis was planned (as in the case of the Taiwan Strait in 1995–1996), anticipated, or unanticipated (like the EP-3 incident). Regardless of the circumstances, Beijing's main goal in each of the crises was to insure party survival and protect party unity at all cost. Therefore, the PLA might have been used by the civilian leadership to show resolve or to placate nationalist sentiments. However, as has been discussed above, in these crises, as in general foreign policy decision making, the PLA is but one actor in a consensus-oriented process involving a plethora of bureaucratic and geographic interests. During periods of crisis, the role of the PLA is better understood as restricted to providing information (relying on its own intelligence gathering) and advice to the civilian party and government leadership.

It is important to note that there is no cohesive, clearly defined set of military interests as embodied by the PLA per se vis-à-vis the civilian institutions and no pattern of continuing pressure by the officer corps on their senior civilian colleagues. Therefore, the problem of a military-civilian disconnect is found at the operational as opposed to the strategic level. At the lower levels of the hierarchy, there is a lack of both close and continuous civilian oversight over the military and communication and coordination between the two, which can lead to solo runs by the PLA, as in 2004, when a Chinese nuclear-powered submarine entered Japanese waters, or in 2007, when a Chinese submarine surfaced near a US carrier. Military tests, such as maiden flights by Chinese stealth fighter aircraft in 2010 and 2012 during visits by US Secretaries of Defense Robert Gates and Leon Panetta, should also be regarded primarily as evidence of a civil-military disconnect at the operational level rather than a well-planned provocation.

China's past behavior in its territorial disputes and patterns in the use of force have been well researched and may provide some hints about the risks involved in China's present-day conflicts in the South and East China Seas.[90]

In general, territorial disputes are the single most likely reason for a country to use military force. China has been party to more territorial disputes (twenty-three) than any other country. However it has settled seventeen of them through bilateral agreements, often involving compromises over the territorial claims.[91] The six outstanding territorial disputes are with India (use of force in 1962, 1967, and 1986), Bhutan, Taiwan (use of force in 1952–1955, 1954, 1958, and 1995–1996), Vietnam (use of force in the South China Sea in 1974 and 1988), and Japan.[92] Cases when China did use military force were rather status-quo oriented; Beijing aimed not to expand territory but to defend claims China has maintained since the founding of the PRC and to protect the country's core interests (Taiwan and the integrity of its ethnic minority border areas). Looking at China's past record in territorial conflicts, M. Taylor Fravel has identified the following pattern: With its rising economic power, China is not now more prone to confrontation. Times of radical politics at home did not lead to a more assertive or belligerent foreign policy in most of its territorial disputes. In contrast to popular wisdom, internal instability, especially threats to regime security (e.g., by minorities), was important in terms of China's willingness to compromise and did not lead to adventurism abroad. China did use force primarily due to a sense of a relative decline in the strength of its claim or its bargaining power; ironically, it engaged militarily most often when facing a powerful opponent that could weaken its position (India, Russia, or Vietnam) and not against weaker neighbors (Mongolia or Nepal) or when the opponent controlled little or no land claimed by China. Individual leaders, ideology, and China's relative position in the international system have had no causal influence on the PRC's behavior. With regard to China's outstanding conflicts, observers consider those with India and Bhutan frozen, whereas the maritime claims to the Spratly, Paracel, and Diaoyu Islands are still cause for concern. But there is at least some reason for optimism since China has shied away from using force in territorial disputes when it felt strong or in a position to prevail.[93] Studies that analyze China's general propensity for the use of force support this pattern.[94]

However, we should not take at face value the PRC's official statements to counter the China threat theory by referring to the peace-loving character of its people or to its pacifist culture. Andrew Scobell explains that it is a myth to interpret Confucianism as a foundation for a pacifist or defensive strategic culture.[95] On the contrary, traditional Chinese military thinking completely accepts the use of force as a legitimate and often necessary option. Successful Chinese war fighting against Japan during World War II and the United States during the Korean War reinforces this reasoning. The argument goes that the weaker side can prevail against a stronger, more powerful adversary. More remarkably, China retrospectively interprets even its failures (e.g., in the case of Taiwan in the 1950s or Vietnam in 1979) as successes because the country acted defensively to fend off worse results. This record of actual or putative successful use of force for purely defensive reasons might encourage the PRC to take undue risks and lead to misunderstandings in crisis situations. Blinded by a "cult of defense," China might actually believe that its steps are defensive in nature, even though others regard them as threatening and aggressive.[96]

Before putting forward answers to the question of whether China poses a military threat, we should take heed of some analytical traps:

1. Many studies focus on past geopolitical power balancing or military rivalries to predict China's future behavior and thus fail to appreciate the fundamental changes in China's external context.[97] Rivalries in the twenty-first century will likely play out in vastly different forms and patterns than they did in the past. In today's world a complex, shifting web of transnational nonstate agents (e.g., global professional groups, business and civic groups, standards-setting groups, terrorist groups, corporations, and so forth) has superseded the dominance of states, making it more difficult to differentiate between friends, allies, and enemies. States and other actors are linked in a variety of global networks, and these connectivities and "networked dependencies" lead to increasing and cascading vulnerabilities. In such a context, where the sources of national power are fluid, nonmilitary instruments to achieve goals will probably be more desirable, making military competition less optimal than it was in the past.
2. The topic of China as a military threat is highly politicized, with rumormongering, sensationalism (driven by Hong Kong and Taiwanese

media and Chinese social media), and vested interests (e.g., defense contractors), making any sober analysis even more challenging.

3. With regard to new weapons systems, not a few observers fail to differentiate between research, development, testing, deployment, and operability. In fact, many years, if not decades, lie between the first research-and-development steps and the combat readiness of weapons platforms (e.g., in the case of stealth aircraft).

4. International experts have illustrated that weapons are black boxes.[98] No one knows their strengths or weaknesses until they are used in actual combat. It is relatively easy to count the observables (number of missiles, tanks, and so forth), but it is impossible to make judgments about the software systems in Chinese weapons, which are the backbone of any modern war-fighting machine. Blasko has rightly criticized Western fascination with the introduction of single weapons systems.[99] More important are the training, doctrine, and personnel because those determine the actual use of the hardware.

5. In addition, it is not useful to compare single items on the Chinese side with single items on the other side (e.g., a Chinese versus a US submarine) since they are never employed singularly in this way; weapons systems are used together to accomplish a mission.[100]

6. There is also the dual-use problem. Some platforms (e.g., satellite programs) can serve civilian and military purposes at the same time. Chinese engagement in peacekeeping operations abroad can provide the PLA with needed training in the far seas or indicate Beijing's commitment to UN norms, signaling a new concept in the use of force and the PRC's willingness to present itself as a responsible great power.[101]

7. The lack of transparency with regard to the capabilities, intentions, and procedures of the Chinese military remains a central issue in PRC security policy. With regard to strategic thinking within the PLA, much information derives from open-source literature in Chinese. However, we do not know what the top leadership thinks about the use of force or the role of cyber warfare; in addition, much of what is written concerns aspirations that do not translate into actual capabilities.

8. Despite all the analytical rigor, ultimately it is highly subjective whether one stresses China's (sense of) vulnerabilities and constraints[102] or highlights its improving military capabilities, coercive power (especially vis-à-vis Taiwan), or confidence and assertiveness;[103] whether one believes the role of the PLA remains focused primarily on regime survival and border defense or stresses China's global reach; or whether one looks at capabilities for asymmetric warfare or thinks that, for example, space and cyber-warfare capabilities reflect global ambitions to project power.[104] Finally, it makes a difference whether one compares the PLA in 2012 with the PLA in 1990 or with the US

armed forces, which observers still consider twenty years ahead technologically.[105]

With these caveats in mind, we propose the following conclusion (see box 4.1).

1. The PLA is no longer the bloated, ill-trained, technologically backward, ground-force-dominated army that it once was. The balance of power in East Asia has changed markedly to China's advantage, and both the PLA's capabilities and its missions have increased.
2. The farther away from China's shores we move, the less threatening China's armed forces become.[106] With regard to Taiwan, there is no longer a balance of power. During a military crisis in the Taiwan Strait, PLA air superiority, combined air, naval, and missile strikes, and a blockade against the island are all realistic scenarios today.[107]
3. China is not engaged in a global strategic competition with the United States as the Soviet Union once was. It is not pursuing a strategic arms race or building an alliance structure, and it does not host bases abroad. Much of the literature in Chinese discusses the lessons of other rising powers. China fears the overstretch that brought the Soviet Union to its knees. Thus, China does not seem to be striving for global power projection capabilities within the next two decades.[108]
4. Worrisome with regard to Chinese intentions and capabilities is a possible willingness and propensity to use preemptive strikes, as warranted by "active defense." China might miscalculate by overestimating US vulnerabilities (overdependence on C4ISR, overuse and overconsumption of US forces in multiple engagements, dependence on allies) and underestimating US willingness to risk casualties to defend its interests.[109] Chinese planners might delude themselves in their conviction that crisis escalation (e.g., using massive missile attacks) can be controlled.[110]
5. As the most prominent danger, we identify the high potential for accidents, undesired conflicts, and incidents in the near seas and disputed territorial waters crowded with vessels belonging to various claimants. The lack of institutionalized crisis mitigation procedures among the contestants compounds this problem.
6. However, the ability of the Chinese leadership to respond and adapt to deteriorating regional relationships is reassuring. When the China threat theory first appeared in the mid-1990s (as a result of Chinese assertiveness in the Taiwan Strait and the South China Sea), Beijing responded with an active regional diplomacy and stepped up reassurances to the outside world and propagation of its "peaceful rise" concept. Similar steps, or at least tactical concessions, to placate neighbors appear possible, and even likely, in future cases of serious tensions.

BOX 4.1. IS CHINA A MILITARY THREAT?

Category	Yes	No
Capabilities	(Strengths)	(Weaknesses)
PRC defense budget	• Defense expenditures have grown over twenty years; actual spending is unknown.	• Defense expenditures remain a fraction of those in the United States. • There is no intention to become involved in an arms race
Military hardware	• There are niche capabilities for A2/AD, as well as state-of-the-art weaponry in the PLAN, modern cruise missiles, ballistic missiles, and counterspace weapons.	• The army is still primarily land based; there is a lack of jointness; only between 25 and 50 percent of its systems are considered modern; it has limited power-projection capabilities • The soldiers have no combat experience.
Training	• Advances have been made toward Western standards (more realistic and standardized).	• The quality of the "human factor" is unknown. • There is a lack of joint training.
Recruitment	• Ambitious programs for officer and NCO corps	• Competition from the private economy
Defense industry/ technological know-how	• There is access to Western (dual-use) technology. • Mass production of indigenous modern weapons systems has begun.	• Some of the military (e.g., the PLAAF) is still heavily dependent on imports; acquisition of technology from abroad is limited due to export restrictions

General intentions	• Intentions are deliberately obscured. • Nationalism (often anti-Japan, anti-US) is widespread.	• Elite consensus: economic development is the number one priority; party commands the gun; officers do not challenge military subordination.
Military doctrine	• "Active defense" with a potential for preemptive strikes	• Main mission: to uphold CCP one-party rule and to defend borders and sea lanes
Crisis behavior	• There is bifurcation between civilian and military behavior at the operational level and a lack of coordination.	• PLA not an independent actor at the strategic level; its role is restricted to information and advice.
Behavior in territorial disputes/use of force	• High number of conflicts; record of use of force • Maritime claims with potential for conflict	• Record of compromising • Orientation toward maintaining the status quo

Sources: Blasko 2012; Cordesman and Kleiber 2007; Kamphausen and Scobell 2007; Mitchell 2006; Mohr 2006; Nodskov 2009; Shambaugh 2002; Tellis and Tanner 2012.

NOTES

1. Blasko 2012; Scobell and Nathan 2012.
2. Blasko 2012.
3. Kiselycznyk and Saunders 2010b; Li Nan 2010; Shambaugh 2002.
4. For example, Li Nan 2010; Swaine 2012a, 2012b.
5. Swaine 2012b.
6. Mulvenon 2012.
7. Mulvenon 2012.
8. Shambaugh 2002.
9. Blasko 2012; Mulvenon and Yang 2002; Shambaugh 2002.
10. Halloran 2012.
11. Fravel and Liebman 2011; Saunders et al. 2011.
12. Stokes and Cheng 2012.
13. Chambers 2007; Craig 2007.
14. Swaine 2012c; Xiang Lanxin 2012.

15. Blasko 2012; Cheng 2012; Cliff et al. 2007; Cordesman and Kleiber 2007; Finkelstein 2007; Nodskov 2009; Shambaugh 2002.
16. Blasko 2012; Cheng 2012; Kiselycznyk and Saunders 2010a.
17. Cheng 2012; Nodskov 2009.
18. Blasko 2012; Li Nan 2011; Mulvenon 2009.
19. National Air and Space Intelligence Center 2010.
20. Chase and Erickson 2012.
21. Chaffin and Erickson 2012a, 2012b.
22. Blasko 2012; International Institute for Strategic Studies 2012; Li Nan 2010; Nodskov 2009; Shambaugh 2002.
23. Blasko 2012.
24. Zhonghua Renmin Gongheguo Guowuyuan Xinwen Bangongshi 2011a.
25. Nathan and Scobell 2012; Tellis 2012; Tellis and Tanner 2012.
26. Blasko 2012.
27. Shambaugh 2002.
28. Blasko 2012; Shambaugh 2002.
29. Halloran 2012.
30. For exceptions, see Blasko 2012; Kamphausen 2012.
31. Kamphausen 2012.
32. Blasko 2012; Kamphausen 2012.
33. Chaffin and Erickson 2012b; Chase 2010; Erickson 2012; Erickson and Collins 2012; Li Nan 2010; Office of Naval Intelligence 2009; O'Rourke 2012; Saunders et al. 2011.
34. Chase 2010.
35. Chase 2010; Erickson 2012; Erickson and Collins 2012; Li Nan 2011.
36. Erickson and Collins 2012.
37. Erickson 2012; Erickson and Collins 2012.
38. Erickson and Collins 2012.
39. Erickson 2012; O'Rourke 2012.
40. O'Rourke 2012.
41. Erickson, Denmark, and Collins 2012.
42. Cliff 2010; Cliff et al. 2011; Halloran 2012; National Air and Space Intelligence Center 2010.
43. Halloran 2012.
44. Cliff 2010.
45. Chase and Erickson 2012; Kristensen and Norris 2011; Kulacki 2011; Stokes 2012.
46. Fravel and Medeiros 2010.
47. Chase and Erickson 2012; Stokes 2012.
48. Chase and Erickson 2012.
49. Kristensen and Norris 2011; Kulacki 2011.
50. International Institute for Strategic Studies 2012; Stockholm International Peace Research Institute 2012.
51. Cheng 2012; Pollpeter 2012; Stokes and Cheng 2012.
52. Cheng 2012.
53. Pollpeter 2012.
54. Pollpeter 2012.

55. Cheng 2012.
56. Friedberg 2011; Friedberg and Ross 2009; Mearsheimer 2006.
57. For example, Blumenthal 2010.
58. Dobbins 2012.
59. Burles and Shulsky 2000; Johnston 1998; Scobell 2003; Scobell and Wortzel 2005; Swaine 2012a.
60. Fravel 2005, 2007–2008, 2008, 2010.
61. Hu Jintao 2012.
62. Zhonghua Renmin Gongheguo Guowuyuan Xinwen Bangongshi 2011b.
63. Nathan and Scobell 2012.
64. Saunders and Wiseman 2011.
65. Kamphausen 2012.
66. Cliff 2010; Cliff et al. 2011.
67. O'Rourke 2012.
68. Holmes 2012.
69. Blasko 2012.
70. Chaffin and Erickson 2012b.
71. Shambaugh 2002.
72. Blasko 2012.
73. Shambaugh 2004.
74. Chaffin and Erickson 2012b.
75. Krekel, Adams, and Bakos 2012; US-China Economic and Security Review Commission 2012.
76. Ball 2011.
77. A. Segal 2012.
78. A. Segal 2012.
79. Rid 2012.
80. Krekel, Adams, and Bakos 2012.
81. Ball 2011.
82. A. Segal 2012.
83. Ball 2011.
84. For this discussion, see, in particular, Chase 2012; Christensen 2012; Kristensen and Norris 2011; Kulacki 2011; Lewis and Xue 2012.
85. Christensen 2012; Mazza and Blumenthal 2012.
86. Lewis and Xue 2012.
87. Christensen 2012; Lewis and Xue 2012.
88. Swaine 2010; Wei Da 2010.
89. F. Miller and Scobell 2005; Scobell and Wortzel 2005; Swaine 2012a, 2012b.
90. Foot and Walter 2011; Fravel 2005, 2007–2008, 2008; Johnston 1998; Scobell 2003.
91. Fravel 2010.
92. Fravel 2010.
93. Fravel 2008.
94. Johnston 1998.
95. Scobell 2003.
96. Scobell 2003.
97. Mazarr 2012.

98. For example, Holmes 2012.
99. Blasko 2012.
100. Blasko 2012.
101. Foot and Walter 2011.
102. Gompert and Saunders 2011, 2012; Nathan and Scobell 2012; Ross 2012.
103. Tellis 2012.
104. Pollpeter 2012; Tellis 2012.
105. Friedberg and Ross 2009; Nathan and Scobell 2012; Scobell and Nathan 2012.
106. Erickson 2012; Twomey 2013.
107. Erickson 2012.
108. Erickson 2012.
109. Blumenthal 2010; Whiting 2001.
110. Chase and Erickson 2012.

5

China in the World Economy

OVERVIEW: TRADE

Never before in history has a country transformed itself from a largely isolated economic backwater into one of the biggest trading nations and investment destinations of the global economy in less than thirty years. In 1980, at the outset of the People's Republic of China's (PRC) economic opening, its trade (then US$38 billion) amounted to only a fraction of global trade, and the country ranked twenty-sixth among the world's trading nations. By 2009 the country had become the world's biggest exporter of goods (ahead of Germany) and the second-biggest importer (after the United States). Its merchandise trade of US$3,642 billion in 2011 represented 10 percent of global trade.

China's spectacular rise to the top of the global trade ladder, its deep integration into the world economy, and its role as a center for transnational Asian production processes (see below) are strikingly evident when we examine the world's largest container ports in 1989 and 2011 (see table 5.1). In 1989, except for the China-related trade cleared through Hong Kong (then a British Crown colony, but with traditional hub functions for China's external economy), no PRC port ranked among the world's top fifteen container ports. By 2011, seven of the fifteen largest ports in the world were located in the territory of the PRC.

Table 5.2 provides more detailed information on China's trade performance and makes clear why China's trade is so remarkable. With a trade ratio (i.e., trade as a percentage of GDP) of more than 66 percent at its peak in 2006, China was one of the most open large economies in the world.

Table 5.1. The Great Shift in Global Trade: The Rise of Chinese Ports, 1989–2011

1989	2011
1. Hong Kong (4.5) (British Crown colony until 1997)	1. Shanghai (China) (31.7)
2. Singapore (4.4)	2. Singapore (29.9)
3. Rotterdam (Netherlands) (3.9)	3. Hong Kong (24.4) (PRC SAR)
4. Kaohsiung (Taiwan) (3.4)	4. Shenzhen (China) (22.6)
5. Kobe (Japan) (2.5)	5. Busan (South Korea) (16.2)
6. Busan (South Korea) (2.2)	6. Ningbo (China) (14.7)
7. Los Angeles (United States) (2.1)	7. Guangzhou (China) (14.4)
8. New York/New Jersey (United States) (2.0)	8. Qingdao (China) (13.0)
9. Keelung (Taiwan) (1.8)	9. Dubai (13.0)
10. Hamburg (Germany) (1.7)	10. Rotterdam (Netherlands) (11.9)
11. Long Beach (United States) (1.5)	11. Tianjin (China) (11.5)
12. Yokohama (Japan) (1.5)	12. Kaohsiung (Taiwan) (9.6)
13. Antwerp (Belgium) (1.5)	13. Port Klang (Malaysia) (9.6)
14. Tokyo (Japan) (1.4)	14. Hamburg (Germany) (9.0)
15. Felixstowe (United Kingdom) (1.4)	15. Antwerp (Belgium) (8.6)

Notes: Rankings are based on container freight volume. Figures in parentheses are in millions of twenty-foot equivalent units (TEUs).
Sources: *The Economist* 2010; City of Hamburg Port Authority (www.hafen-hamburg.de).

Only small economies, such as Singapore, Taiwan, and the Netherlands, registered such a high trade ratio. After this ratio declined to 45 percent in 2009 in the context of the global financial crisis (India's fell to 31 percent, Japan's to 22 percent, the United States' to 19 percent, and Brazil's to 18 percent), China once again reached more than 53 percent in 2011 due to its fast-growing foreign trade (+22 percent).

Trade and current account surpluses have increased enormously since China joined the World Trade Organization (WTO) in 2001, triggering widespread criticism of China as a "mercantilist" trading nation and a "currency manipulator" in reckless pursuit of national economic interests at the expense of other countries (see also below).[1] However, based on widely used yardsticks—such as the import share of gross domestic product (GDP) or duties as a percentage of imports—we cannot simply call China a closed "mercantilist" economy.[2] Moreover, its trade and current account surpluses have diminished as a result of the 2008 global financial crisis, mainly due to exports falling faster than imports in 2008–2009 and to faster-rising imports since 2010 (2011: imports +25 percent; exports +20 percent).

The national Chinese data do not reveal the huge variation in regional contributions to trade.[3] Although the five leading provincial-level jurisdictions (Guangdong, Jiangsu, Shanghai, Beijing, and Zhejiang) jointly account for almost 75 percent of China's trade volume, the bottom five (Ningxia, Guizhou, Qinghai, Tibet, and Hainan) constitute a mere 0.5 percent.

Table 5.2. Selected Data on China's Trade Performance, 1980–2011 (in US$ Billions)

	1980	1985	1990	1994	1998	2002	2005	2006	2007	2008	2009	2010	2011
Trade	38.1	69.6	115.4	236.6	323.9	620.8	1,421.9	1,760.4	2,173.8	2,563.3	2,207.2	2,972.7	3,641.9
Share of world trade (%)	0.9	1.8	1.6	2.7	2.9	4.7	6.7	7.2	7.7	7.9	8.8	9.9	10.1
Exports	18.2	27.3	62.1	121.0	183.7	325.6	761.9	968.9	1,218.0	1,430.7	1,201.7	1,577.9	1,898.4
Imports	20.0	42.3	53.3	115.6	140.2	295.2	660.0	791.5	955.8	1,132.6	1,005.5	1,394.8	1,743.5
Balance	–1.8	–15.0	8.8	5.4	43.5	30.4	101.9	177.4	262.2	298.1	196.2	183.1	154.9
Trade/GDP (%)	12.5	22.9	29.7	42.2	31.8	49.6	63.5	66.8	66.3	59.2	45.0	50.6	53.2
Current account/GDP (%)	n/a	n/a	0.3	1.4	3.1	2.4	7.2	9.1	11.3	9.8	5.8	4.0	2.8

Sources: IMF; Ministry of Commerce of the PRC; World Bank; WTO; Zhonghua Renmin Gongheguo Guojia Tongjiju 2012.

If the European Union—the PRC's biggest trading partner—and the Association of Southeast Asian Nations (ASEAN) (ranked third in 2011) are omitted as collective trading entities from the calculations, then China's ten most important export destinations in 2011 were (in declining order) the United States, Hong Kong, Japan, South Korea, Germany, the Netherlands, India, the United Kingdom, Russia, and Taiwan (see figure 5.1). Its top import suppliers in 2011 were (also in declining order) Japan, South Korea, Taiwan, the United States, Germany, Australia, Malaysia, Brazil, Saudi Arabia, and Russia (see figure 5.2).

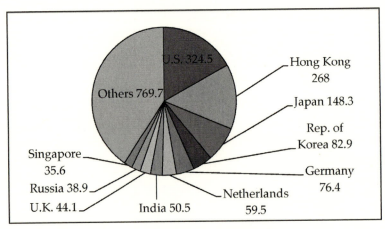

Figure 5.1: Ten top export destinations in 2011 (in US$ billions).
Source: Ministry of Commerce of the PRC.

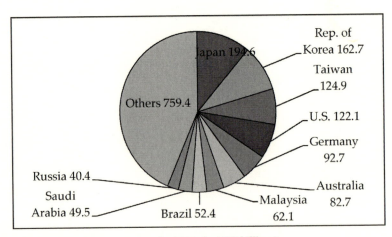

Figure 5.2. Ten top import sources in 2011 (in US$ billions).
Source: Ministry of Commerce of the PRC.

When we look at China's most popular traded commodities, it comes as no surprise to find apparel, furniture, and footwear among the top export items and mineral fuel, oil, plastics, iron, steel, and copper among the top imports. It stands out, however, that China's number one import and export product in 2011 was electrical machinery and equipment.

The breakdown of China's most important trade partners and the prominence of electrical machinery among both its imports and exports reveal a central feature of Chinese trade.[4] China is at the center of transnational Asian production networks in which electronic components, such as hard drives, computer chips, and displays, are first imported from Japan, South Korea, and Taiwan (countries with which China therefore has a trade deficit) and then assembled in China. The final products (laptop computers, cameras, DVD players, and so forth) are eventually shipped to the United States and Europe (with which China consequently has a trade surplus).

This export-processing regime constituted more than 40 percent of China's trade in 2008 (47 percent of exports and 33 percent of imports), but it has recently decreased somewhat[5] (the share in 2011 was 36 percent). The assembly process on the Chinese mainland often involves foreign-funded enterprises, which contributed about 52 percent to China's total exports and imports in 2011, a huge increase compared with the 5 percent of the 1980s.

One remarkable aspect of the processing trade regime is the extremely low degree of value added in China. An exemplary study that looked into the case of Apple's iPod (selling for US$299 at the time) found that the labor costs of assembly in China (US$4) constituted only a tiny fraction of the total input costs (then about US$150).[6] The authors concluded that the US trade deficit with China increased by US$150 (the factory costs) with each iPod sold on the US market, even though only a few dollars remained in China. Assembling the iPods in the United States would reduce the trade deficit figure with China, but the deficit would increase with those other economies where the components originated (such as South Korea and Taiwan). This example highlights how careful one has to be when looking at national trade statistics and bilateral trade deficits or surpluses in the context of transnational production processes, which exploit comparative price advantages.[7]

CURRENCY POLICY AND FOREIGN EXCHANGE ACCUMULATION

The Chinese exchange rate regime has undergone several transformations since 1978 (see figure 5.3). We can identify the following stages:[8]

- Until China began opening up to the outside world in the late 1970s, the Chinese yuan (CNY) was fixed at a highly overvalued level as part of China's import substitution industrialization strategy (the reduction of dependence on imported finished goods) under the economic planning system. As was the general pattern in other socialist countries, China's central bank (then called the Bank of China) allocated foreign exchange according to a central plan, and all foreign exchange earnings had to be surrendered.

- From 1979 to 1994 China engaged in a gradual process to change the existing exchange rate regime by taking the following measures: The official CNY exchange rate declined from 1.5 ¥/US$ in 1980 to 5.8 ¥/US$ by the end of 1993. In 1980, Chinese authorities began experimenting with local foreign exchange markets; foreign-funded enterprises and a limited number of Chinese state-owned companies were allowed to swap foreign exchange (hence the name "swap centers"). The prices of the foreign currencies at these swap centers were market determined and showed a premium over the official exchange rate. Thus, in effect, China had a dual exchange rate system during this period. By the end of 1993, swap markets had spread across China and conducted the majority of foreign exchange transactions.

- In January 1994, China abolished the secondary swap market and introduced a unified exchange rate at what was then the prevailing swap market rate (8.7 ¥/US$). From 1994 to 1996, access to foreign currency was liberalized for all trade-related transactions. This current account convertibility of the CNY means that every importing/exporting company can now buy/sell foreign exchange if it documents a trade flow.

- Due to the 1997–1998 Asian financial crisis and the economic turbulence on China's periphery, Beijing did not embark on full convertibility of its capital account at this time, and it still has yet to do so. Again in the context of the Asian financial crisis, the Chinese authorities fixed the CNY at 8.28 ¥/US$ in October 1997, where it remained basically stable until July 2005. From 1997 to 2002, the CNY thus appreciated in tandem with the dollar, but when the dollar began to depreciate (as of 2002), the value of the CNY also fell.

- On July 21, 2005, China ended the dollar peg and introduced a new currency regime under which the CNY fluctuated against a basket of currencies within a small daily range (at first this was 0.3 percent, but it was increased to 0.5 percent after May 2007). After an initial one-step revaluation of 2.1 percent on July 21, 2005, the CNY appreciated by approximately 20 percent from 2005 to mid-2008, when, in the course of the global financial crisis, China returned to a dollar peg at the rate of 6.83 ¥/US$.

- This peg remained in place until June 19, 2010, when the Chinese authorities again returned to the 2005–2008 crawling peg within a limited daily trading range (first 0.5 percent and then later extended

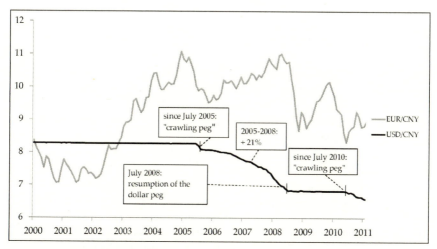

Figure 5.3. Exchange rate of the CNY in relation to the euro and the dollar, 2000–2011.
Source: Oanda—Forex Trading and Exchange Rates Services.

to 1.0 percent) for a basket of currencies. The idea of managing one's own currency in relation to a basket of foreign currencies was adopted from the Singapore model. The exact composition of this basket is kept secret to make it more difficult for foreign speculators to anticipate changes in the CNY exchange rate.

How does China's current exchange rate regime work in practice?[9] Technically, every dollar or unit of a foreign currency can make its way to China through one of the following channels: export earnings (the vast majority of China's exports are settled in foreign currencies, especially the US dollar), foreign direct investment (FDI), or capital flows aimed at the Chinese equity or real estate markets. Since China operates a "closed capital account"—that is, private capital flows to and from China in either CNY or foreign currencies are highly restricted—the latter category is called "hot money."

Chinese exporters take their dollars to local commercial banks, which a "surrender requirement" then demands that they sell to the People's Bank of China (PBoC) more or less completely as required by changing regulations. Under China's fixed or crawling peg, the PBoC buys these dollars in exchange for CNY at the rate it sets every day. The PBoC sells CNY at this given rate in return for the foreign exchange needed by Chinese importers or companies seeking to invest abroad, for example. Since there is an excess supply of foreign exchange on the Chinese mainland foreign exchange market, the PBoC ends up buying much more foreign exchange (primarily US dollars) than it sells, effectively keeping the value of the CNY from rising.

Since the commercial banks receive CNY in return for the foreign exchange sold to the PBoC, the amount of liquidity in the commercial banking system could increase tremendously and result in rising inflation. To prevent this, the PBoC engages in offsetting domestic operations, a process known as "sterilization," whereby the central bank takes the money back from the commercial banking system by either forcing the banks to buy central bank debt or requiring the banks to keep a certain amount of their assets at the central bank (a "required reserve ratio").[10]

Contrary to standard economic theory and expectations, the PBoC has successfully mopped up the liquidity resulting from the foreign exchange inflows. Over the last several years, the PBoC has bought between US$1 billion and US$2 billion in foreign exchange daily, thereby dramatically increasing the official reserves under its control to US$3,181 billion by the end of 2011. This represented 43.5 percent of China's GDP and 30 percent of all global foreign-currency reserves; it equaled the combined reserves of all advanced economies and accounted for almost 50 percent of all the foreign exchange reserves held by the emerging and developing countries combined (see figure 5.4).[11]

The exact composition of China's foreign exchange holdings is considered a state secret. Most analysts believe that 60 to 70 percent is held in US dollars, 20 to 30 percent in euros, and the remainder in Japanese yen, South Korean won, British pounds, and Swiss francs. But the official reserves constitute only part of China's actual foreign exchange holdings;

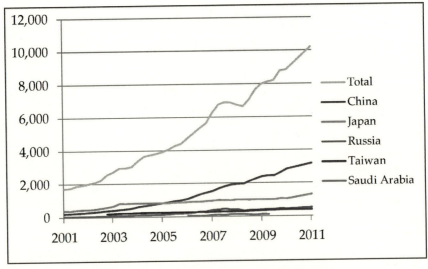

Figure 5.4. World currency reserves, 2001–2011 (in US$ billions).
Sources: IMF and the central banks of China, Russia, and Saudi Arabia.

"other foreign assets" of the PBoC should also be included, such as assets under the authority of the large state-linked commercial banks and the those of China's sovereign wealth fund, the China Investment Corporation (CIC), together valued at US$482 billion in 2011).[12] As of mid-2012, China's actual foreign exchange holdings were estimated to be approximately US$3,900 billion.[13]

China's official reserves are managed by a division of the PBoC, the State Administration of Foreign Exchange (SAFE), which is tasked with making sure these funds are safe, liquid, and profitable. China has invested a high proportion of its forex holdings in US Treasury bonds, making it the biggest foreign investor in these types of assets, ahead of Japan (see chapter 10).

Since the outbreak of the global financial crisis in 2007–2008 and the lurking danger of US inflation due to the Federal Reserve's expansionary monetary policy, there has been growing frustration and mounting public criticism in China about the country's exposure to the dollar and broad discussions about how to diversify its foreign exchange holdings away from that currency. Suggestions by leading Chinese politicians, economists, and journalists have included buying nondollar assets (denominated in euros or yen), using the money for domestic development, supporting outgoing Chinese companies, or buying commodities needed for China's continuous development.

However, all these proposals are either impractical or will have negative side effects of one sort or another. Increasing the amount of yen or euro assets would drive up the value of these currencies and provoke resistance from the source countries. After the crisis, in 2010 and 2011 the euro did suffer, showing that it is not immune from such situations. One cannot easily exchange forex holdings for CNY for domestic use. Chinese companies face considerable hurdles in their global investment activities, and buying up commodities drives up global market prices and is not welcomed by international competitors. Thus, at least until the United States lost its AAA credit rating in August 2011, the Chinese government saw no viable large-volume alternative to buying US debt.

An innovative Chinese initiative was launched with trial schemes aimed at gradual internationalization in the use of the CNY through currency swap agreements, pilot programs to settle trade in CNY, and issuance of CNY-denominated bonds in Hong Kong.[14] However, many additional prerequisites (such as full CNY convertibility, deep and liquid financial markets, secure property rights, and a trustworthy legal infrastructure) still have to be met before the CNY is in a position to rival the dollar as an international reserve currency.[15]

Three interconnected questions are frequently raised regarding the mounting international controversy over China's management of the CNY's exchange rate:

- Can the CNY be judged purposely and severely undervalued such that the term "currency manipulation" is warranted?
- What are the consequences of the currency misalignment for China and the outside world?
- What is the best strategy for dealing with this problem from the standpoint of the Chinese authorities, foreign governments/central banks, and international institutions?

Answering the first question is tricky because there is no precise and generally accepted economic definition of undervaluation.[16] Economists use different models and data to measure the phenomenon. In China's case, for example, undervaluation estimations vary from virtually 0 to 50 percent.[17] Even after the significant appreciation of the CNY against the dollar (see figure 5.3) of more than 12 percent in June 2010 or 40 percent in 2005 (adjusted for inflation in both cases), economists still consider the CNY to be undervalued by 3 to 23 percent.[18]

In addition, the exchange rate is only one factor that influences the price of any given product on the world market. Other sources that decide the competitiveness of a country's goods or services abroad are its inflation rate, productivity gains and losses, and domestic wages. Therefore, it is difficult to determine with any confidence how much a currency is actually over- or undervalued.

This is even more difficult with regard to the term "currency manipulation," which can be traced back to two origins. One is Article IV, Section 1 of the Articles of Agreement of the International Monetary Fund (IMF). This document stipulates that "each member undertakes to collaborate with the Fund and other members to assure orderly exchange arrangements and to promote a stable system of exchange rates." In particular, each member state should "avoid manipulating exchange rates or the international monetary system in order to prevent effective balance of payments adjustment or to gain unfair competitive advantage over other members." The problem here is that, although legally binding, the terms "manipulating exchange rates" and "unfair advantage" are ambiguous and therefore subject to differing interpretations. Thus, it comes as no surprise that the issue has often divided the IMF Executive Board, and China has thus successfully avoided pressure regarding its currency at the IMF's biannual meetings.

The second source of the term "currency manipulation" is the 1988 US Omnibus Trade and Competitiveness Act, which requires the secretary of the US Treasury to analyze annually "whether countries manipulate the rate of exchange between their currency and the United States dollar for purposes of preventing effective balance of payments adjustments or gaining unfair competitive advantage in international trade." Here, again, the wording is imprecise and gives the US Treasury secretary large discretion.

Research by Jeffrey Frankel and Wei Shang-Jin has made clear that political variables, for instance unemployment and the US bilateral trade deficits, play as important a role in manipulation of the findings as hard economic variables, such as global current account imbalances, calculated currency misalignments, or foreign-reserve buildups, especially during election years.[19] Publication of the Treasury's report in 2010 was postponed from April to July because at the time the United States was seeking China's support for the UN resolution on Iran.

When viewed against this backdrop, one finds that the Chinese positions (see box 5.1) and those put forward abroad in response to the above three questions differ enormously. At the same time, however, it is not simply a juxtaposition of China versus the West (or the United States); as boxes 5.2 and 5.3 indicate, the argument also pits scholars and policy makers in the West against one another.

When putting forward their positions, Chinese authorities apply adroit tactics. One standard procedure is to cite foreign central bank officials (e.g., Jürgen Stark, former chief economist of the European Central Bank [ECB]) or leading foreign economists critical of official US positions (e.g., Joseph Stiglitz and Robert Mundell) as proof that this is just a political ruse. In addition, the Chinese press regularly highlights the possible costs for small and medium-size private Chinese businesses that might fall victim to a rapid CNY appreciation.

Although there is a high degree of homogeneity in the official positions in the Chinese case, the situation is less clear-cut in the United States. Basically, two camps can be juxtaposed against one another. On the one hand we have Keynesian economists and commentators (Paul Krugman of the *New York Times*, Martin Wolf of the *Financial Times*), as well as domestic US manufacturers' associations (e.g., the Alliance of American Manufacturing), labor unions, members of Congress, and individual research institutes (e.g., the Peterson Institute of International Economics). These voices claim that the CNY is undervalued by up to 50 percent and that a substantial rapid appreciation of the currency is warranted (see box 5.2). On the other hand, we find that large multinational corporations with production sites in China, the American Chamber of Commerce, the US-China Business Council, former US trade representatives, and think tanks promoting free trade (e.g., the Cato Institute, the Heritage Foundation, and the Carnegie Endowment) are basically sympathetic to the Chinese position and counsel caution when it comes to reforming Chinese currency (see box 5.3).

The European point of view is almost completely absent in this argument due to the fact that the euro-CNY exchange rate is a function of the general euro–US dollar exchange rate. For example, when the euro massively depreciated against the US dollar as a result of the sovereign default crisis in the spring of 2010, European criticism of the CNY exchange rate stopped.

BOX 5.1. STANDARD CHINESE POSITIONS
ON THE CNY EXCHANGE RATE

- The direction of its currency policy is a matter for China alone to decide; adjustments should be made according to China's own agenda (to support economic development).
- China will continue its exchange rate reforms to allow greater flexibility, while at the same time safeguarding a "reasonable" and "balanced" exchange rate.
- Any unreasonable appreciation of the CNY would cause serious economic and social problems (collapse of growth, rising unemployment).
- This is because Chinese exporters are at the low end of the industrial value chain and have only a small profit margin; any significant appreciation in the value of the CNY would wipe them out.
- An appreciation of the CNY would lead to cheaper imports of agricultural products, which would be disastrous for the country's 500 million farmers.
- Deficits or surpluses in a country's current account reflect structural trade patterns. Thus, China has a trade surplus with the EU and the United States, but it has a trade deficit with Japan, the ASEAN members, and South Korea.
- China is not responsible either for the global imbalances or for the global financial crisis.
- Western countries accuse China of using its exchange rate to subsidize its exports. However, these very same countries also engage in protectionist measures.
- Western countries are responsible for the global imbalances due to their fiscal profligacy and ultraloose monetary policies.
- The United States is trying to make China a scapegoat for current US economic problems and unemployment. It should stop politicizing the currency issue.
- China will never give in to foreign pressures, as Japan did with the Plaza Accord of 1985. This agreement forced the Bank of Japan to cut interest rates, which led to bubbles in the financial and property markets with disastrous consequences for Japan to this day.

Only since the summer of 2010 have other countries (e.g., Brazil and India) adopted a position critical of the PRC, albeit without joining together to form a common anti-China front.

The Chinese and their critics do agree that in the long term an appreciation of the CNY will be in China's own interest—by making Chinese

BOX 5.2. STANDARD CRITICISMS
OF CHINESE EXCHANGE RATE POLICIES

- There is a clear case for a manipulated Chinese exchange rate—that is, massive intervention by the PBoC, which has been buying US$1 billion per day for a number of years and has amassed US$3.2 trillion in foreign exchange reserves (i.e., 45 percent of GDP).
- China has not lived up to its promises; it has been very reluctant to allow the CNY to appreciate.
- So far, the US strategy of upholding free trade and relying on dialogue with China has led nowhere. It is now time to get tough and put credible pressures on China.
- China, the world's biggest capital exporter, is primarily responsible for the current global imbalances. These cannot be reduced because of ongoing Chinese currency-market interventions.
- China played a major role in causing the global financial crisis because it flooded financial markets with cheap money that led to the mortgage bubble.
- The United States should not fear that China will no longer buy US debt since the United States is already awash with liquidity.
- Appreciation of the CNY could generate hundreds of thousands of jobs in the United States.
- In addition to the United States and Europe, the emerging market economies and developing countries that compete with Chinese exports pay the price for Chinese currency manipulation.
- Fears of a Japanese scenario (the "lost decade") in China after a CNY appreciation are totally unfounded. Japan suffered a deflationary recession not because of the Plaza Accord but rather because of untouched structural reforms. For example, the German mark appreciated against the US dollar after the Plaza Accord, but Germany did not experience the economic calamities that befell Japan.

exports more expensive and Chinese imports cheaper.[20] An appreciation would be an integral part of rebalancing China's economy away from its hitherto investment-driven and export-led growth to a path more dependent on domestic consumption. This has been an important policy goal of the Chinese leadership since 1998 (and it is in line with the notions of "harmonious society" and "scientific outlook on development" supported by the Hu-Wen administration). Many observers outside China consider this an indispensable step in rebalancing the global economy.

In addition, a more flexible exchange rate would be beneficial to China's monetary policy since it would enable the PBoC to rely more on interest

BOX 5.3. STANDARD POSITIONS FAVORING A GRADUAL APPRECIATION OF THE CNY

- China's position regarding the potential costs of rapid and substantial appreciation is persuasive: a successful rebalancing of the Chinese economy toward more consumption will take time. Rushing the process would exact a high cost. As a result of rising unemployment caused by the closing down of exporting companies, household consumption would decline.
- The risk of a Sino-American trade war sparked by the US obsession with the Chinese exchange rate should not be considered negligible. A tangible scenario of tit-for-tat bilateral protectionist measures could easily spiral out of control, with disastrous consequences for the world economy.
- A substantial revaluation of the CNY would not have major consequences for the US current account deficit because it would simply lead to a shift to imports from other Asian countries. Therefore, it would not lead to any significant improvement in the US employment situation.
- China has only marginal influence on any rebalancing of the global economy. Rather, the United States should do more to increase household savings and domestic investments.

rates and less on direct intervention (credit quotas or capping lending) to influence the macro economy. The PBoC could then reduce the amount of outstanding central bank bills and cut the required reserve ratio. Chinese commercial banks could then pay a higher interest rate on private deposits. In turn, this would increase household wealth and limit the incentives for making speculative investments in China's real estate and equity markets, a situation that is all too prevalent in a context where actual interest rates are frequently negative.

If there is indeed a medium- to long-term gain from an appreciation of the CNY, why do we see so much Chinese resistance to any outside pressure? In fact, there is no single homogenous position, as implied in box 5.1. Since 2009, representatives of the PBoC have often indicated that more CNY flexibility (a code word for appreciation) might be just around the corner. This is because the PBoC (or rather, SAFE) has the most to lose if the present exchange rate regime is maintained: the longer it continues to buy up foreign exchange (in practice, mostly dollars), the bigger its balance sheet losses will be if the CNY appreciates over time.

The Chinese Ministry of Commerce has contested these PBoC initiatives, however, acting as a powerful agent for all those who in the short term would suffer from a rapid, substantial appreciation of the CNY: the powerful lobby of the coastal provinces (where most exporters are based) and the large state-owned enterprises (which are forced to export their excess capacity). Faced with a situation of squaring short- and long-term losses or gains, the State Council—the ultimate decision maker in exchange rate policy—has opted to take the more cautious reform path.[21]

INBOUND AND OUTBOUND FOREIGN DIRECT INVESTMENTS

In the context of China's opening up to the outside world, FDI has played a dual role: the Chinese government has been trying to attract FDI flows from abroad since 1979, while it has also actively promoted overseas direct investments by Chinese companies since the early 2000s. Like its trade relations, China's role as a recipient and provider of foreign capital has changed dramatically over the last thirty years. China has continuously been the second most prominent target of inward foreign direct investment (IFDI) behind the United States.[22] After a relatively modest decline in IFDI in 2009, FDI going to China, according to Chinese statistics, increased to US$106 billion in 2010 and US$116 billion in 2011. Thus, more than US$1 trillion had been invested in China by the end of 2011.

Even more remarkable is the growth rate of China's outbound FDI (OFDI). Chinese OFDI grew annually by 50 percent from 2002 to 2009. China even registered small growth in OFDI flows in 2009, when global OFDI dropped by 43 percent.[23] In 2011 Chinese OFDI grew to almost US$75 billion. By 2013 the Chinese Ministry of Commerce expects China's OFDI flows to increase to US$100 billion, reaching a cumulative US$500 billion. However, these annual flows should not obscure the fact that China is still a minor player when it comes to the stock of global OFDI: its stock of OFDI is just 9 percent that of the United States and a mere 2 percent of the total global stock (see table 5.3).[24]

IFDI

The opening to and promotion of FDI became a central element in China's reform policy as of the late 1970s and went hand in hand with the expansion of trade, in which foreign-invested enterprises played a crucial role, as noted above.[25] Beijing gradually extended the initial preferential conditions applicable to investments by foreign companies in the special economic zones (SEZs) to coastal cities and export and technology zones in the mid-1980s. After Deng Xiaoping's "southern journey" in 1992, the government further eased existing restrictions (e.g., foreign manufacturing companies wishing to tap into the Chinese

Table 5.3. FDI to and from China, 1985–2011 (in US$ Billions)

	1985	1990	1995	2000	2005	2008	2009	2010	2011
Inward Foreign Direct Investment (IFDI)									
IFDI (per year)	1.9	3.5	37.5	40.7	60.3	92.4	90.0	105.7	116.0
IFDI (share of GDP) (%)	0.6	0.9	5.2	3.4	2.7	2.1	1.8	1.8	1.5
IFDI (stock/year end)	6.0	20.7	134.9	348.3	654.5	852.6	942.6	1,048.4	1,164.4
Outward Foreign Direct Investment (OFDI)									
OFDI (per year)	n/a	0.9	2.0	1.0	12.3	55.9	56.5	68.8	74.7
OFDI (stock)	0.9	4.4	10.0	20.3	57.2	184.0	245.7	317.2	424.8

Note: China's reported IFDI/OFDI figures on yearly flows and stocks at the end of the year often do not add up.
Sources: Zhonghua Renmin Gongheguo Guojia Tongjiju 2011; Zhonghua Renmin Gongheguo Shangwubu, Guojia Tongjiju, and Waihui Guanliju (annual).

market received limited access) and opened new sectors (e.g., real estate) to foreign investors for the first time.

Since the mid-1990s, the existing investment regime has generally been characterized by outside observers as favorable for foreign investors, with moderate taxes, investment-protection agreements, current account convertibility, and solid repatriation provisions. As a benchmark for its economic openness, China's FDI as a share of GDP (which was up to 6 percent until 2008–2009) was much higher than that of Japan, South Korea, or Taiwan (which was always less than 2 percent).

Over the last decade, the State Council has published a number of provisions to guide the direction of FDI. Typically, these guidelines list the projects that encourage, restrict, or prohibit foreign investments. The most recent guidelines, for example, aim at attracting FDI to support high-tech companies, to assist the service-outsourcing industry, and to encourage labor-intensive industries in central and western China. These guidelines take a medium- to long-term perspective and are embedded in the national five-year plans, the "national industrial restructuring and revitalization plans," or the "central China foreign investment plans." In total, sixteen government departments are involved in implementing the provisions set forth in the respective guidelines and plans, including the National Development and Reform Commission (NDRC), the Ministries of Commerce and Finance, and the securities and banking regulatory bodies.

In contrast to these central government initiatives, a prominent feature of China's investment regime is its decentralized nature, which allows local governments a high degree of discretion to decide utility rates, tax exemptions, and land-rent conditions. However, it is difficult for outside investors to identify the regional or local authority in charge of FDI approvals and regulations. Against this backdrop and in view of the variable quality of local governments, Western investors regularly complain about the lack of transparency, unclear responsibilities, fuzzy decision making, tiresome bureaucratic procedures, and discriminatory treatment.

In reaction to the sharp critical comments in 2010 by several major Western companies (including General Electric and Siemens of Germany) and business associations (e.g., the European Chamber of Commerce in China), leading Chinese politicians (Premier Wen Jiabao and Vice President Xi Jinping) tried on several occasions to reassure foreign investors about China's commitment to an open, fair environment for FDI. Indeed, China has a stake in safeguarding FDI, since foreign companies are responsible for 22 percent of tax revenue, 28 percent of industrial value added, and 55 percent of foreign trade and provide 45 million jobs.[26]

If one examines the sources, contractual forms, and composition of Chinese FDI, some noteworthy features become apparent.[27] Among the top countries providing FDI to China in 2011, the biggest groups of investors by far (with a combined share of about 70 percent) were from Hong Kong and Taiwan (see figures 5.5 and 5.6). From 2008 to 2010, Taiwan's share of FDI jumped more than threefold, reflecting the improved status of cross-Strait relations; not until 2011 did its share decrease somewhat, from 6.3 percent in 2010 to 5.8 percent. The large proportion of FDI originating in Greater China (including Hong Kong and Taiwan) is due to geographical proximity, common language, and low transaction costs. Hong Kong and Taiwan have been able to shift most of their labor-intensive production to the Chinese mainland (first footwear and garments, then the electronics industry). Tax havens, such as the British Virgin Islands, the Caymans, and Western Samoa, which for years ranked high among top Chinese FDI suppliers, have gradually lost their importance. Chinese economic legislation has cut preferential tax treatment for foreign investors, the so-called round-tripping investments (whereby Chinese companies transfer export earnings to offshore financial centers, the money is then reinvested in China, and the companies enjoy preferential tax treatment). The four industrialized nations—Japan (FDI share in China, 5.5 percent), the United States (2.6 percent), the United Kingdom (1.4 percent), and Germany (1.0 percent)—have declined in importance.[28]

Since 2000, wholly foreign-owned companies have dominated the contractual modes of FDI in China (with almost 80 percent of all realized FDI in 2011), whereas since 2000 joint ventures have declined in importance (18.5 percent of inflows in 2011). The sectoral composition of FDI reveals a high degree of manufacturing (in 2011, 45 percent) and a low degree of

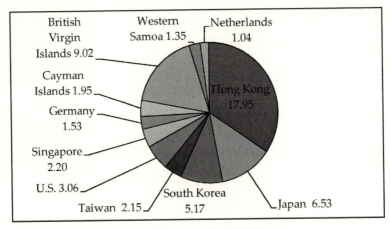

Figure 5.5: The origins of Chinese FDI, 2005 (in US$ billions).
Source: Ministry of Commerce of the PRC.

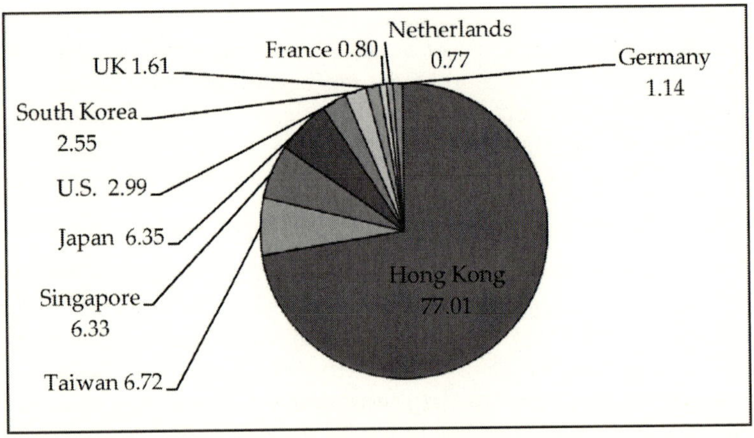

Figure 5.6. The origins of Chinese FDI, 2011 (in US$ billions).
Source: Ministry of Commerce of the PRC.

services, even after the service sector (i.e., wholesale trading, banking, and insurance) opened up as a result of WTO accession. Unlike in other emerging market economies, in 2011 real estate investment, with 23 percent, was the most important category in the service sector. Despite ongoing efforts to redirect FDI to western and central China, these regions still clearly lag behind the coastal areas. There are some signs that rising labor costs and a lack of qualified workers in coastal China may bring about a change in this pattern.

FDI has played a pivotal role in helping China gain access to foreign technology, achieve structural changes, and expand trade. In fact, it has been the dominant source of foreign capital. In contrast, short-term portfolio investments and bank lending have been negligible. Beyond FDI flows to China, Chinese economic policy can draw on an exceptionally high domestic savings rate (above 50 percent of GDP). When compared with the mid-1990s, the importance of FDI as measured against GDP has declined. However, foreign-owned companies still dominate research and development in the high-tech industries.

OFDI

Active Chinese promotion of OFDI is a comparatively recent phenomenon. In the 1980s and early 1990s, state-owned companies mostly undertook OFDI and directed the negligible OFDI flows primarily toward Hong Kong. Only after the Asian financial crisis, and especially after WTO accession, did the Chinese central state begin to encourage outward investment.[29] Since then, however, OFDI flows have increased dramatically, leading to the impression, widely held abroad, that Chinese state-owned companies are following the orders of the state (or rather, the Communist Party) by buying up assets, equity stakes, or commodities all over the world (hence the derogatory term "China Inc.").

However, it is not easy to assess the role that Chinese OFDI actually plays. The first caveat is the problem of obtaining reliable data.[30] The bulk of Chinese spending goes to Hong Kong, which then acts as a transit point. In many cases, the billions of dollars that the Chinese media announce with great fanfare as part of large cross-border deals are later downsized by up to 90 percent. The Western media often report nonbinding future project contracts as actual investment spending.

In addition, in view of China's huge financial resources and the absence of transparency with respect to most Chinese OFDI, many Western observers believe that Chinese investments are driven primarily by political interests rather than commercial goals. However, the purposes and motives behind the new Chinese OFDI offensive vary greatly, depending on the actors involved (ranging from small private enterprises to large state-owned companies), the sector in question (extraction of natural resources, manufacturing, or the services sector), and the targeted country (whether in the Western Hemisphere, one of the developing countries, an authoritarian state versus a democracy, and so forth).

The list of drivers behind Chinese OFDI is relatively long and subject to various interpretations.[31] One motive, of course, is China's search for secure access to overseas sources of energy and raw materials (petroleum, natural gas, mineral ores, and timber) in countries such as Australia,

Brazil, Canada, the central Asian states, Russia, Iran, and Angola. Furthermore, OFDI reflects efforts by Chinese manufacturers to acquire new production technologies, established brand names, and marketing know-how. Often enough, going abroad is not a sign of commercial power (as in the case of Japanese companies entering global competition in the 1970s) but a result of excessive supply capacities due to overinvestment, fierce domestic competition, and declining domestic revenue. This is especially true of the small and medium-size Chinese textile enterprises that moved to African production sites (Mauritius and Zambia) in order to ensure their survival.[32]

A study of Chinese OFDI in Europe finds that Chinese companies use much the same parameters as their Western counterparts: market potential (targeting the most populous countries, like Germany, Italy, France, and the United Kingdom) and access to distribution networks and advanced technology drive their selection of investment destinations.[33]

There is definitely heavy state involvement in Chinese OFDI. This begins with the drafting of plans and guidelines intended to direct such investments. As such, China's Tenth Five-Year Plan (for 2000–2005) formalized the directive for Chinese companies to go abroad to find new markets and establish fresh trade links. In order to strengthen coordination and avoid duplication and competition, the NDRC and the Ministries of Commerce and Foreign Affairs published a list of preferred target countries/regions in 2004 and 2009 (that included Southeast Asia, Saudi Arabia, South Africa, Russia, Canada, and Australia), along with key industries (oil drilling and refining, farming, manufacturing, and various service industries, such as shipping, construction, and research and development). The Ministry of Commerce and Chinese embassies around the world provide detailed information about business opportunities and the associated risks. Because of their state backing, Chinese state-owned commercial banks (especially the China Development Bank and the Export-Import Bank of China) play an important role by offering financial conditions that other commercial banks cannot match. Chinese companies can therefore offer comprehensive packages that their competitors regard as state subsidized and unfair. This applies especially in areas such as mineral extraction and railroad construction. The following illustrates a typical case of this "China cycle," as it is known: in 2010, Chinese state-owned banks granted a loan to Vale, a Brazilian iron ore company, to buy cargo ships from a Chinese shipyard to transport iron ore from Brazil to China.

The Chinese government nurtures some of its biggest multinational companies to become so-called dragon heads, or national champions, able to compete with the leading transnational corporations. However, there are several related caveats. First, some of today's Chinese business giants (e.g., Huawei or TCL) were not initially designated to become national champions. In other cases (e.g., in the bidding process for the Potash Group in 2010), Chinese state companies (specifically Sinochem in this case) were reluctant to follow bidding orders of the central state agencies because they feared the economic risks involved in a takeover. State-owned Chinese companies under regional or local jurisdictions are fierce competitors. Shanghai Automotive Industry Corporation (SAIC) is said to have worked actively behind the scenes to stifle its rival, Beijing Automotive Industry Corporation (BAIC), in its attempt to buy GM's German subsidiary, Opel, in 2009.

Chinese embassies and the Ministry of Foreign Affairs (MFA) in Beijing have lodged numerous complaints about Chinese state-owned companies behaving abroad in ways that are detrimental to Chinese foreign policy goals. There is also more media coverage when Western legislative intervention stops attempted Chinese takeovers (e.g., the failed attempt by China National Offshore Oil Corporation [CNOOC] to buy California-based Unocal in 2005). However, Chinese institutions have also denied a number of foreign acquisitions by Chinese companies (e.g., Sichuan Tengzhong's bid to buy US carmaker Hummer and China Development Bank's planned takeover of Germany's Dresdner Bank).

One final aspect of state involvement occurs in the process of OFDI approval procedures, which involve a plethora of actors.[34] The State Council plays a leadership and coordinating role, directly deciding on large projects (i.e., those involving more than US$200 million for resource projects or more than US$50 million for others and any projects that involve Taiwan). The NDRC must grant approval for projects of more than US$10 million, whereas the Ministry of Commerce must grant approval in every case (this is done through its local foreign-trade offices). Applicants then must obtain from SAFE the necessary foreign exchange. If state-owned companies are involved, then the State-Owned Assets Supervision and Administration Commission (SASAC) must also be consulted at the central or subnational level. Depending on the specific case, the Ministries of Finance and Foreign Affairs may also play roles, as will the usual regulatory bodies if the OFDI involves the insurance or banking sectors.

With so many bureaucratic players, each with its own agenda and bureaucratic interests, one can hardly speak of a single unified "China Inc." Chinese companies regularly complain about time-consuming approval procedures, discretionary local policies that often contradict official policy guidelines, and the lack of policy coordination. As a result, a considerable amount of OFDI is channeled out of China without any official approval or support.

Similar to the incoming FDI, China's outgoing FDI also has some noteworthy characteristics. When it comes to OFDI's regional distribution, North America and Oceania have declined in importance, whereas Asia,

Latin America, and Europe have become more important.[35] China's most prominent OFDI target regions in 2011 were Asia (61 percent), Latin America (16 percent), the EU (11 percent), Oceania (4 percent), Africa (4 percent), and North America (3 percent).[36]

On a country-by-country basis, in 2011 OFDI flows to Hong Kong were far ahead those to the tax havens (the Caymans and British Virgin Islands, which often serve as conduits to channel FDI to third-party countries), Singapore, and Australia (see figure 5.7). The Grand Duchy of Luxembourg, which appeared on the list of Chinese OFDI flows for the first time in 2007, was the most important Chinese OFDI destination in Europe in 2009 and 2010 (attracting almost 50 percent of all Chinese OFDI going to Europe) due to its preferential tax regime. Since OFDI flows to a specific country can vary enormously from one year to the next, we should also look at OFDI stocks. Again, at the end of 2011 Hong Kong led the tax havens and Australia by a huge margin. Chinese OFDI stock in Singapore was only slightly ahead of that in Luxembourg, which ranked sixth and ahead of the United States.[37]

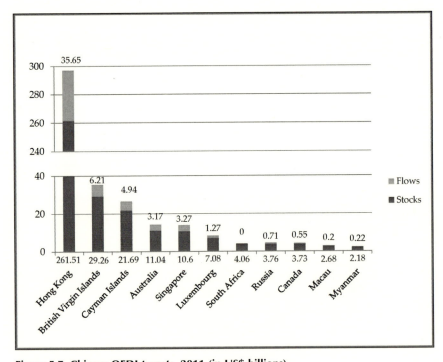

Figure 5.7. Chinese OFDI targets, 2011 (in US$ billions).
Sources: Ministry of Commerce of the PRC; Zhonghua Renmin Gongheguo Shangwubu, Guojia Tongjiju, and Waihui Guanliju 2011.

With regard to sectors or industries, contrary to popular belief and media attention, leasing, business services, and finance have generally dominated Chinese OFDI. Mining held an important share for the first time in 2009, making up almost 25 percent of all OFDI, but by 2011 it had dropped to 19 percent.

If we look at the types of companies that engage in foreign investment, we find that state-owned enterprises lead in terms of the amount of money involved (63 percent of OFDI stock in 2011), but they are only responsible for a small percentage of the actual cases (11 percent of OFDI stock in 2011). This means that state-owned enterprises are responsible for the large, headline-grabbing Chinese OFDI projects. Limited companies and private firms conduct the vast majority of investments.[38]

THE CONSEQUENCES OF CHINA'S OPENING TO THE OUTSIDE WORLD

China's increasing participation in the world economy has had important implications for the growth and direction of trade and investment flows, the economic fate of individual countries, global financial and commodity markets, and economic management in multilateral settings (for instance, the IMF and the Group of Twenty [G20]). In addition, beyond purely economic variables, such as the growth of GDP, export/import statistics, and stock of investments, the opening to the outside world has also played a vital role in transforming both China's political system and the direction of its foreign policy.

Impact on the Outside World

China's roles in the global economy and in global economic governance have changed considerably over the last several years. At the same time, China has been both praised as a growth engine and castigated as a possible threat to the outside world, especially since the outbreak of the global financial crisis.

After 2000, and even against the backdrop of shrinking world trade in 2009, China was able to increase its share of foreign trade with many partners significantly. By the end of 2011, it was the most important trading partner with Japan, Australia, South Korea, Taiwan, Vietnam, South Africa, Brazil, and Russia (see table 5.4).

Its smaller role as a trading partner with EU member countries is due to the high degree of intra-EU trade that already exists. But huge changes have been taking place even here, as highlighted by the case of Germany. In the course of only four years, China went from a medium-size export destination for German industry (ranked eleventh in 2007) to Germany's fifth-largest export recipient in 2011. Germany's manufacturing and automobile industries have benefited greatly from Chinese demand, which in turn has helped Germany recover from the 2008–2009 global crisis (see chapter 11).

In many ways, China's growing integration into the global economy has been positive for high-income countries (the United States, the EU states, Japan, and South Korea). They have benefited from a growing market for consumer and capital goods as well as from imports of cheap, labor-intensive goods made in China. Observers can also identify positive results in some East and Southeast Asian countries involved in China's processing trade as exporters (Malaysia and Singapore) and in countries that provide resources (Australia, Canada, Angola, Congo, Saudi Arabia, Peru, Chile, and Brazil). However, China has presented a challenge to those countries that compete directly in labor-intensive sectors (e.g., Mexico, Pakistan, Vietnam, and Bangladesh).[39]

Overall, there is a growing probability that trade frictions with China will increase. If China is able to move up the value chain and produce more high-tech manufactured goods, this could place it in direct competition with established Western producers. There is already growing concern among producers of railroad technology and power equipment (e.g., Germany's Siemens and Japan's Kawasaki Heavy Industries) that China is

Table 5.4. China's Importance as a Trading Partner, 1980–2011 (as a Percentage of the Exporting Country's Overall Trade)

	1980	1990	2000	2009	2011
United States	1.0	2.3	6.1	14.2	13.9
Japan	3.5	3.5	10.0	20.5	20.6
Germany	0.5	1.0	2.4	5.6	6.1
United Kingdom	0.3	0.5	1.6	6.0	5.6
Russia	n/a	n/a	4.6	7.6	9.9
Argentina	1.2	1.5	3.8	10.5	10.6
Brazil	0.8	1.1	2.0	12.4	16.0
Australia	2.4	2.6	6.8	19.8	23.2
India	0.5	0.1	2.4	8.9	9.7
South Korea	n/a	n/a	9.4	20.4	20.3
Philippines	1.9	1.1	4.7	11.8	11.2
Vietnam	n/a	0.2	9.8	13.9	18.0
Hong Kong	13.4	30.7	38.8	48.7	48.4
Taiwan	1.1 (1984)	4.2	10.7	22.9	22.8

Sources: Arora and Vamvakidis 2010, 17; 2009 data: *IMF Direction of Trade Statistics Yearbook 2012*; data for Taiwan: Taiwan Mainland Affairs Council.

about to emerge as a competitor that will win lucrative deals (e.g., railroad construction in the Balkans) or discriminate against Western companies in the Chinese market (in the wind-power sector, for instance). European complaints about a new Chinese assertiveness and arrogance following the financial crisis have featured constantly in newspaper headlines since 2010.

Furthermore, China is already a "market mover" in crucial commodities, such as gas, oil, iron ore, and copper. If it were to buy big chunks of these commodities in the global market and thereby drive up their market prices, there would definitely be a backlash from the West. As indicated in 2010, China's state control over mining, prices, and exports of rare earths (crucial for the production of a plethora of high-tech goods and currently primarily obtained in China) may at any time lead to conflicts with Western trading partners.

In multilateral settings such as the G20 or the IMF, China already has a reputation for hiding behind its status as a developing country and shying away from shouldering systemic responsibilities. As the failure of the Doha Round demonstrated in July 2008, much will depend on whether other emerging economies join China, effectively creating a new South-South cooperation, and whether China will be able to rally support for its positions.[40]

Impact on China

China's opening to the outside world is usually discussed internationally in terms of its consequences for the outside world. The West is closely scrutinizing and viewing with mounting suspicion the negative side effects of China's economic rise, such as the "offshoring" of jobs, intellectual property rights (IPR) violations, inadequate product-safety standards, greenhouse gas (GHG) emissions, and so forth.

Less attention is paid in the West to other areas, however, which also result from China's increasing integration into the world economy—far-reaching power shifts and fundamental changes in the rules (both formal and informal) of China's domestic politics that the Chinese leadership did not deliberately initiate.

When China began its policy of opening up in 1979, it had no intention to expose state-owned companies to global competition. On the contrary, the heart of the state-controlled economy was to be shielded and protected. Within the PRC's fast-growing export sector, however, new forms of entrepreneurship began to emerge (most of the time with the support of foreign or overseas Chinese investors), and this put state industries under increasing pressure to adapt and become more competitive.

With the integration of coastal China into transnational production networks, the authority of the central leadership changed in unexpected ways. Decentralized networks of shared interests connecting local governments and foreign investors gradually found ways to evade central government orders, thereby curbing the central government's ability to enforce compliance.

The exploding number of international contacts during the reform era has dramatically increased the number of players and complicated the Chinese foreign policy playing field. Most Chinese state bodies are now involved in permanent—and, in part, extremely extensive—exchange routines with foreign institutions (both governmental and nongovernmental) and transnational companies. These transnational networks among political, bureaucratic, economic, and scientific actors play an important role in diffusing administrative, judicial, and technical know-how, as well as in articulating interests regarding lawmaking and administrative regulation. Advice from foreign legal specialists has gone into the formulation of a considerable number of China's commercial laws.

The necessity of administrative cooperation with numerous foreign economic actors has led to organizational changes within Chinese state organs, even in terms of funding and daily operations. Foreign financial assistance and experts support a number of policy programs (such as poverty reduction, local elections, and environmental-protection schemes). Leading Chinese officials regularly participate in transnational cooperation and policy networks. Regional government bodies have also established close relations with foreign investors. Thus, novel transnational lobbies that have a viable stake in safeguarding and deepening China's integration into the world economy have emerged within China. These unintended consequences of economic interdependence constrain the Chinese leadership's ability to exert its power indiscriminately in international politics.

NOTES

1. Bremmer 2010.
2. Branstetter and Lardy 2008.
3. Naughton 2007.
4. Bergsten et al. 2006; Brandt, Rawski, and Zhu 2007; Naughton 2007.
5. Lemoine 2010.
6. Linden, Kraemer, and Dedrick 2009.
7. C. Freeman 2013.
8. Burdekin 2008; Das 2009; Frankel 2010; Goldstein and Lardy 2009.
9. Anderson 2009; Setser 2008.
10. Anderson 2009; Frankel 2010.
11. US Department of the Treasury 2012a.
12. China Investment Corporation 2012; Setser 2008; Setser and Pandey 2009.
13. US Department of the Treasury 2012a.

14. For details on the internationalization of the CNY, see Gao and Yu 2012; Ma, Liu, and Miao 2012; K. Miller 2010; Yu Yongding 2012.
15. Chin and Helleiner 2008; Eichengreen 2011; Murphy and Yuan 2009; Prasad and Ye 2012.
16. Frankel 2010.
17. Das 2009.
18. US Department of the Treasury 2012a.
19. Frankel 2010; Frankel and Wei 2007.
20. Goldstein and Lardy 2009.
21. Yi Jingtao 2007.
22. United Nations Conference on Trade and Development 2010.
23. United Nations Conference on Trade and Development 2010.
24. United Nations Conference on Trade and Development 2012.
25. Branstetter and Lardy 2008; Naughton 2007.
26. Xi Jinping 2010.
27. Branstetter and Lardy 2008; Naughton 2007.
28. Yao and Zhang 2012.
29. Cheung and Qian 2009.
30. Scissors 2009, 2010.
31. Brautigam 2009; Brandt, Rawski, and Zhu 2007; Cernat and Parplies 2010; Ohashi 2005; Pan Chengxin 2009; F. Wu 2005a, 2005b; Zweig 2010.
32. Brautigam 2009.
33. Cernat and Parplies 2010.
34. Luo, Xue, and Han 2010.
35. Cheung and Qian 2009.
36. Zhonghua Renmin Gongheguo Shangwubu, Guojia Tongjiju, and Waihui Guanliju 2012.
37. Zhonghua Renmin Gongheguo Shangwubu, Guojia Tongjiju, and Waihui Guanliju 2012.
38. Zhonghua Renmin Gongheguo Shangwubu, Guojia Tongjiju, and Waihui Guanliju 2012.
39. Arora and Vamvakidis 2010; Bergsten et al. 2006; Branstetter and Lardy 2008; D. Park and Shin 2010; Zweig 2010.
40. Bergsten et al. 2008.

6

China's Role in International Environmental and Climate Policy

China currently faces numerous serious environmental problems, some of which are already producing global repercussions. The country's extensive industrial expansion is a highly significant factor in accelerating climate change.

CHINA'S ENVIRONMENTAL PROBLEMS
AND THEIR TRANSNATIONAL EFFECTS

During the period from 1980 through 2000, China had the largest worldwide increase in carbon dioxide (CO_2) emissions, and by 2006 it had overtaken the United States as the world's most prolific emitter. Its status as the biggest producer of greenhouse gases (GHGs) is due to its dependence on coal for two-thirds of its domestic energy. With regard to per capita CO_2 emissions, since 2008 China has exceeded the global average, but it has not yet reached the levels of the advanced industrialized nations (see figure 6.1).

In addition to producing the GHG CO_2, the burning of coal also produces sulfur dioxide (SO_2), a major contributor to air pollution and acid rain. Acid rain affects 30 percent of China's land area, especially south of the Yangtze River. Several neighboring countries, in particular South Korea and Japan, have addressed the issue of acid deposits from China in talks with the Chinese government.

China itself already faces the serious detrimental effects of climate change. According to the Chinese Ministry of Environmental Protection,

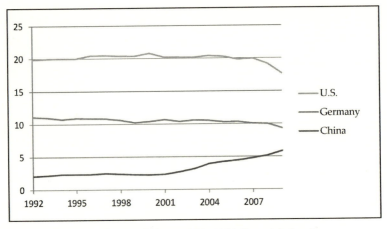

Figure 6.1. Per capita carbon emissions, 1993–2011 (in metric tons).
Sources: US Energy Information Administration; EDGAR—Emission Database for Global Atmospheric Research (http://edgar.jrc.ec.europa.eu).

the average annual air temperature in mainland China has increased by about two degrees since 1950. Furthermore, there has been an increase in severe weather conditions. Since the 1990s, flooding, heavy rains and snow, tropical storms, and droughts have occurred with increasing frequency. The rising sea levels along Chinese coasts (currently 1.4 to 3.2 millimeters per year) may create serious problems since the coastal regions, where the country generates a large proportion of its gross domestic product (GDP), are also China's most densely populated areas. The interior of the country is affected by glacial melting. Approximately one-fifth of the glacial area in western and northern China (the Himalayas, the Qinghai-Tibetan Plateau, and the Tian Shan and Altai Mountains) has melted since the beginning of the twentieth century.

With respect to water supply, many regions in China face serious water scarcity and contamination. Per capita availability of water is only a one-quarter the global average. The situation in the arid region of northern China is particularly serious. Although the supply of water has always been precarious in this area, climate change and desertification have further exacerbated the problem.

ENVIRONMENTAL POLICY: INSTITUTIONS AND AMBITIONS

Not until the end of the 1970s did the Chinese central government begin to systematically monitor and regulate the ecological side effects of industrialization. In the 1980s environmental pollution became subject to selective statistical monitoring, and in individual cases sanctions were imposed. The National Environmental Protection Agency under the central government was largely ineffective initially. But during the 1990s it was upgraded to the State Environmental Protection Administration (SEPA). At the same time, there was an increase in government spending on measures to prevent or counteract environmental destruction.

Beginning in 2003, the Hu-Wen administration initiated a change of direction. Greater care in using environmental and energy resources is now a key element of national development strategy. SEPA, which lacked political influence, was upgraded to the Ministry of Environmental Protection. At a national conference on environmental protection in 2006, Premier Wen Jiabao stated that grave errors had been made during China's growth process. If long-term harmonization of economic progress and environmental protection were to be achieved, he said, then resolute administrative, legal, economic, and technical measures were required to rectify these mistakes. In the aftermath of his speech, the central government introduced a series of programs aimed at reducing emissions and restoring ecosystems. Since 2006, there has been a fundamental move away from the earlier skeptical attitude regarding findings on global climate change toward implementation of a more active climate policy.[1]

As part of its National Climate-Change Program (2007), China resolved to increase the share of nonfossil fuels in its primary energy mix to 15 percent by 2020. By 2009, China produced substantially more electricity from renewable sources of energy (including hydropower) than either the United

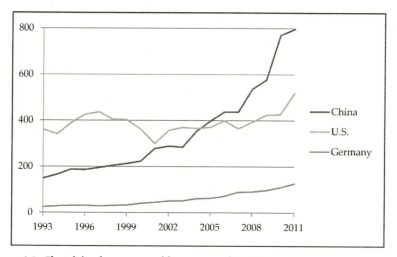

Figure 6.2. Electricity from renewable sources of energy, 1993–2011—a comparison (in kWh billions).
Source: US Energy Information Administration.

States or Germany (see figure 6.2). At the same time, the forestry sector
initiated an action plan for large-scale campaigns to counter the effects of
climate change. Based on satellite analysis, China's forest cover as a share
of its total land area has in fact increased over the last decade, in contrast to
trends in other East and Southeast Asian countries.

The five-year plans for the periods 2001–2005, 2006–2010, and
2011–2015 designated a series of stringent objectives to cut down on
pollutant emissions and reduce energy consumption. Some of these
programs brought about significant progress in specific sectors and regions. However, aggregate national emissions and energy consumption
remained high due to the extremely fast-paced industrialization. Thus
there is a fundamental conflict between the ambitious objectives of China's environmental policy and the imperatives of industrial growth—a
conflict that will be extremely difficult to resolve.

INTEGRATION IN INTERNATIONAL CLIMATE POLICY

Bilateral and Multilateral Collaboration

The People's Republic of China (PRC) collaborates closely with the United
States in climate policy matters, notably with the US Department of Energy,
which has an office in Beijing. In the context of this cooperation, energy-
efficiency standards have been launched on a broad range of household ap-
pliances, and the US-China Clean Energy Research Center was established.
The Chinese government is keen to further institutionalize its collaboration
with other nations on environmental and climate policies through, for example, joint research initiatives and regular dialogue.

Bilateral relations with the emerging nations and developing countries
have become increasingly important in terms of China's climate policy.
Brazil, South Africa, India, and China (the BASIC Group countries) have
agreed to coordinate their positions more closely prior to UN climate-
change conferences and to cooperate in the fields of climate science and
environmental technology.

The Kyoto Protocol (1997)

China signed the Kyoto Protocol in 1998 and ratified it in 2002. The protocol entered into force in 2005. Like all developing countries, however,
China is not legally bound to meet specific emission-reduction targets. Under the principle of "common but differentiated responsibilities," the main
burden for reducing emissions falls on the long-established industrialized
nations that for over 150 years have been principally responsible for the
high levels of GHG emissions.

Additional multilateral mechanisms accompanied national adaptation programs aimed at implementing the agreements in the Kyoto Protocol; of these, the Clean Development Mechanism (CDM) is especially relevant to China. Under the CDM, developing countries can earn "certified emission-reduction credits" for emission reductions in relation to the "business-as-usual" scenario. Industrialized nations bound by the Kyoto Protocol to emission reductions can purchase these credits, which they can count toward meeting their Kyoto targets. These transfers thus provide a financial reward for developing countries that implement emission-reduction measures. China is the world's largest beneficiary of the CDM schemes, having participated in 52 percent of all CDM projects.[2]

The UN Climate-Change Conferences in Copenhagen (2009) and Cancún (2010)

The Copenhagen Accord was drafted at the controversial UN Climate-Change Conference in Copenhagen.[3] However, the document was merely "taken note of," and not formally adopted, by the conference delegates. Therefore, it is not binding under international law. Still, a key outcome of the Copenhagen conference is the commitment to implement measures to reduce GHG emissions in order to limit increases in global temperatures to a maximum of 2°C above preindustrial levels. For this purpose, Appendixes I and II of the Copenhagen Accord list the emission-reduction pledges by the conference participants. China committed to three voluntary national mitigation actions:[4]

- To lower carbon dioxide emissions per unit of GDP by 40 to 45 percent by 2020 (compared to 2005 levels)
- To increase the share of nonfossil fuels in its primary energy consumption to about 15 percent by 2020 (compared to 2005 levels)
- To increase forest cover by 40 million hectares and forest stock volume by 1.3 billion cubic meters by 2020 (from 2005 levels)

Although China was not bound to implement these measures under international law, following the Copenhagen conference the Chinese government firmly upheld all three objectives, both in the context of diplomatic negotiations and in its domestic programs.

The Twelfth Five-Year Plan for the 2011–2015 period dispelled doubts about China's willingness to implement its pledges. In accordance with the Copenhagen concessions, the plan proposes reducing carbon dioxide intensity by 17 percent by 2015 (compared to 2010 levels), increasing the share of nonfossil fuel sources in primary energy consumption to 11 percent, raising forest cover to about 22 percent of China's total land area, and increasing forest stock by 600 million cubic meters.

Delegates to the 2010 UN Climate-Change Conference in Cancún reached a set of formal decisions, known as the Cancún Agreements. A total of forty-two industrialized nations accepted legally binding emission-reduction targets in accordance with their different responsibilities and capabilities. The developing countries announced "nationally appropriate" actions on a voluntary basis. Even though the Chinese government reiterated the three pledges it had made in Copenhagen, it consistently emphasized the voluntary nature of its domestic mitigation measures.

CHINESE ATTITUDES TO CLIMATE DIPLOMACY

Traditional Approach

During the period from 1992 through 2008, Chinese delegations at international climate-change conferences categorically rejected any obligation to commit to legally binding emission reductions. China's chief negotiators pointed to the historical responsibility of the Western industrialized nations and Japan. They argued that as a developing country, China was a victim and not a perpetrator of climate change and continued to have low per capita carbon dioxide emissions. Consequently, the industrialized nations had to bear the main burden of emission reductions, and the developing countries could only be expected to contribute within the scope of their economic development. Their right to catch up in terms of economic growth was irrefutable.

The Chinese government defended the sovereignty and interests of the developing countries and stated that intervention in domestic affairs in the name of climate policy was unacceptable. The government would not be pressured into taking an active, transparent, and therefore potentially compromising leadership role on the international stage of climate diplomacy. This foreign policy doctrine, traced back to Deng Xiaoping, shaped the participation of Chinese delegations at climate-change conferences until 2009. Despite the country's rapidly growing global importance and rise as the biggest emitter of GHGs, for a long time the Chinese government still took a passive or evasive approach toward international climate negotiations.

Changes in China's Approach to Climate Policy

Given international research and dialogue on the causes and effects of global climate change as well as parallel research being carried out in China, since the early twenty-first century the Chinese government has been growing increasingly concerned about the consequences of climate change for future stability in the country. Key Chinese officials are becoming more aware of their vulnerability vis-à-vis climate change. The revised domestic economic development strategy also had a direct impact on China's climate policy: following two decades of expansive growth with intensive use of resources and enormous damage to the environment, the introduction of sustainable, energy-saving, efficiency- and technology-driven economic development is now a key political task.

These new strategic considerations include international climate negotiations. The Chinese leadership has continued to firmly advocate the establishment of mechanisms to transfer environmental technology to the developing countries so as to promote domestic development objectives from the outside. Having obtained half of all CDM-financed projects, China has benefited in terms of both energy and the environment from this type of technology-transfer scheme.

China's role and vested interests in international climate policy have come under increasing criticism from other developing countries. Although for decades the Chinese government had fostered a self-image as an advocate for the Third World—without any direct responsibilities or obligations—the developing countries now increasingly call China's role as advocate into question. Its status as the world's biggest industrial producer of carbon emissions is incompatible with its self-image as a developing country, arousing general doubts about the credibility of China's display of solidarity with poorer nations. The country's economic rise and the resultant consequences for the climate now undermine the Chinese government's traditional conduct with regard to foreign policy issues.

China's Climate-Policy Dilemmas

China's new interest in international climate policy now clashes with its traditional behavior patterns and foreign policy positions. The PRC faces a series of conflicting objectives that became particularly apparent in the context of the UN Climate-Change Conference in Copenhagen.

Dilemma 1: Climate Change versus Growth Targets

In the medium to long term, the PRC's domestic economic and environmental policy objectives are essentially compatible with the aims of the United Nations Framework Convention on Climate Change (UNFCCC).

Regime legitimacy in China, however, remains based primarily on improving in the short term the living conditions of politically significant sectors of the population. Although binding emission reductions are important for the medium term, they are likely to compromise short-term economic growth and therefore challenge vested interests.[5] Stressing the voluntary nature of its domestic efforts, China continues to oppose international agreements that impose binding targets. At the same time, the government, under the climate-policy principle of "common but differenti-ated responsibilities," has called upon the industrialized nations to reduce their emissions by 40 percent by 2020. But because the Chinese govern-ment is unwilling to make legally binding commitments, it does not have any bargaining power to convince the United States or the European Union (EU) to make any drastic concessions.

There was obvious disagreement within the Chinese delegation in Co-penhagen over potential compromises. Whereas climate-policy experts in the delegation recommended binding commitments even for quantitative targets, general advocates of international law advised against any such type of obligation. In the end, the Chinese delegation placed its traditional foreign policy approach of rejecting binding obligations above its emerging interests in a significant and cooperative reduction of global GHG emis-sions. Interest in economic and environmental flexibility and avoidance of accountability under international law overshadowed the threats posed by climate change.

Dilemma 2: China's Self-Image as a Developing Country versus Its Status as a De Facto Superpower

The second dilemma focuses on China's self-conception with respect to international relations. Foreign policy debates have revealed deep divisions over whether China can still regard itself as a developing country in accor-dance with its decades-long foreign policy practices or must accept and ac-tively take on the role of a superpower in line with its actual global profile. Both Western observers and an increasing number of developing countries that regard China's cultivation of its "Third World" image as implausible have raised this particularly critical question.

The following example illustrates this situation: In the run-up to the UN Climate-Change Conference in Copenhagen, the least developed countries (LDCs) and the Association of Small Island States (AOSIS) called for a cli-mate agreement to restrict atmospheric CO_2 levels to a maximum of 350 ppm and to limit global warming to 1.5°C. China promptly rejected this initiative, thereby hurting its reputation in these countries. The Thai delega-tion openly criticized China, arguing that it was time for China to assume a greater degree of responsibility. Several African countries maintained that China had already benefited disproportionately from the CDM and there-fore had an obligation to help other developing countries.[6]

The Chinese delegation attempted to mitigate any diplomatic damage by supporting transfer payments from the industrialized nations to the devel-oping countries. The conference ultimately agreed upon annual payments of US$30 billion to assist the developing countries in reducing deforestation, acquiring environmental technology, and cushioning the negative effects of climate change. The aim was to increase these payments to US$100 billion by 2020. At every opportunity, the Chinese delegates emphasized that the payments were primarily intended to benefit the developing countries in Africa and the small island states that faced particularly serious threats from rising sea levels. Despite the changes in its general economic situation and these obvious credibility issues, the PRC continued to cultivate a self-image as an advocate for the Third World.

Dilemma 3: Sovereignty versus Transparency

Defending the sovereignty of nation-states is one of the guiding principles of Chinese foreign policy. Beijing has always categorically rejected international intervention in domestic affairs. When it comes to implementing global climate agreements, however, this principle comes into conflict with the necessity for external verification of national emissions-reduction measures. At the Copenhagen Climate-Change Conference, US delegates specifically stated that their country would only accept binding emission targets on the condition that an international body verified implementation of these goals and subsequent compliance. They called for establishment of a measuring, reporting, and verification (MRV) system for this purpose.

The Chinese delegates were extremely skeptical about setting up such an MRV system. On the one hand, they feared intervention in China's domestic affairs. On the other, the government was fully aware of its many shortcomings regarding implementation of environmental directives at local levels and feared that an MRV mechanism would damage its international credibility. Additional pressure was generated due to the fact that, to ensure the funds were used for the intended purposes, the United States was calling for transparency as a precondition for providing increased financial aid to the developing countries. The United States was also demanding full transparency with respect to technology transfers.

The Chinese delegation actually succeeded in overcoming this dilemma in Copenhagen. The PRC agreed to a mechanism whereby there is regular reporting by national authorities on implementation progress of the agreed measures. But measuring and verification by supranational authorities are only to be carried out for projects subsidized by international funds or involving technological assistance. This means that the measuring and verification processes essentially remain under the control of the nation-states, with supranational checks only in specific instances. These mechanisms also create an incentive for the industrialized countries to provide financial aid or to participate in technology-transfer schemes, since these are potential means to bring about a greater degree of transparency.

CHINESE CLIMATE-POLICY REQUIREMENTS

The Copenhagen Climate-Change Conference disclosed a number of discrepancies and inner conflicts within China's foreign policy. Traditional PRC behavioral patterns on the international stage have frequently proven an obstacle when it comes to achieving newly defined or changing targets and interests. In the end, Beijing will have to revise its doctrine of self-restraint with respect to foreign policy issues. If China wants to fulfill its medium-term targets, it must develop appropriate leadership qualities and shed its reservations concerning international obligations, international cooperation, and transparency, even if this means weakening its own state sovereignty. To encourage other countries to make concessions, China too will have to make them. Only by becoming actively involved in the international climate regime will China be able to effectively safeguard its own interests.

The trade-off between growth targets and climate risks inevitably involves inconsistencies and readjustments. Diplomatically, economically, and ecologically, China certainly will benefit substantially from enhanced initiatives and cooperation in global climate policy. Chinese climate policy has undergone a number of adaptations since 2009. As far as domestic policy is concerned, the Chinese government has set extremely ambitious environmental and energy targets under the Twelfth Five-Year Plan. If successfully implemented, these targets might improve China's credibility and provide a fresh impetus to its participation in international climate diplomacy.

NOTES

1. Conrad 2012; Edmonds 2011.
2. United Nations Framework Convention on Climate Change (UNFCCC) 1997, 1998, 2012.
3. UNFCCC 2009.
4. UNFCCC 2010.
5. Conrad 2012; Grunow 2011.
6. Economy 2010.

7

China and International Human Rights Policy

Beijing's selective commitment to cooperation and its tactical flexibility in international politics are particularly obvious in issues that involve human rights. China's international integration within the legal framework of the United Nations is at the heart of its strategy of dealing with the issue of human rights. By seeking the country's admittance to the United Nations, which it obtained in 1971, the Chinese government accepted the general obligation to uphold human rights as contained in the UN Charter. Until the early 1980s, however, the Chinese leadership rejected any notion of universal human rights, claiming it was a "bourgeois" ideology, and avoided being drawn into international human rights activities.

In 1982, only several years after adopting its reform and opening policy, the People's Republic of China (PRC) became a member of the United Nations Commission on Human Rights (UNCHR), vowed to respect human rights, and began to ratify a series of special human rights conventions. The PRC is an elected founding member of the UN Human Rights Council, which succeeded the UNCHR in 2006 (see figure 7.1). In total, by 2011 China had joined twenty-five human rights conventions, many of which, though not all, China's National People's Congress had already ratified.

Even though the comprehensive "social pact" (the International Convention on Economic, Social, and Cultural Rights) was ratified in 2001, the most important agreement from a Western perspective, the "civil pact" (the International Convention on Civil and Political Rights) has still not been ratified. The PRC claims the delay is because it first has to make a number of adjustments to its legal system.

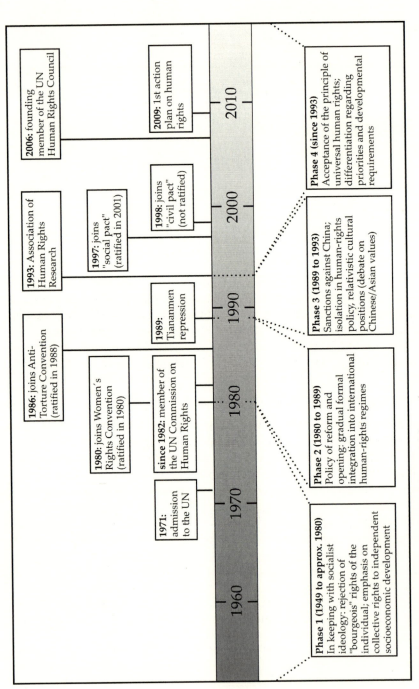

Figure 7.1. China and the international human rights regime.

1960   1970   1980   1990   2000   2010

1971: admission to the UN

1980: joins Women's Rights Convention (ratified in 1980)

since 1982: member of the UN Commission on Human Rights

1986: joins Anti-Torture Convention (ratified in 1988)

1989: Tiananmen repression

1993: Association of Human Rights Research

1997: joins "social pact" (ratified in 2001)

1998: joins "civil pact" (not ratified)

2006: founding member of the UN Human Rights Council

2009: 1st action plan on human rights

Phase 1 (1949 to approx. 1980) In keeping with socialist ideology; rejection of "bourgeois" rights of the individual; emphasis on collective rights to independent socioeconomic development

Phase 2 (1980 to 1989) Policy of reform and opening; gradual formal integration into international human-rights regimes

Phase 3 (1989 to 1993) Sanctions against China; isolation in human-rights policy, relativistic cultural positions (debate on Chinese/Asian values)

Phase 4 (since 1993) Acceptance of the principle of universal human rights; differentiation regarding priorities and developmental requirements

In addition to human rights cooperation with a number of other countries through its involvement in the United Nations, the Chinese government has also been developing its own position regarding the human rights debate. This position, which first emerged in the 1990s, emphasizes its different values and political priorities, as well as its different cultural traditions and levels of socioeconomic development.

In response to sharp criticism from the West about political repression in China (especially in the wake of the violent suppression of the urban protest movements in June 1989), the Chinese government attempted to counter Western reproaches with its own interpretation of human rights. It argued that a more discriminating independent position should replace the West's "monopoly" on interpreting the notion of human rights. To this end, China took the following steps: In 1993 it set up the China Society for Human Rights Studies (CSHRS), which runs China's official website on its human rights developments (www.chinahumanrights.org), hosts regular human rights forums (e.g., the Beijing Forum on Human Rights), and releases the *Blue Book on Human Rights* (the first volume was published in 2011). In addition, since 1991 the State Council Government Information Office has issued a series of white papers containing programmatic statements on the development of human rights in China. As a reaction to the international criticism due to Chinese suppression of unrest in Tibet prior to the Beijing Olympic Games, in 2008 China published an action plan for 2009–2010 and, in 2012, an additional plan for 2012–2015. On the one hand, specific goals in the plans (e.g., with regard to improvements in prison conditions and interrogation methods) met with cautious approval abroad. On the other hand, however, they retained a clear, substantive focus on collective, nonpolitical, and unenforceable human rights (such as the right to development and social and economic rights) based on the modernized socialist and culturalist interpretation that has characterized the human rights positions of the Chinese government since the 1990s.

Since the final years of the twentieth century, the Chinese government has taken the positions listed in table 7.1 vis-à-vis the relevant UN institutions, but not merely as a passive means for protecting China's national sovereignty and fending off Western meddling in China's domestic affairs. Rather, Chinese diplomats have actively stepped up their campaigns for approval among the developing and emerging economies.[1] The Chinese government was instrumental in establishing the UN Human Rights Council in 2006 and intensified its efforts to legitimize and popularize its own understanding of human rights.[2]

In addition to its efforts in the United Nations, Beijing maintains a number of bilateral and multilateral human rights dialogues, for instance, with the United States, the European Union (EU), and Germany. Institutionalized rounds of talks, depending on the parties involved, have been

Table 7.1.   Official Chinese Positions in the International Human Rights Debate

Principles	• China pursues a "socialist path of human rights development with Chinese characteristics." This means the following:
	  ▪ The universality of human rights is acknowledged but human rights priorities and needs that vary from nation to nation (such as the right to development, social and economic rights, civil and political rights), based on different cultural traditions and notions of political order, are legitimate.
	  ▪ Human rights standards will be raised gradually over the long term, in consideration of the level of socioeconomic development.

The Chinese situation	• Historically, China has been a victim of human rights abuses by the Western powers and Japan. • The human rights situation in China has never been better than it is today (in terms of growth in per capita GDP and disposable income; reduction in the rural poverty rate; rule of law; and improvements to the judicial system). • China is limited by its natural, historical, cultural, economic, and social conditions in realizing the target that all citizens can completely enjoy human rights. • Challenges remain, especially with regard to imbalances in the development process (the growing gap in income distribution and regional disparities, the quality of education and health care, housing prices, food safety).

Steps to be taken by the Chinese government	• China must focus on the following:
	  ▪ "Prioritizing the people": safeguarding the people's economic, political, social, and cultural rights (to meet material and cultural demands; to improve the democratic system with expanded elections, management, and supervision; to safeguard people's rights for information and participation).
	  ▪ Improving people's well-being (expansion of public services in education, health care, and the pension system).
	  ▪ Shifting from "policy-oriented administration to law-oriented administration" in order to respect the rule of law (protection of human rights in the constitution, establishing a "multilayered and all-around legal system").

International cooperation	• The United Nations plays a key role in promoting human rights worldwide. • China is willing to learn from abroad based on principles of full equality and mutual respect. • International human rights policy cannot be pursued via confrontation and sanctions. • The Western powers, with their own records of historical and current human rights transgressions, cannot lay claim to moral or political superiority when it comes to human rights issues.

Sources: Wang Chen 2011; Zhonghua Renmin Gongheguo Guowuyuan Xinwen Bangongshi 2010, 2012b.

held at varying intervals since the mid-1990s. These talks, usually called at China's initiative, take place behind closed doors. They have come to constitute the primary instrument for Western human rights policy toward diplomacy with China.

Confrontational measures by the West are largely a thing of the past. A total of eleven petitions were submitted to the United Nations Commission on Human Rights between 1990 and 2004 to censure China for human rights violations. But only one of these actually made it onto the agenda, and in 1995 a vote ultimately decided the matter in China's favor. Differences of opinion among European states over the treatment of China by the Commission on Human Rights surfaced in 1997. As a consequence, since 1998 the Europeans, as well as the Australians and Canadians, have not supported further initiatives to censure the country. In response, China has declared its willingness to engage in a human rights dialogue with the EU that encompasses academic and technical legal exchanges. As a result, the only Western criticism of China's actions during the unrest in Tibet in 2008 took place on the sidelines of a meeting of the UN Human Rights Council; the council issued no statement, and certainly no resolution.

To this day, the United States is the only major country that officially delivers systematic and frank criticism of China—in the form of documented cases and condemnations appearing periodically in human rights reports issued by the State Department. Other Western states refer to criticism of the human rights situation put forward during human rights dialogues conducted behind closed doors and to specific successes, such as those achieved with the release of individual political prisoners or improvements in prison conditions.

Evaluations of Western human rights strategy are ambivalent. Critics point to improvements inside China that are rudimentary at best. They criticize the fact that the West is currently forgoing resolutions critical of China in the United Nations and, in doing so, carelessly relinquishing a vital lever of influence. A distinctive feature of the human rights dialogue between the EU and China, argue critics, is the lack of tangible results. The only purpose thus far has been to bypass awkward discourse at high political levels and to provide an opportunity to cite the dialogue on rights whenever society voices criticism.[3]

After the failure of earlier confrontational strategies, other observers refer to the lack of alternatives with respect to human rights dialogues.[4] Outsiders argue that any change in China's human rights policy will be induced first and foremost by way of inner-societal dynamics. The prospects for success from sanctions or incentives from the outside are dim.[5] The most important step, therefore, is to analyze and purposefully influence those internal processes that might contribute to tangible improvements, for example, in the judiciary and penal systems.

In summary, a look at the official positions of the Chinese government on human rights policy reveals that any changes will be primarily on the declarative and procedural/organizational levels. After ratification of a number of human rights conventions, China has fulfilled its UN obligations by introducing the relevant international standards into its legal system, complying with the specific reporting requirements, allowing special observers from the United Nations into the country for fact-finding trips, and cooperating with the UN High Commissioner for Human Rights. A department of human rights, including a special envoy responsible for international human rights dialogue, was specially created in the Ministry of Foreign Affairs (MFA).

This openness with respect to cooperation in international human rights policy, however, contrasts sharply with the PRC's human rights practices on the ground, which are often repressive, and with its intransigence in the face of Western criticism. Harsh diplomatic attacks on other countries and repressive measures at home formed the backdrop for the reaction to the case of Liu Xiaobo, the dissident who was imprisoned at the end of 2008 for "undermining state security" and awarded the Nobel Peace Prize in absentia in December 2010. At home, the government reacted to this unwelcome honor with added reprisals against regime critics and harassment of foreign journalists accredited in China. It also condemned the award in the harshest of terms, calling it a political provocation and national defamation. In a vehement diplomatic campaign, China urged other states—for the most part nondemocratic states or those dependent on China for economic aid—to boycott the award ceremony. Nineteen of the fifty-eight nations invited to attend the event subsequently chose not to participate. These included such countries as Russia, Cuba, Vietnam, Sudan, and Iran, most of which have traditionally supported China's human rights policy in international human rights committees. The conflict surrounding Liu Xiaobo is symptomatic of the degree to which Chinese foreign policy relegates regard for international esteem and positive demeanor to the background as soon as core political interests, such as containing domestic opposition to Chinese Communist Party (CCP) dominance, come into play.

When it comes to political influence from abroad, China is an extremely difficult case not just because of the intransigence of its leadership. Recent research has unveiled a widespread lack of understanding, and even indifference, among the Chinese population concerning political topics such as rights and freedom of participation.[6] Data from the World Values Survey, a global survey with adjustments for cultural particularities, indicate that even young, well-educated Chinese rank economic development and social stability considerably higher than do their European counterparts, for whom freedom of speech and participation in democratic processes are more important. The conclusion to be drawn from representative, random surveys is that Americans and Western Europeans, on the one hand, and Chinese, on the other, differ greatly when it comes to understanding and weighing political rights of freedom, defense, and codetermination (even when accounting for the possibility that political restrictions, self-restraint, or tactical responses bias interviewees' survey answers).

This finding directly affects Western policy toward China. In diplomatic confrontations over violations of the political rights of Chinese citizens or ethnic minorities, the majority of the Chinese populace reacts to Western reproaches with a lack of understanding or outright rejection and, if anything, identifies even more strongly with the Chinese government position. A confrontational approach to topics related to political and civil rights may earn Western governments the approval of their own media and public, at least in the short term, but in China itself—at its current stage of development—such an approach does not meet with broad support among the populace. It may even be counterproductive if it engenders solidarity with the positions of the Chinese government.

NOTES

1. T. Chen 2010.
2. D. Freeman and Geeraerts 2011.
3. Kinzelbach and Thelle 2011.
4. Chan 2006.
5. Chen Dingding 2009.
6. Shi and Lou 2010.

8

The Taiwan Issue

The Taiwan issue represents a fundamental problem in Chinese politics that dates back to the Chinese Civil War and the Cold War. It is intimately intertwined with the overall security structure in the Asia-Pacific region as well as with the role of the United States in the region.

The present-day situation in the Taiwan Strait shows elements of both inertia and dynamism. On the one hand, for decades in some cases, there have been few substantial deviations from positions of principle on either side of the strait regarding the status quo and a solution to the conflict. On the other hand, however, trade and investment are leading the way to more economic interdependence, albeit in a highly asymmetrical form. The political gap between the two sides appears to be unbridgeable as far as the core issues of national unity and identity and the forms of government are concerned. Taiwanese nationalism fostered under President Chen Shuibian (2000–2008) only served to widen this gap.

Multifaceted improvements in bilateral relations since President Ma Yingjeou took office in May 2008 have done little to alter this basic situation. Controversies over Taiwan's claim to substantive participation in international matters and independent membership in multilateral organizations continually nourish the lack of trust on both sides.

OPPOSING STANCES ON THE STATUS QUO AND THE FUTURE

We should not underestimate Taiwan's importance to the People's Republic of China (PRC). The island country occupies a highly symbolic and geostrategic place in China's way of thinking on security policy,[1] an attitude reinforced by China's maritime ambitions in competition with those of the United States and Japan. Above all else, the Taiwan issue is a central theme in Chinese nationalism. For instance, the PRC considers the island's recovery and reunification with the "mother country" a prerequisite for ending the "century of humiliation" as a historic episode, for enabling China's return to the community of major world powers, and for realizing the "great revival of the Chinese nation."[2] In other words, Taiwan is not merely a territorial problem; Beijing views it as a matter of national destiny and as a central political mission, as well as an important touchstone for the esteem in which the Chinese leadership is held.[3] Seen against this backdrop, the stances taken in shaping relations in the Taiwan Strait take on a particular volatility.

Box 8.1 summarizes the basic positions of each side on key aspects in the conflict (notwithstanding the wide range of positions found in Taiwanese politics and society).

The core of the dispute between the two sides involves the status of Taiwan. In the past several years, the PRC has been quite flexible in this regard (a stance known as the "one-China principle"). Beijing softened the rhetoric it had used for decades—namely, that Taiwan is a province of the PRC—in order to bring Taiwan back to the negotiating table. Beijing still espouses absolute adherence to the one-China principle, as in the Chinese Anti-secession Law of 2005, for example. However, the concrete form of "one China" today is more open to discussion. The only insistence is common acknowledgment of a "one-China framework."[4]

During President Chen Shuibian's term of office, domestic political dynamics in Taiwan resulted in an overwhelming variety of proposals for dealing with the one-China principle.[5] There were preparations to take steps toward achieving a two-country solution through the use of the "one country on each side" slogan (2002) and advocating a name change whereby the name "Republic of China" (2007) would be dropped.

A modus vivendi between the PRC under Hu Jintao and the Taiwanese government under Ma Yingjeou was established when both sides accepted the Consensus of 1992, the outcome of an informal November 1992 meeting in Hong Kong between representatives from the PRC Association for Relations across the Taiwan Strait (ARATS) and Taiwan's Strait Exchange Foundation (SEF). In the consensus, both sides agreed that there was only one China, but each insisted on its own interpretation of the one-China principle.[6] In the meantime, the PRC government attempted to adopt a more differentiated view of the domestic political realities in Taiwan, conceding that defending Taiwan's separate identity was not the same as advocating Taiwanese independence.

BOX 8.1. CONTRASTING CHINESE AND
TAIWANESE FUNDAMENTAL POSITIONS

	PRC	Taiwan
Roots of the conflict	• Taiwan reverted to China when Japanese occupation ended in 1945. • The PRC government has been the sole government of China since 1949.	• The Republic of China (ROC) government was transferred to Taiwan in 1949. • The ROC claims territorial control over Taiwan, Jinmen, Matsu, and Penghu.
Present status	• The PRC government claims sole representative authority (the "one-China principle"). • Recognition of the "one-China principle" is the prerequisite for all negotiations. • Strengthening of political, economic, cultural, and social cooperation will create better conditions for achieving peaceful reunification.	• Taiwan has been governed as a territory separate from the PRC since 1949. • The constitution of the ROC is the basis for all exchanges with the PRC. • The Taipei government's policy vis-à-vis the mainland is "No unification, no independence, no use of force." • The ROC aims to uphold the status quo in the Taiwan Strait while pursuing common interests.
Solution to the conflict	• Complete reunification of China is an irresistible historical process. • Reunification will be based on the (Hong Kong) formula of "one country, two systems." • Moves toward independence are the result of manipulation by nonrepresentative secessionist forces.	• Final settlement of the bilateral relationship hinges on the mainland's moving toward greater freedom, democracy, and equitable wealth. • The wording "one country, two systems" implies the subordination of Taiwan. • Any decision on future relations must be based on free and democratic elections.

Sources: Authors' summaries are compiled from (for the PRC side) Hu Jintao 2005b, 2007, 2008, 2012; Wang Yi 2012; Zhonghua Renmin Gongheguo Guowuyuan Xinwen Bangongshi 2000; (for the Taiwan side) Chao Chien-min 2011; Lai Shin-Yuan 2010a, 2010b, 2011; Ma Yingjeou 2008, 2010, 2012.

Although the PRC leadership has projected an image of flexibility in its rhetoric on specific issues, the notion of "one country, two systems" has consistently pointed the way to the future solution of the Taiwan issue. According to former PRC president Hu Jintao, Hong Kong demonstrates that this scenario might indeed be a credible and practical strategy for resolving the Taiwan conflict.[7] Taiwan might even expect rights of autonomy considerably broader than those in Hong Kong: in addition to a separate economic, monetary, and customs territory, a separate government structure and a separate armed forces are also conceivable, so the PRC's promise goes.

However, Taiwan's populace sees this offer to grant Taiwan the status of a special administrative region (SAR) under Communist rule as a strategy of subjugation, and it thoroughly distrusts Beijing's promises of autonomy. The consensus across political parties in Taiwan is that the future of the Taiwan issue has yet to be resolved and will depend solely on the will of the Taiwanese people; reunification is out of the question, except within the framework of a democratic, free, and prosperous China. In fact, when polled in surveys, 70 to 80 percent of Taiwan's populace regularly rejects the Chinese principle of one country, two systems. A large majority—over 60 percent—approves of adhering to the status quo. A significant minority of over 20 percent favors independence. The number of advocates of unification with the PRC has continued to decline over the last decade. Improvements in the atmosphere between the two governments since 2008 and the growing number of visitors back and forth have so far failed to change these opinions (see figure 8.1).

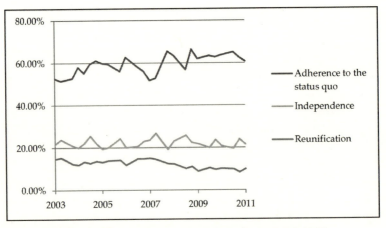

Figure 8.1. Attitudes in Taiwan regarding the Taiwan issue, 2003–2011.
Source: Taiwan Mainland Affairs Council.

The PRC relies on a number of typical instruments to achieve the longer-term goal of reunification and to curb independence efforts in Taiwan. These include increasing the island's economic dependence on the mainland; intensifying social exchanges and administrative and technical cooperation; imposing diplomatic restrictions on Taiwan; creating a backdrop of military threat; and, finally, actively influencing Taiwan's most important partner, the United States.

ECONOMIC CONVERGENCE AND ADMINISTRATIVE COOPERATION

Despite their political differences, economic exchanges between mainland China and Taiwan have gathered momentum in the fields of trade and investment since the early 1990s, representing the equivalent of economic unification and deeply rooted integration. Table 8.1 sheds light on the central aspects of the economic dynamics.

Taiwan generates a large foreign-trade surplus in its trading activities with the PRC, and it is heavily dependent on its supply relationship with the mainland for its exports. Conversely, Taiwan's significance in relation to the PRC's foreign trade has generally declined. The first drop in trade in 2009 occurred in the context of the global financial and economic crisis, but it balanced out in 2010 and 2011 when new trade records were set.

We can also discern a similar pattern of growing Taiwanese dependence on the PRC in the case of investments. Official Taiwanese statistics (from

Table 8.1.   Trade between the PRC and Taiwan, 1990–2011 (in US$ Billions)

Year	Overall Trade*	Exports PRC*	Imports PRC*	Share of the PRC's Trade (%)**	Share of Taiwan's Trade (%)**
1990	2.6	0.3	2.3	4.5	4.2
1994	16.3	2.3	14.0	7.6	9.9
1998	20.5	3.9	16.6	7.4	11.0
2000	30.5	5.0	25.5	6.6	10.7
2002	44.6	6.6	38.0	6.4	15.9
2004	78.3	13.5	64.8	5.7	18.7
2006	107.8	20.7	87.1	5.0	20.6
2007	124.5	23.5	101.0	4.7	22.0
2008	129.2	25.9	103.3	4.1	21.2
2009	106.2	20.5	85.7	3.9	22.9
2010	145.4	29.7	115.7	4.9	23.0
2011	160.1	35.1	125.0	4.4	22.9

Sources: *Ministry of Commerce of the PRC; **Taiwan Mainland Affairs Council.

the Mainland Affairs Council) indicate that up until the end of 2011, enterprises from Taiwan made investments in the PRC amounting to over US$110 billion. In effect, approximately one hundred thousand Taiwanese enterprises employ over 14 million Chinese workers on the mainland, concentrated mainly in the coastal regions of Guangdong, Shanghai, Jiangsu, and Fujian. Approximately 1 million Taiwanese businessmen, together with their families, live permanently on the mainland. The asymmetric cross-Strait investment flows become apparent when we consider that the mainland has received approximately 75 percent of all Taiwanese outbound foreign direct investment (OFDI), whereas, since 1979, inward foreign direct investment (IFDI) from Taiwan has amounted to less than 5 percent of the PRC's total IFDI.

Much of Taiwan's information technology production has been transferred to the mainland.[8] Given the turbulent "network integration" being privately promoted, the multifaceted efforts by several successive Taiwan governments to diversify investment flows and limit the economic focus on the Chinese mainland have been ineffective.

Long-term political considerations on the part of Beijing are behind these developments. Since the 1980s, the PRC government has promoted close economic interactions with Taiwan by granting special privileges to private Taiwanese investors. The purpose of this policy was—and still is—to entangle Taiwan in a web of economic dependence in order to create a lever for exerting political influence. However, numerous studies have shown that so far this plan has not worked.[9] Taiwanese businesspeople in China (the *Taishang*) are almost exclusively interested in local commercial success. They disregard Beijing's wishes that they become involved in Taiwanese politics and work for political reunification or other goals of the PRC government. In their skepticism of reunification, the people of Taiwan thus far have refused to be swayed by the growing economic dependence on the mainland or by Beijing's posturing or promises.

In view of the fact that economic and tourist exchanges have been growing since the 1990s, it has become necessary to coordinate certain technical and administrative matters. To this end, semiofficial organizations (ARATS for the PRC and SEF for Taiwan) have held unofficial talks since 1992. These talks have improved the political climate and led to solutions to some substantive issues, such as regulating postal and telecommunications traffic, tourism, and air and sea transportation links. An abrupt general deterioration in relations resulted in temporary suspension of the talks in 1999.

Talks between ARATS and SEF resumed in June 2008, after the inauguration of Taiwan's new president, Ma Yingjeou, when there were calls on both sides to restore the Consensus of 1992. In all, up to the end of 2012, eight meetings (the so-called Chen-Chiang talks), with venues alternating between mainland China and Taiwan, were held; eighteen agreements were reached on topics ranging from direct air and sea traffic to postal and telecommunications services, food safety, finances, fishery matters, product standards, protection of intellectual property, investment protection, and currency clearing.

The development of tourism has also been highly dynamic. Before 2008, tourism from China to Taiwan was subject to restrictive requirements due to security concerns in Taiwan (fears of espionage from the mainland, illegal economic migrants, and so forth). Since then, the number of visitors to Taiwan from the mainland has increased dramatically (see figure 8.2).

The pinnacle of this intensified cooperation was reached in June 2010 with the Economic Cooperation Framework Agreement (ECFA), signed in Chongqing following negotiations between ARATS and SEF. Both sides agreed to accept a gradual reduction of their import customs duties, with the long-term goal of one day forming a free trade zone. The very favorable conditions granted to Taiwan reveal the ECFA's importance to the PRC government. The first steps taken to reduce customs duties have greatly eased the burden on Taiwanese shipments to the mainland. Furthermore, at least until now, Taiwan has not had to open its markets to agricultural products and workers from the mainland.[10]

Beijing wanted to demonstrate tangible progress toward institutionalized cooperation with Taiwan. At the same time, the PRC leadership favored strengthening President Ma Yingjeou's position by offering prospects for revitalizing Taiwan's trade with the mainland. Ma Yingjeou clearly took a more conciliatory stance toward Beijing than his predecessor. During the ECFA negotiations, the Taiwan government faced pressure from critical

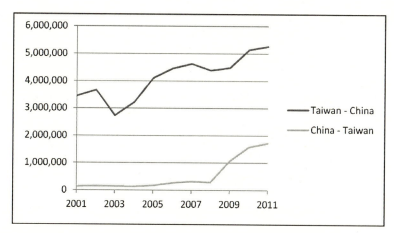

Figure 8.2. Visitor traffic between mainland China and Taiwan, 2001–2011.
Source: Taiwan Mainland Affairs Council.

opposition voices and public opinion that accused the government of betraying Taiwan's interests. Against this backdrop, Taiwan's leadership justified the ECFA as absolutely necessary to maintaining the competitiveness of Taiwanese enterprises in trade with the mainland because a free trade agreement between China and the Association of Southeast Asian Nations (ASEAN), which had already entered into effect in January 2010, threatened to give Taiwan's Southeast Asian competitors—especially enterprises in Singapore and Malaysia—the edge in business dealings with China. At the same time, the Taipei government presented the ECFA as a first step to reach an entire series of additional free trade agreements between Taiwan and other nations in the Asia-Pacific region.

On the whole, administrative and technical cooperation has rapidly intensified since 2008.[11]

- *Expansion of areas of cooperation*: For many years exchange relations were restricted to a few special economic and social areas. Since 2008, agreements have moved beyond these areas, and they now include previously sensitive issues such as judiciary cooperation and fighting crime.
- *Intensifying exchanges in both directions*: Prior to 2008, flows of goods, investments, and visitors from Taiwan to mainland China primarily characterized exchanges. Since then, however, there has been a marked increase in mainland flows to Taiwan. The number of high-ranking political and economic delegations from the PRC visiting Taiwan has grown by vast proportions. The first banks from the PRC opened branches in Taiwan in 2010.
- *Establishing new communications channels*: In addition to the semiannual unofficial rounds of talks between ARATS and SEF, since 2005 there have also been regular contacts between the Chinese Communist Party (CCP) and Taiwan's Kuomintang (KMT). The PRC government has even lifted its strict ban on contacts with politicians from Taiwan's Democratic Progressive Party (DPP). Consequently, travel to the mainland is no longer uncommon among prominent DPP politicians.

Official negotiations between government representatives from both sides are still not possible, however, due to the unresolved status of the Taiwan issue and because of sensitivities on the part of Taiwan (maintaining a separation of economic and political relations). However, on an unofficial level (known as "track two"), "talks among experts" behind closed doors now deal with a large number of topics that call for consensus. On the sidelines of the Asia-Pacific Economic Cooperation (APEC) summits, Chinese president Hu Jintao and Lian Zhan, the leader of the Taiwanese delegation, have held consultations. The Chinese minister of commerce and the Taiwan minister of economic affairs have also exchanged views at APEC ministerial meetings. In 2011 the most important newly institutionalized communications mechanism was established with the Cross-Strait Committee for Economic Cooperation. This body deals with key issues of bilateral cooperation at the level of deputy ministers under the auspices of the ARATS and SEF.

Despite this tangible progress, there continues to be large scope for setbacks in the economic and administrative cooperation between Beijing and Taipei.[12] On the one hand, development of the atmosphere surrounding relations depends on the political constellation in Taiwan. A substantial part of the population is skeptical about too close a relationship between the CCP and the ruling KMT. Advocates of independence still have considerable political clout, and future changes in government could cause relations with the PRC to deteriorate abruptly. On the other hand, Beijing's current flexibility will be put to a hard test in the long run if Taiwan fails to continue moving forward to show its willingness to take up political talks aimed at solving the Taiwan problem.

POLITICAL DIVERGENCE AND DIPLOMATIC COMPETITION

Despite ever-increasing economic interdependence and the rounds of talks that resumed in 2008, the two sides have as of yet achieved no convergence or clarification with respect to the politically contentious issues involving the international legal and diplomatic status of Taiwan. The greater scope of action in international relations sought by all successive Taiwanese governments has at best only partially become a reality.

For Taiwan, which still clings to its status as an alternative system of government, relations with mainland China are vital. Conflicting interests within the party system and the Taiwanese populace impede the development of a coherent mainland policy on which the PRC could also depend in the long term.[13]

The political activities of President Chen Shuibian at home and abroad between 2000 and 2008 led to particularly open tensions and animosities in the island's relations with the PRC. To mobilize his constituency, Chen resorted to symbolic acts unacceptable to Beijing, such as removing the word "China" from official titles (e.g., the *Taiwan Post* instead of the *China Post*). During his second term of office, Chen went even further and took steps that Beijing could only interpret as signs of a forthcoming change in the status quo or even preparation for Taiwan's declaration of official independence. In 2006, Chen disbanded the National Unification Council, which had existed since 1991, and announced that Taiwan was to become a "normal country" or a "second republic" by way of referenda and amendments to the constitution.

The KMT, which resumed control in 2008, rescinded several of Chen's initiatives, once again focusing on universal Chinese traditions.[14] At the same time, however, the new president, Ma Yingjeou, supported Taiwan's autonomy, the priority interests of the Taiwanese populace, and protection of Taiwan's democratic system and free values.[15] No future government in Taiwan will be able or willing to abandon the island's status as a de facto autonomous state. As far as this fundamental issue is concerned, Beijing cannot expect any concessions from either political parties or the general public of Taiwan.

The citizens of Taiwan expect symbolic and diplomatic success with regard to elevating the international status of the island. They also expect practical improvements in international and business travel. But before 2009 Beijing was not willing to compromise on these matters. More than anything else, an understanding that intractable positions by Beijing would only drive more voters in Taiwan to the DPP, which is critical of China, probably motivated the change in 2009.

The PRC leadership insists that Taiwan cannot join any international or regional organization that makes—from Beijing's perspective—status as an independent state under international law a precondition for membership. Below this threshold, however, Taiwan can take part in special organizations, such as the Asian Development Bank and the International Olympic Committee, or high-ranking economic forums such as APEC, provided it goes by the name of "Chinese Taipei." However, it may never refer to itself as the Republic of China in international organizations or forums. Beijing unrelentingly forbids any international activities by Taiwan that might give the impression that there are "two Chinas" or "one China and one Taiwan."

The Taiwanese side sees the restrictions imposed by Beijing diplomacy as a hostile curtailment of the international leeway necessary for its survival. Between 2006 and 2008, President Chen sought to obtain Taiwan's admittance to the United Nations by way of a referendum—a call accompanied by harsh warnings from Beijing. President Ma's administration, in contrast, has chosen to take a different stance. In 2008, for instance, for the first time in fifteen years, Taiwan did not submit a new petition for UN membership. Instead, the government redoubled efforts toward acceptance into specific UN agencies. In 2009 Beijing tolerated Taiwan's acceptance into the World Health Assembly, a decision-making body of the World Health Organization, as an observer. The PRC leadership acknowledged having granted Taiwan "fair and reasonable arrangements" in light of opportunities for international cooperation.[16] In contrast, however, the PRC has not yet ceded to Taiwan's aspirations to become a member of the United Nations Framework Convention on Climate Change (UNFCCC) or the International Civil Aviation Organization (ICAO).

There are also tensions regarding diplomatic treatment of Taiwan by other countries. Most states adhere to the one-China policy in favor of the PRC and maintain merely informal representations, referred to as "economic promotion agencies," in Taiwan. Until the beginning of 2008, Beijing's claim to sole representation led it to break diplomatic ties with those states that had diplomatic relations with Taipei. An unofficial "diplomatic ceasefire" initiated by Ma Yingjeou has replaced this practice. As a result, now neither side attempts to lure the diplomatic partners of the other side away with financial incentives or other privileges.

Under this arrangement, the number of states that maintain diplomatic relations with Taiwan—mostly smaller states in Oceania and Central and Latin America—has not dropped below twenty-three since 2008, despite the substantially increased diplomatic influence of the PRC. When Paraguay, which maintains diplomatic relations with Taiwan, made advances toward Beijing in August 2008 with the aim of establishing official diplomatic relations, the Chinese government rejected this request behind closed doors. Taiwan and the PRC are clearly attempting to avoid a resurfacing of their hostile diplomatic contest.[17]

THE POTENTIAL FOR CONFLICT IN THE TAIWAN STRAIT

Aside from the conflict on the Korean Peninsula, the Taiwan issue represents the greatest challenge to security policy in Asia. It could even trigger an armed confrontation between China and the United States.[18] The PRC leadership remains unwilling to abandon the military option with respect to the Taiwan issue. In official commentaries (e.g., the 2000 Taiwan white paper "The One-China Principle and the Taiwan Issue") and legislation (the Anti-Secession Law of 2005), it has enumerated those events that might trigger the use of military force: (1) nuclear armament of Taiwan, (2) the collapse of internal order in Taiwan, (3) Taiwan's formal secession, (4) concrete steps toward independence by Taiwan's rulers, (5) and exhaustion of all peaceful attempts to achieve reunification.

The latter two items in particular, which are very vaguely formulated, give PRC leaders a broad scope for interpretation. However, this does not necessarily mean that such flexibility will heighten the risk of armed conflict, for Beijing could also use it to avoid internal party or societal calls for a hard stance toward Taiwan.[19] Moreover, because the PRC claims to have won a decisive victory with regard to Taiwan's independence since 2008, it has recently stepped up its rhetoric for peaceful development across the Taiwan Strait, bringing Taiwan policy more in line with its general foreign policy of peaceful development.

As explained in chapter 4, the Chinese army focuses its organization, doctrine, and tactical orientation heavily on a Taiwan scenario. The long-standing military balance of power in the Taiwan Strait has shifted in favor of the PRC (see figure 8.3), due in particular to what now amounts to approximately twelve hundred short-range missiles stationed in the coastal area across from Taiwan and to the Chinese modern arsenal of submarines and combat aircraft.

Defense experts judge Taiwan's military capabilities to repel an attack by China, especially an amphibian invasion, to be still adequate, but the general trend is clearly moving in China's favor. Taiwan's military budget has been declining for a number of years due to internal political conflicts and the 2008–2009 economic difficulties. The United States has provided Taiwan with some modern weaponry, such as missile-defense and anti-submarine systems, but so far it has only been ready to upgrade, and not replace with newer versions, Taiwan's existing fighter aircraft.

Recurrent People's Liberation Army (PLA) maneuvers that simulate the conquest of Taiwan make clear that China still takes the military option seriously. These exercises have been below the threshold of the missile tests conducted by the PRC in 1995 and 1996, which it intended as threatening gestures. Nevertheless, they clearly serve to apply political pressure on the Taiwanese leadership and public.

The stereotypical view that internal conflicts between hawks in the army and moderate forces in the civilian party characterize the PRC's Taiwan policy is untenable according to recent research findings (see chapter 4). A broad consensus exists among civilian and military leaders in the PRC regarding underlying Taiwan strategy: there is absolutely no room for com-

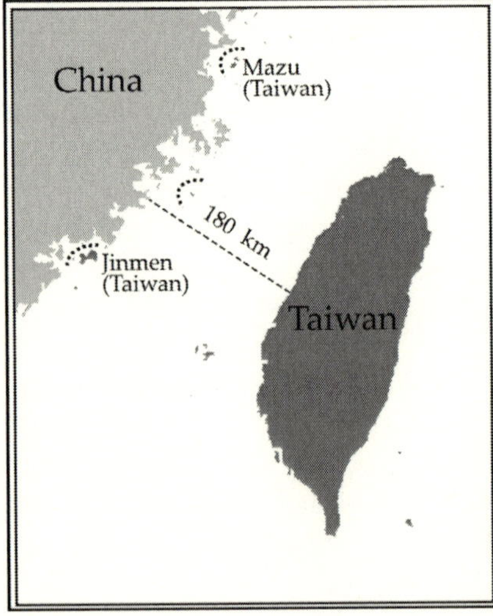

	China	Taiwan
Army		
troops	400000	130000
tanks	3100	1100
artillery	3400	1600
Air force		
combat aircraft	490/2120*	410
Navy		
submarines	32/53*	4
destroyers	16/26*	4
frigates	44/53*	22
Missiles		
short- and medium- range (300 - 1750km)	1385 - 1745	n/a

Figure 8.3. Military strength in the Taiwan Strait.
Note: An asterisk indicates number of weapons systems near Taiwan Strait as part of total PRC forces.
Source: US Department of Defense 2012.

promise on any steps taken by Taiwan toward independence. Despite the government's acknowledgment of the priority of a peaceful solution, it has not categorically ruled out military action.[20]

The development of relations between mainland China and Taiwan is hampered by historical and emotionally charged issues of identity and status, by pronounced political instrumentalization on both sides of the strait, and by fragile communications and conflict-solving mechanisms that up to now have been only weakly institutionalized and will probably prove unsustainable during periods of tension.[21] Therefore, there is a high risk of misperceptions and misinterpretations arising on either side.

Beijing tends to look at Taiwan's entire domestic politics through the prism of reunification. For this reason, it often senses betrayal of the national cause, even if the political initiatives are only minor. Those in charge in Taiwan, on the other hand, are inclined to overestimate the rationality of Beijing's weighing of interests. At the same time, they underestimate Beijing's determination to bring about reunification. Ultimately, neither side can fathom the future role of the United States, particularly during a crisis situation. Security-policy circles in Beijing have growing doubts about America's willingness to intervene militarily. Their colleagues in Taipei, however, continue to place trust in American intervention, at least in their public statements, believing the United States will intervene much as it did in 1995–1996, when the US president, in response to Chinese missile tests and maneuvers, ordered two groups of aircraft carriers and supporting craft into the area near the Taiwan Strait in order to send Beijing a clear signal. Considerable risks adhere to the very different perceptions and expectations that exist in light of present and future constellations of power—especially when viewed in conjunction with the military power amassed on each side.

At the same time, since 2008 new opportunities have opened up for creating solutions, or at least solutions of a nonmilitary nature, by mutual agreement. After the PRC's Eighteenth Party Congress and the reelection of Ma Yingjeou in Taiwan in 2012, both sides appear to have come to terms with the current modus vivendi. Both refer to the Consensus of 1992 (one China with differing interpretations) as the guideline for bilateral relations and express a willingness to continue their institutionalized dialogue (in the ARATS-SEF and ECFA contexts) to expand economic and practical cooperation while shelving sensitive matters of sovereignty.

THE ROLE OF THE UNITED STATES IN THE TAIWAN ISSUE

The United States plays a key role in the Taiwan issue. Since establishment of diplomatic relations with the PRC in 1979, the United States has been committed to a one-China policy in favor of the PRC. Despite this, however, the United States maintains a wide range of special relations with Taiwan below the diplomatic level, based on the Taiwan Relations Act (TRA) passed by Congress in 1979. This legislation is not a defense agreement as defined by international law, but it is understood in Washington to be a "political commitment" in support of Taiwan. The main US interest lies in maintaining the status quo—that is, securing "peace and stability" in the Taiwan Strait.[22]

To achieve this goal, the United States practices "strategic ambiguity," known in American studies as a strategy of "dual deterrence," since it includes not only warnings but also reassurances to both Beijing and Taipei.[23] For instance, the US government warns the PRC about using force against Taiwan; at the same time, Washington assures the PRC that it does not support the creation of an independent state of Taiwan under international law. With respect to Taipei, Washington warns against taking unilateral political action that Beijing could interpret as a provocation and use as an excuse for an attack; at the same time, Washington promises to take Taiwan's interests into consideration whenever relations with the PRC are involved.

The practical consequences of this dual strategy are well documented. In view of the Chinese military threat to Taiwan's security, the United States, citing the TRA, has provided several shipments of modern defensive weapons to Taiwan despite vehement objections and diplomatic intervention by Beijing. Nevertheless, in 2004 and 2008 the United States supported Beijing's position by harshly criticizing President Chen Shuibian's political advances to change the status quo in Taiwan.[24]

The challenge for the United States is to determine the extent to which one of the two sides is moving to change the status quo and how it should respond. The difficulty is that the line between acceptable and unacceptable measures brought about by Taiwan's domestic politics is rarely clearly defined. Accordingly, the PRC and Taiwan are both endeavoring to win the United States over to their respective positions and initiatives. In this respect, close historical and political ties, the commitment to stand by an endangered young democracy, an influential pro-Taiwan lobby in the US Congress, and the orientation of the American system of alliances in the Asia-Pacific region all give Taiwan a clear advantage over the PRC. Even though there has been some talk in the United States about abandoning Taiwan in exchange for better relations with the PRC, for the time being there are no signs of a fundamental shift in official US policy toward Taiwan.[25]

NOTES

1. Wachman 2007.
2. Hu Jintao 2008.
3. Rigger 2013.

4. Hu Jintao 2007, 2008, 2012.
5. Fell 2012.
6. Chen Qimao 2011; Chu Shulong 2006; Kan 2011; Lin Chong-Pin 2008.
7. Hu Jintao 2012.
8. Rigger 2011.
9. Lee Chun-yi 2010; Schubert 2010; Tanner 2007; Tung Chen-Yuan 2007.
10. Lai Shin-Yuan 2010b.
11. Xin Qiang 2010.
12. Chen Qimao 2011.
13. Fell 2012.
14. Ma Yingjeou 2011.
15. Ma Yingjeou 2012.
16. Hu Jintao 2008.
17. Xin Qiang 2010.
18. Bush and O'Hanlon 2007; Carpenter 2005.
19. Shirk 2007.
20. Bush and O'Hanlon 2007.
21. Xin Qiang 2010.
22. Christensen 2007; Hickey 2011; Kelly 2004; Rigger 2013.
23. Bush and O'Hanlon 2007.
24. Dumbaugh 2008.
25. Rigger 2013; Tucker and Glaser 2011.

9

China's Relations with Japan and Korea

From its own perspective, the People's Republic of China (PRC) is still primarily a regional power in Asia (at least at present). In this context, its relations with Japan and North and South Korea occupy a special position. The importance of Northeast Asia for China stems from its geographical proximity and a tradition of active cultural exchange, as well as from historical pressures (between China and Japan), alliances (between China and North Korea), densely interwoven economies, and the strong presence of the United States in the region.

SINO-JAPANESE RELATIONS

After the devastating conflict during World War II, strategic considerations drove the resumption of contacts between China and Japan. The Soviet threat, feared equally by both sides, suggested the utility of closer Sino-Japanese harmony. As of the mid-1960s, unofficial visits by political delegations and limited economic exchanges were taking place. The Sino-American rapprochement that had begun in 1971 facilitated the establishment of diplomatic relations in September 1972. The Chinese government regarded the US-Japanese alliance as a contributing factor to the containment of Japanese militarism. After the breakup of the Soviet Union, however, Beijing has increasingly criticized the alliance as a Cold War institution directed against China.

Strong reactions to internal political events in Japan—which, against the backdrop of bloody conflicts of the past, Beijing has denounced as nationalist provocations, displays of contempt for the victims of war, or evidence of a lack of a historical sense of responsibility and remorse—shape China's relations with Tokyo. According to widely held Chinese views, Japan has not adequately apologized for its wartime atrocities against the Chinese people; nor has it come to terms with the past by means of research, education, and raising awareness. (In this connection, Chinese often cite Germany's open discussions of and extensive research into Nazi war crimes as a positive reference model.) Comments from individual Japanese politicians, activities by marginal radical nationalistic groups, and even school textbooks—which, according to Chinese understanding, trivialize or justify Japan's role in the war, especially in China—have triggered recurrent crises in bilateral relations. Japanese politicians from the Liberal Democratic Party have occasionally undertaken symbolic acts that Chinese observers feel honor convicted Japanese war criminals and therefore can be considered anti-Chinese provocations. Nationalist organizations, such as the Japanese Youth Federation, have provoked strong reactions from Beijing regarding territorial conflicts (see below regarding the dispute surrounding the Diaoyu/Senkaku Islands). By the same token, since the 1990s, in addition to governmental actions, politically tolerated citizen initiatives and Internet campaigns in China have also determined the dynamics of Sino-Japanese relations. These groups have called for compensation for Chinese victims of the Japanese occupation in Japanese courts and have mobilized the public to defend the Diaoyu Islands against Japanese claims.[1]

In essence, virulent political rivalry over leadership in Asia characterizes Sino-Japanese relations. This competition has entered a new phase due to the recent shifts favoring China in terms of relative economic and military strengths. The remainder of this section briefly discusses the key factors that repeatedly feed mutual mistrust and political tensions.[2]

The Long Shadows of History

The "century of humiliation" (1842–1949) constitutes the key point of reference in the collective Chinese memory to this day, and it also continues to affect China's foreign policy behavior. In China's view, no other country has inflicted greater suffering on the Middle Kingdom than Japan.[3] The forced handover of Taiwan to Japan by the Treaty of Shimonoseki in 1895, Japan's acquisition of the former German territories in Shandong after World War I, Japan's incursion into Manchuria beginning in 1931, and then the Second Sino-Japanese War after 1937 (with its numerous casualties) are all evidence of Japan's aggression and its continuing efforts to dominate China. From China's perspective, Japan's unwillingness to face up to responsibility for its own history is reflected in a variety of ways: Japanese textbooks in which Japan does not refer to its war crimes in China, recurrent visits by Japan's prime minister to the Yasukuni Shrine (a symbol honoring executed Japanese war criminals), and inadequate apologies by the Japanese government during bilateral state visits.

The Chinese Communist Party (CCP) still celebrates the nation's "victory in its war of resistance against Japan" as a basic element of its authority to rule, and it exploits widely held anti-Japanese sentiment in society to defend China's national dignity. However, the Chinese leadership treads a fine line here because it repeatedly faces pressures from nationalistic citizen movements that demand tougher action from the Chinese government regarding Japan. In 2005, for instance, on the occasion of Japan's efforts to become a permanent member of the UN Security Council, online Chinese calls for action led to street protests directed against Japanese businesses and diplomatic missions, which Chinese security forces ultimately had to quash.[4]

Territorial Disputes

One of the most volatile maritime territorial conflicts in the Asia-Pacific region today involves China and Japan in the East China Sea. In addition to rights to exploit extensive natural resources on the continental shelf east of Shanghai (oil and gas fields as well as fisheries), this dispute involves control over the Diaoyu Islands (known as the Senkaku Islands in Japanese) (see figure 9.1).

These eight unpopulated islands and reefs, situated approximately 112 miles northeast of Taiwan and covering an area of just over 2.3 square miles, fell to Japan in 1895 after the First Sino-Japanese War; the United States then occupied them, along with Okinawa, after Japan's capitulation in 1945.[5] Since their restitution in 1972, Japan has exercised control over the islands. Like the Taiwanese government, the Chinese government regards the islands as its sovereign territory based on historical, geographical, and judicial claims and criticizes the United States for its part in causing the dispute.[6]

The parties are slugging this conflict out by means of more than disputes over historical claims and international law. In fact, the archipelago has also been the site of direct confrontations on a number of occasions, particularly in 1990, 1996, 2004, 2005, 2010, and since 2012.[7] The Japanese Coast Guard has forcibly stopped Chinese fishing boats or research vessels (no doubt exploring for raw material deposits in this maritime region), and in repeated incidents, Japanese, Taiwanese, or Chinese activists have attached national emblems or navigational lights to the reefs (on the islets). The most recent deterioration in Sino-Japanese relations occurred when the Japanese government purchased three of the islets (which had been leased to a private citizen) in September 2012, setting off mass anti-Japanese

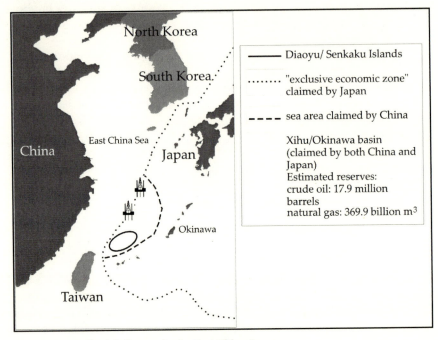

Figure 9.1. Territorial disputes in the East China Sea.

protests across China.[8] Since then, China has begun routine patrols by its marine surveillance and fisheries law enforcement command vessels in the waters near the disputed islands to challenge the Japanese position, which denies any conflict over sovereignty. The more recent incidents prove that previous steps toward conflict resolution have failed.[9] These steps included an understanding from 2001 on providing notification before making boat trips into the disputed territory and a declaration of intent from 2008 regarding shared exploitation of resources.

Differences in Security Policy

China evaluated Japan's alliance with the United States critically following the end of the Cold War and has criticized it increasingly since the end of the 1990s. The reason for this criticism is the US request that Japan "share its military burden." A more active role by the Japanese armed forces became apparent in several deployments abroad (e.g., the provision of naval units for military exercises in the Indian Ocean and the posting of ground troops to Iraq—albeit without a combat mission—in 2003). The Chinese media depicted Japanese discussions on amendments to the Peace Constitution of

1947 (largely drafted by legal experts under US General Douglas MacArthur) and on the inclusion of Australia and India in the Japanese-US security cooperation as indicators of a "resurgence of Japanese militarism."

The development of a joint US-Japan regional missile defense shield since 1998, intended to prevent North Korean attacks or provocations, has been the major target of Chinese mistrust. The PRC insists that such a defense shield should under no circumstance include Taiwan. Japan, for its part, considers the accelerated modernization of the Chinese air force and navy a challenge to the openness of the sea routes in the surrounding area.

Japan and the Taiwan Issue

The Taiwan issue is of critical importance not only to Sino-American relations but also to Sino-Japanese relations as well. Taiwan's past as a Japanese colony (1895–1945) partly explains this. Special connections continue to exist today between the two states due to their recent history. Although there are no intergovernmental diplomatic relations, prominent Taiwanese politicians (such as former president Li Denghui) take many so-called private trips to Japan. There, they often meet high-ranking Japanese politicians who generally exhibit great sympathy for Taiwanese democracy and skepticism toward the PRC. The Chinese government observes these contacts with mistrust as they have the potential to encourage Taiwanese claims to state and diplomatic autonomy.

Economic Interdependence

Conflict-ridden aspects of Sino-Japanese relations stand in the way of important common interests and efforts—in particular economic exchanges—that have time and again ensured a stabilization of the relationship.[10] Even before the establishment of diplomatic relations in 1972, Japan was China's most important trading partner. Japanese corporations specifically used the two countries' economic complementarity and geographical proximity, as well as China's orientation toward Japan's model of development after 1978, to tap into the Chinese market. The development of economic relations took precedence over historical and political tensions. The Chinese leadership's violent suppression of the urban protest movement in 1989, which led to coordinated sanctions by the Western democracies and Japan, is an example of economic relations taking priority over history and politics, as Japan was the first of the Group of Seven (G7) nations to renormalize relations with China in 1990. Since then, trade and investment flows have developed dynamically despite sporadic political tensions (in particular during Prime Minister Junichiro Koizumi's 2001–2006 term of office) and an interim slump in 2009 (see figure 9.2).

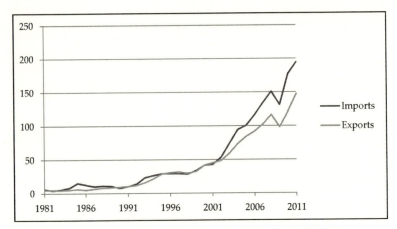

Figure 9.2. Overview of Sino-Japanese trade, 1981–2011 (in US$ billions).
Source: IMF.

As described in chapter 5, Japan is currently China's most important source of imports (US$194.4 billion in 2011) and its third most important export destination after the United States and Hong Kong (US$147.3 billion in 2011). At the same time, Japan has long been one of the most important sources of foreign direct investment (FDI) going to China (ranked fifth after Hong Kong, Taiwan, the European Union, and Singapore in 2011).

By the same token, China's importance to Japan has grown rapidly in recent years. Since 2008 China has overtaken the United States as Japan's biggest export destination. In 2010 Japan's economy benefited greatly from the high demand for Japanese investment goods, boosted also by China's 2008–2009 stimulus programs. In addition to businesspeople, Chinese tourists have become a major economic factor in Japan, as they look to purchase popular consumer goods (primarily electronics) due to Japan's greater safeguards against counterfeiting.

Some of the especially sensitive business topics in the Sino-US relationship (see chapter 10) are less problematic in Sino-Japanese relations. Unlike the United States, Japan does not have a trade deficit with China, and Japanese investors hold 95 percent of Japanese government bonds. Indirect restrictions by Chinese government departments regarding access of Japanese companies to specific markets and public invitations to tender on the mainland might, however, be the source of increasing tensions in the future. China's growing export ratio in traditionally Japanese-dominated fields (such as household electronics, vehicle construction, and high-speed trains) might also give rise to intensified competition and trade disputes.

Involvement in Regional Organizations

Joint membership in regional organizations has helped maintain dialogue between China and Japan during periods of tension (between 2003 and 2006, for instance). Leading politicians from each side have met for bilateral talks on the margins of Asia-Pacific Economic Cooperation (APEC) and Association of Southeast Asian Nations + China, Japan, and South Korea (ASEAN+3) summits for years. The need for mutual support to overcome regional and global challenges—such as stabilization of the Korean Peninsula, maintenance of the security of established sea routes, support for the world trade regime, and resistance to protectionist trends—is also strengthening cooperative relations.

Rivalry, Resentment, and Pragmatic Cooperation

Sino-Japanese relations are subject to a multitude of contradictory historical, political, economic, and international factors that may abruptly propel the bilateral relationship from cooperation to conflict (or vice versa). The PRC government thereby faces the serious challenge of balancing China's pronounced rivalry with and resentment of Japan with pragmatic cooperation with a view to maintaining its long-term economic and security interests.

RELATIONS WITH NORTH AND SOUTH KOREA

Several factors similar to those in Sino-Japanese relations exist in China's relations with South and North Korea. Historical determinants are also of great importance in China's relationship to the Korean Peninsula.[11] The Korean Yi dynasty was a tributary state of the Chinese Empire for many centuries. This close relationship only ended with the encroachment of Japanese imperialism into Korea at the end of the nineteenth century. This experience has had various impacts. On the one hand, Korea's historical subordination under Chinese rule fuels the concern of both Korean nations facing unilateral dependence on China and China's new hegemonic role in the region. In addition, certain territorial disputes (e.g., over Korean territories that Japan handed over to China in 1910) and historical disputes regarding Korean nation building (primarily the status of the Korean kingdom of Koguryo) also date back to this period.

Korea and China share the traumatic experience of Japanese occupation. Japan's war guilt, war crimes, and reparation claims also remain in the collective memory of Korean citizens and play a role in politics, the media, and education. The political division that occurred on the Korean Peninsula after Japan capitulated to the Allies at the end of World War II and Soviet and US armed forces occupied the areas north and south of the thirty-eighth parallel, respectively, has dramatically influenced China's relationship with the two Korean states that emerged: the Democratic People's Republic of Korea (DPRK) in the north and the Republic of Korea (ROK) in the south.

Close political, ideological, and personal connections have existed between PRC and DPRK leaders since revolutionary times (between Mao Zedong and Kim Il Sung). In October 1949, North Korea was one of the first nations to establish diplomatic relations with the newly formed PRC. Chinese historians write that this alliance was "sealed in blood" by the Korean War (1950–1953), when the PRC entered into a direct armed confrontation with the United States. In the course of this war, approximately nine hundred thousand Chinese soldiers, who had "volunteered" alongside North Korean troops under the banner of socialist solidarity to avert a feared American advance into China, lost their lives. In 2010, on the sixtieth anniversary of the outbreak of the Korean War, Vice President Xi Jinping designated Chinese intervention as "a just war to defend an invasion." To date, the Treaty of Friendship, Cooperation, and Mutual Assistance signed in 1961 forms the official basis of PRC relations with the DPRK. This alliance, pledging mutual assistance in the event of a military attack, is unique in the PRC's present-day foreign relations.

The Korean War helped to establish in Korea an alliance and influence structure with third countries (the Soviet Union and China with the North; the United States with the South). These remained essential to China's involvement on the Korean Peninsula until the early 1990s. From the end of the 1950s, the DPRK used Sino-Soviet rivalry to play each power against the other and to maximize its own military and economic support. The North Korean leadership after 1979 initially rejected China's reform and opening policy as revisionism, leading to a noticeable cooling of Sino–North Korean relations. The collapse of the Soviet Union in 1991, however, opened up completely new options for the PRC's Korea policy. Beijing no longer had to consider Pyongyang as a wedge between China and the USSR and could tap the potential for economic cooperation with South Korea in a targeted way (China and South Korea established diplomatic relations in August 1992). North Korea was forced to accept a rapid increase in Sino–South Korean exchanges over the course of the 1990s.

Due to the presence of its military bases, the United States has guaranteed South Korea's security with respect to North Korean aggression ever since the Korean War. Despite an economic "China fever" in South Korea and rapidly developing transnational industrial production networks, nothing suggests that the PRC might supersede the United States as South Korea's ally in the near future. In fact, since the 1990s North Korean missile and nuclear tests have strengthened the US–South Korean military alliance. The Chinese government regards this alliance very critically, viewing it as a relic of the Cold War (much as it does the US-Japanese military alliance). Furthermore, US–South Korean naval exercises at the end of 2010 off the western coast of the peninsula gave rise to vocal protests in Chinese Internet forums. However, there is also much criticism among the South Korean public of China's continued support of North Korea's political system through economic and financial aid. The forced repatriation of North Korean refugees picked up in Chinese border areas is another point of contention.

We can identify the following basic characteristics in the overall structure of Chinese relations with North and South Korea, all of which have been largely consistent to date.

Primacy of the Political Status Quo

Maintenance of stability on the Korean Peninsula is China's key interest.[12] The PRC has a shared border of over 870 miles with North Korea, and a large ethnic Korean minority lives in China's northeastern province of Jilin. In the event of a collapse of the DPRK, China would expect a massive flood of refugees into its northeastern region. The flight into China of tens of thousands of North Koreans on account of the famine in 1996 demonstrates the likelihood of this scenario.

As a result of North Korea's geographical proximity, particularly to the Chinese capital of Beijing, stability or instability on the Korean Peninsula is of direct importance to China's security policy. In the event of a North Korean collapse and Korean reunification under the leadership of Seoul, the Chinese anticipate the danger that American troops stationed in South Korea might advance to the Chinese border and that China would find itself confronted with an East Asian alliance consisting of Japan, Taiwan, and a united Korea led by the United States. Following this logic, North Korea is an indispensable buffer zone to keep American forces in South Korea and away from Chinese land borders, allowing China's armed forces to remain focused on the Taiwan Strait.[13]

Beijing has repeatedly supported the North Korean government diplomatically (in the event of critical requests and resolutions in the United Nations), economically (by sending deliveries of food and raw materials during periods of crisis), and militarily (by supplying arms and providing secret service cooperation), all with the goal of maintaining the status quo. The Chinese government reacted passively and strategically in response to the North Korean aggression against South Korea in 2010 (the sinking of the *Cheonan*, a South Korean warship, and the shelling of the South Korean island of Yeonpyeong).[14] The PRC expressed sympathy for South Korea and called on both sides to show restraint and resume the Six-Party Talks (see below).

In what manner, and to what effect, Chinese politicians attempt to influence the North Korean leadership behind closed doors remains a mystery. Since the 1990s, the Chinese government has repeatedly sent reminders about the introduction of economic reforms in the DPRK, but so far these have largely been ineffective. Over the past several years, the number of documented high-level visits and return visits between Chinese and North Korean leaders has increased markedly, yet without any breakthroughs in economic reforms or in North Korea's foreign relations.

The Nuclear Issue on the Korean Peninsula

The PRC has only criticized the DPRK openly in cases where Beijing has regarded actions taken by the North Korean state and military leadership as a direct threat to stability on the Korean Peninsula. This was the case after the North Korean nuclear tests in October 2006 and May 2009 when the Chinese government even approved two UN Security Council resolutions critical of North Korea.

After North Korea pulled out of the multilateral Treaty on the Nonproliferation of Nuclear Weapons (NPT) in 2003, the Chinese leadership called for the convening of Six-Party Talks, with the objective of resolving the nuclear crisis triggered by its Korean neighbor. It also offered to host the meetings and to act as a mediator. Aside from China and the two Koreas, the United States, Russia, and Japan also participated. However, the talks were suspended in 2009.[15] China deliberately used these negotiations to present itself as a responsible regional power. At the same time, Chinese foreign affairs and security politicians wanted to prevent an arms race in the region, which had the potential to expand the US-led alliance system or might even lead to a nuclear arming of Japan or South Korea.

Meanwhile, the Chinese leadership appears to have grudgingly accepted the nuclear status of the DPRK. In China's assessment, Pyongyang will not voluntarily abandon its nuclear weapons by way of negotiations, for these serve as a security guarantee against the United States and as a means of threatening South Korea and Japan.[16] Since North Korea's abandonment of the Six-Party Talks in 2009, the US-DPRK relationship remains deadlocked. Nuclear upgrading in the region has the potential to spiral out of control.

Trade and Investment

China's economic relations with the two Koreas reflect the developmental stage of their respective political relations over the course of time.[17] This obviously applies to South Korea, which has been attractive to China in the context of its economic reform policy only since the 1980s. The Chinese government regards the South Korean modernization experience as a successful model of state control of industrialization and world-market integration. Like Japanese or Taiwanese companies, South Korean businesses have used the opening of the Chinese market to transfer labor-intensive industries to Chinese coastal locations and then to supply global markets. After China's accession to the World Trade Organization (WTO), Korean companies have also been able to dramatically boost sales on the Chinese domestic market (the most conspicuous firms being Hyundai and Kia in the automotive industry and Samsung and LG in the information technology and communications sectors).

China has now become South Korea's most important trading partner, export destination (South Korea has a very high export surplus in its trade with China), and foreign investment destination. By the same token, South Korea has also become one of China's most important trading partners, accounting for more than 4 percent of the PRC's exports and almost 10 percent of its imports in 2011 (see figure 9.3).

The same frictions that affect China's economic relations with the United States, Japan, and Europe characterize its economic exchanges with South Korea.[18] With the steady increase in trade and investment, South Korea fears an erosion of its own economy due to job losses in the industrial sector and its growing dependence on the Chinese market. South Korean farmers complain that the glut of Chinese agricultural products threatens their existence. Since 2000, there have been repeated open trade conflicts involving unilateral increases in customs tariffs or import restrictions on individual goods; however, these have generally been swiftly resolved. A series of reciprocal complaints were dealt with or remain pending with the WTO. Like those

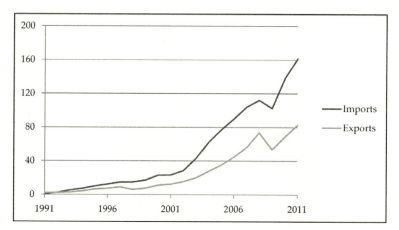

Figure 9.3. China's trade with South Korea, 1991–2011 (in US$ billions).
Source: IMF.

voiced in Europe and the United States, South Korean complaints relate to quality problems with imported Chinese goods, price dumping, and forced technology transfers in exchange for access to the Chinese market. South Korean politicians also worry about a loss of value added and employment in view of Chinese competition with key industries in South Korea, such as shipbuilding and electronics.

Until its collapse in 1991, the Soviet Union was North Korea's most important economic partner. China subsequently assumed this role. After the mid-1990s, starting from a low level, trade with North Korea increased sharply. Outside observers view North Korea as dependent on China for its economic viability.[19] The PRC's share of North Korean foreign trade reaches 70 percent, with Russia and Japan playing secondary roles. China recently supplied almost all of North Korea's energy imports and delivered the majority of its imported consumer goods, plus almost half of its food imports. Conversely, North Korea plays practically no role at all in China's vast foreign trade. Compared with the PRC's trade with South Korea, the share of North Korea's imports to China was a mere 0.14 percent in 2011, and the share of exports to North Korea vis-à-vis total Chinese exports was 0.17 percent (see figure 9.4).

The usual monetary data for accounting for foreign trade, which serve as a basis for both Chinese trade statistics and International Monetary Fund (IMF) statistics, cannot be trusted implicitly in the case of Sino–North Korean economic exchanges, as the trade statistics do not usually document relief supplies (food, energy sources, and commodities), military armaments, in-kind donations, and politically negotiated compensation

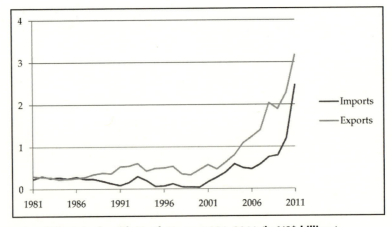

Figure 9.4. China's trade with North Korea, 1981–2011 (in US$ billions).
Source: IMF (incomplete documentation regarding trade flows; see the explanation in the text).

transactions. Both China and North Korea regard these exchange processes as state secrets, and they are much greater than the officially recorded trade. Without doubt, they are critical for the survival of the North Korean regime and thus are in China's strategic interests.

Increasing investments by Chinese state businesses in North Korea over the past decade have now attracted the attention of the South Korean government. Chinese companies doing business in North Korea are not restricted geographically to the specific investment zones that apply to South Korean companies. Chinese firms have therefore gained access to coal and mineral deposits, among other things, and have participated in the modernization of North Korean port facilities. From the perspective of the Chinese government, this should not only stabilize North Korea but also open up new cross-border development opportunities for China's northeastern provinces.[20]

Because relations with the DPRK are subject to complete secrecy in Beijing, they are overseen not by the Ministry of Foreign of Affairs but rather by the International Liaison Department of the Central Committee of the CCP, which is responsible for relations with Communist "sister parties." Chinese state-security and military departments also maintain steady relations with corresponding North Korean institutions. Because of this nearly complete lack of transparency, which is unusual even by Chinese standards, the Western media have repeatedly speculated about potential turnarounds or secret plans in Chinese policy toward Korea (such as possible acceptance of a peaceful reunification of Korea or plans by the Chinese army to invade North Korea in the event of a crisis affecting the regime). But actual Chinese initiatives or actions have not substantiated such speculations.

In summary, the primacy of the status quo has consistently determined China's policy on Korea. Beijing is not likely to abandon this orientation in the absence of a systemic crisis in North Korea. The PRC government is treading a fine line in its Korea policy. In order to prevent any destabilization in the North Korean regime and to stop North Korea from provoking South Korea and the United States, thereby destabilizing the general situation, Beijing has dispensed with exercising direct pressure and tolerated Pyongyang's erratic threats as long as they appear to have a limited impact and to be controllable (as in 2010, for instance). By accepting North Korea's menacing and blackmailing of other nations militarily, the Chinese government is exposing itself to unpredictable advances and actions by the DPRK leadership. In view of the precarious state of North Korea's governance and economy, the Korean Peninsula is likely to remain the focus of ongoing security-policy crisis management for the Chinese government. It is uncertain to what extent Beijing will be able to exercise a moderating influence on Pyongyang in the event of a political crisis.

NOTES

1. Reilly 2009.
2. Mochizuki 2005; Roy 2005; Sutter 2012.
3. Hu Shaohua 2006.
4. Reilly 2009; Wan 2006.
5. On the role of the United States in the conflict, see Manyin 2013.
6. For details, see Zhonghua Renmin Gongheguo Guowuyuan Xinwen Bangongshi 2012a.
7. Beukel 2011; Hagström 2012; Reilly 2009; Smith 2012.
8. Manyin 2013; Przystup 2012.
9. Beukel 2011.
10. Mochizuki 2005; Sutter 2012.
11. Chung 2005; Hao Yufan 2009; Lanteigne 2009; Snyder 2009; Sutter 2012.
12. Gill 2011.
13. Shen Dingli 2006.
14. Bajoria 2010; International Crisis Group 2009, 2011; N. Lewis 2010.
15. Hao Yufan 2009; Twomey 2008.
16. Shen Dingli 2006.
17. Snyder 2009.
18. Snyder 2009.
19. Choo 2008; Snyder 2009.
20. Haggard, Lee, and Noland 2012.

10

Sino-American Relations

During the Cold War, Sino-American relations shifted fundamentally from a climate of confrontation and animosity (from the Korean War in 1950 until rapprochement in 1971) to one of strategic cooperation vis-à-vis the Soviet Union (1971–1989). The end of the Cold War meant an end to a unifying strategic objective on both sides. Since the 1990s, however, Sino-American relations have encompassed other bilateral, regional, and global fields of interaction. Each party is the other's most significant point of reference, not only in terms of superpower rivalry but also with regard to competition and cooperation when defining international relations in the twenty-first century.

Sino-American relations have been subject to extreme fluctuations over the past twenty years, caused by domestic policy dynamics in both countries, economic advances in China and associated shifts in perception, and bilateral political and military tensions in specific areas.

COMMON INTERESTS AND AREAS OF COOPERATION

George W. Bush's administration (2001–2009) initially defined China as less important for US foreign policy than other Asian-Pacific countries and identified the People's Republic of China (PRC) as a "strategic competitor." As a consequence of the foreign policy realignment spurred by the terrorist attacks of 9/11, the Bush administration dropped this characterization, intensified bilateral cooperation efforts, and disregarded earlier conflicts.[1]

In contrast to earlier election campaigns in the United States, the Barack Obama/John McCain presidential campaign of 2008 hardly mentioned

China. The Chinese government showed initial skepticism vis-à-vis newly elected President Obama because the Democrats leaned toward trade protectionism and Beijing considered Secretary of State Hillary Clinton critical of China. In time, however, China's fears were largely alleviated.[2] The Obama administration—initially at least—emphasized shared interests and continued the course of pragmatic cooperation with China.[3] An increase in economic interdependence between both countries—occasionally referred to as symbiotic codependency, or "Chimerica"—and urgent worldwide challenges required closer coordination.[4]

Increasing Economic Interdependence

Both countries are increasingly entwined due to the mutual flow of trade, investments, and currency and their respective dependence on economic growth. However, this intensification in trade ties has also increased the potential for foreign policy conflicts.

In 2011, trade in goods with the PRC comprised 13.6 percent of US foreign-trade volume, making China the second most important commercial partner of the United States (behind Canada but ahead of Mexico). In terms of imports, China was already the largest supplier to the United States, providing 18.1 percent of all imported goods. China was also the third-largest destination for US exports (7.0 percent), after Canada (19.0 percent) and Mexico (13.3 percent).On the flip side, the United States was the PRC's most important trading partner (accounting for 12.3 percent of trade volume in 2011), the largest recipient of exports (17.1 percent), and the fourth-largest source of imports (7.0 percent), following Japan, South Korea, and Taiwan (not counting the European Union [EU] and the Association of Southeast Asian Nations [ASEAN] as collective trading partners).

The United States remains a crucial source of technology and management expertise for China. By the end of 2011, China had received US$67.6 billion in foreign direct investment (FDI) from the United States (almost 6 percent of cumulative FDI stock in the PRC), making the United States by far the most important non-Asian investor (excluding the tax havens) in China. However, since 2010 the United States has been the target of large-scale investments from China in the extractive industries, high-tech manufacturing, and entertainment. Whereas official Chinese statistics at the end of 2011 report a cumulative Chinese outbound foreign direct investment (OFDI) stock in the United States of US$9 billion, research by the Rhodium Group produces much higher figures that may more accurately reflect the reality. China is said to have invested more than US$16 billion and to have created twenty-nine thousand jobs in the United States by 2011. Although thus far Chinese investments in the United States only make up 1 percent of the US FDI stock, current trends are likely to continue. In addition, for years China has financed the United States deficit as its largest creditor and has helped keep interest and inflation rates at historic lows.[5]

Mutual Interests Regarding Global Issues

Both sides share an interest in combating transnational Islamist terrorist groups. As a result, the United States accepted China's classification of an underground Islamist organization in Xinjiang as a terrorist group; similarly, China did not interfere with the Iraq War in 2003 or attempt, despite considerable initial reservations, to thwart US attacks on the Taliban in Afghanistan.

The United States and China also agree regarding prevention of the proliferation of weapons of mass destruction and ending Iran's and North Korea's nuclear programs. In both cases, China has supported sanctions passed by the UN Security Council. In the case of North Korea, between 2003 and 2009 China hosted and mediated the Six-Party Talks (see chapter 9). Furthermore, in April 2010, China participated in the Nuclear Security Summit in Washington.

In order to handle additional traditional and nontraditional security risks, both countries rely on close cooperation. Safeguarding international maritime security (protection against piracy), obtaining access to raw materials and sources of energy, combating cross-border drug trafficking, and preventing the spread of contagious diseases—none of these can be achieved without effective coordination between the United States and China, each of which possess veto rights in the UN Security Council.

Furthermore, as the world's largest economies and the biggest emitters of greenhouse gases (GHGs), the US and Chinese governments are both aware that they must make significant contributions to international efforts to curtail climate change. They agree on definitions of the general objectives for all the problem areas, but opinions on how to achieve these objectives diverge greatly.

The creation of new bilateral communication pathways demonstrates the increase in Sino-American interdependence.[6] For example, during George W. Bush's presidency, both the US-China Senior Dialogue (under the aegis of the US State Department) and the Strategic Economic Dialogue (under the aegis of the US Treasury Department) were created (in 2005 and 2006, respectively). In 2009 these forums were combined to create the Strategic and Economic Dialogue (S&ED), a yearly conference, hosted alternately, covering "economic track" and "strategic track" issues.

Each meeting brings together high-ranking delegations. The secretaries of state and the Treasury represent the United States, and the Chinese state councilor responsible for foreign policy and the vice premier responsible for foreign-trade policy represent the PRC. The US delegation, which traveled to Beijing in May 2010 for the second S&ED meeting, consisted of over two hundred members, making it the largest group of high-ranking American officials to attend such international negotiations.

In the meantime, more than sixty different bilateral dialogue committees, differentiated by topic, envisage regular talks between the two parties.[7] Differences have arisen only in terms of defense policy. Time and again, carefully planned and organized meetings between top US and Chinese officials fall victims to small and not-so-small crises in bilateral relations. From January to September 2010, for example, China broke off its defense consultations as a reaction to the US decision to supply weapons to Taiwan. In contrast, the frequency of meetings between heads of state has increased. In 2009 and 2010, Barack Obama met nearly every three months with Hu Jintao, either at bilateral conferences or within the framework of the Group of Twenty (G20) summits.[8]

DIVERGING INTERESTS AND AREAS OF CONFLICT

A passage in the declaration released on the occasion of President Obama's visit to China in 2009 promises "positive, cooperative, and comprehensive relations in the twenty-first century." This statement does not conceal the fact that old conflicts, diverging interests regarding new issues, and a deeply rooted mistrust have negative effects on bilateral relations. Furthermore, scholars and practitioners on both sides agree that bilateral relations have taken a turn for the worse since 2010.[9] The following sections analyze the sources of these disputes.[10]

Sovereignty

China views Taiwan, Tibet, and Xinjiang as national "core interests" that permit absolutely no "interference" from other nations. China perceives even symbolic actions, such as Barack Obama's reception of the Dalai Lama (in February 2010) or—in particular—US decisions to deliver weapons to Taiwan (as in January 2010 and January 2012), as "interference in domestic affairs" and grave encroachments upon its territorial integrity and national sovereignty. From the Chinese perspective, support for the Tibetan exile movement or for the armed forces in Taiwan hurts the PRC by aiding and abetting "separatist powers."

Political Values and Human Rights

The fact that methods of governance, political values, and concepts of public policy in each country differ entirely gives rise to a slew of latent and manifest conflicts. As a matter of principle, the Chinese government suspects that at least parts of the US administration and US Congress are working to bring about a regime change in China, despite official assurances to the contrary. Human rights issues have lost some of their political explosiveness for bilateral relations since the second half of the 1990s, not because the situation in China has systematically improved but because after 1994 US administrations no longer made economic ties contingent upon improvements in the Chinese human rights situation. The Bush administration eventually ceased its unsuccessful attempts to obtain an official condemnation of Chinese human rights violations by the UN Commission on Human Rights. Instead, US diplomatic efforts focused on applying pressure in specific cases. The Obama administration has continued this policy under the catchword of "principled pragmatism."

Of late, however, the US Congress has increasingly demanded that the PRC eliminate Internet censorship and reprisals against certain religious groups and ethnic minorities and that it release prominent dissidents and political prisoners. Diplomatic tensions also stem from Chinese aid for authoritarian regimes, particularly in Myanmar, Sudan, and Zimbabwe, where there have been severe human rights violations.

Security Policy in the Asia-Pacific Region

Aside from the issue of Taiwan, additional strategic military conflicts of interest in the Asia-Pacific region put a strain on Sino-American relations.[11] In principle, China is not prepared to accept the massive military presence of the United States in this part of the world (about one-fifth of all US armed forces report to the Pacific Command) and the dominant security-policy role the United States plays in the region. In particular, US aerial and naval reconnaissance and military maneuvers within China's two-hundred-mile "exclusive economic zone" harbor a potential for ongoing conflict.

The PRC views US plans to build a missile defense shield (national missile defense) as an attempt to undermine China's nuclear second-strike capability. US intentions to protect Japan or even Taiwan using such a missile defense system (theater missile defense), thereby neutralizing attempts to modernize the People's Liberation Army (PLA), are time and again subject to fierce Chinese criticism.

Closely connected to this issue are conflicts regarding America's military allies. From China's point of view, the Bush and Obama administrations built up US military cooperation with Japan, Australia, Singapore, and other Asian nations with the goal of containing Chinese power.[12] In addition, China perceived US extension of the campaign against terror to include Central Asia (through troops in Afghanistan and covert operations in Pakistan) as part of a "strategy of encirclement." As a countermeasure,

China used the Shanghai Cooperation Organization (SCO) to achieve a reversal in the stationing of US troops in Uzbekistan and Kyrgyzstan. The strategic partnership between China and Russia should be interpreted in this context—that is, as a measure to establish a countervailing power to the United States.

In 2010, an open conflict between the two countries arose over the territorial dispute in the South China Sea (see chapter 3). Rumors that the Chinese government had designated the territories in question as part and parcel of their nonnegotiable "core interests" prompted the United States to designate "freedom of navigation" in the South China Sea as in its own national interest.

Dealings with North Korea have proven a recurring point of contention (see chapter 9). Although China condemned the North Korean nuclear tests conducted in 2006 and 2009 and supported related UN resolutions, Washington criticized inadequate Chinese implementation of the sanctions against North Korea and even accused the PRC of not using all the means then at its disposal to exert pressure on North Korea (i.e., stopping food and fuel deliveries). Two official receptions for Kim Jong Il in China in 2010, coupled with China's halfhearted condemnation of North Korean provocations vis-à-vis South Korea (the sinking of a warship and the shelling of a South Korean island) reinforced such US perceptions.[13]

The United States generally interprets the modernization of the PLA (see chapter 4) as serving to restrict US access to the western Pacific (the so-called antiaccess and area-denial strategy) and, in particular, to prevent US intervention in support of Taiwan.

Global Climate-Change and Security Policy

Despite common objectives to curtail climate change and promote the use of renewable energy, considerable tensions have arisen in this area (see chapter 6). Whereas the United States calls for binding and verifiable commitments from China regarding GHG emissions, China insists that the most developed industrial nations should bear the brunt of emission reductions and that it will implement its ambitious climate goals only via voluntary national measures. Therefore, despite US demands that China assume the position of a responsible twenty-first-century major power, many Chinese Ministry of Foreign Affairs (MFA) officials regard American demands as a strategy to obstruct China's rapid economic progress.[14]

Finally, we turn to another recurring security-policy conflict: Chinese proliferation policy. Chinese deliveries of weapons and missile components to Iran, Pakistan, and North Korea have prompted numerous condemnations from the United States and the imposition of sanctions by the US Congress. Only in the past several years have there been any signs of détente in this area.[15]

Economic Frictions

Economic relations that served as ties to bind the two sides together in recent years have also contributed to rising tensions.[16] In the first decade of the twenty-first century, structural imbalances in bilateral trade relations became a principal source of conflict. For years, the United States has had a considerable trade deficit with China (see table 10.1 for official US data).

Data quantifying the extent of this deficit are contradictory—according to US figures, the deficit in 2011 was US$295.4 billion, whereas Chinese statistics place the number at US$202.3 billion. Therefore, the share of the total US foreign-trade deficit comprised by the trade-balance deficit with China also varies according to the source of the data (see figure 10.1).

On the one hand, the Chinese government alleges that the US deficit merely reflects the division of labor in transnational production networks in the Asia-Pacific region and that the US government increases the deficit by restricting high-tech exports to China for political reasons. On the other hand, the United States claims that Chinese monetary policy and the currency regime are at the root of the trade-deficit problems (see chapter 5). As early as 2003, the United States began to pressure China to considerably revalue the renminbi (RMB) (Chinese yuan, or CNY) to reduce the bilateral trade imbalance.

Despite an incremental and substantial revaluation of the CNY between summer 2005 and autumn 2008 and again since July 2010, US criticism has intensified. In Congress several pending bills denounce China as a

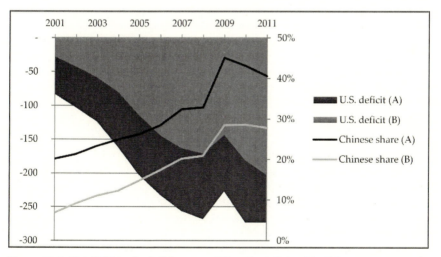

Figure 10.1. Total US trade deficit versus US trade deficit with China, 2001–2011 (in US$ billions).
Source: Ministry of Commerce of the PRC (B); US Census Bureau (A).

Table 10.1.   Trade between the United States and the PRC, 1990–2011 (in US$ Billions)

Year	Total Trade Volume	Chinese Exports	Chinese Imports	US Trade Deficit with China	Share of Total US Trade Deficit (%)
1990	20.0	15.2	4.8	−10.4	10.3
1994	48.1	38.8	9.3	−29.5	19.5
1997	75.5	62.6	12.9	−49.5	27.5
2000	116.3	100.0	16.3	−83.7	19.1
2002	147.3	125.2	22.1	−103.1	21.3
2004	231.4	196.7	34.7	−162.0	24.9
2006	343.0	287.8	55.2	−232.6	28.4
2007	386.7	321.5	65.2	−256.3	32.4
2008	407.5	337.8	69.7	−268.1	32.8
2009	365.9	296.4	69.5	−226.9	45.1
2010	456.8	364.9	91.9	−273.0	43.1
2011	503.3	399.4	103.9	−295.4	40.6

Source: US Census Bureau.

"currency manipulator" and impose punitive tariffs on imports from the PRC. But neither the Bush nor the Obama administration has supported this position. Rather, both have intensified commercial diplomacy efforts to influence the Chinese government.

As a consequence of China's rapid export growth, its central bank has stockpiled foreign-currency reserves (see chapter 5). The bulk of these reserves have been invested in US securities, making China the largest international investor in US debt. At the end of June 2011, China held US$1.73 trillion of public and private US securities, the vast majority of which (US$1.32 trillion) were US Treasury securities (see figure 10.2).[17] There is considerable concern in the United States that China might use its foreign-currency investments to destabilize US and worldwide financial markets and monetary systems so as to extort concessions from the United States.[18] We should not overdramatize this scenario, however. China's holdings of US Treasury securities have declined since their peak in mid-2011 and are now close to the amount held by Japan. At the end of 2011 China accounted for 23 percent of all foreign holdings of US Treasury securities and less than 9 percent of all US federal debt.[19] One can argue that to some extent this also makes China vulnerable because the value of Chinese foreign-currency reserves depends directly on the continued stability of the US dollar. This is also why there has been so much general criticism of America's increasing debt by Chinese economists and official media since 2009. Suspicions have been voiced on a number of occasions that the United States is trying to balance its budget via a loose monetary policy, devaluation of the dollar, and inflation at the expense of China and other creditor countries.

Pressures from the global financial and economic crisis have exacerbated frictions between the two countries since 2008. US government and commerce representatives have accused China of discriminating against foreign competitors when awarding government contracts, setting up nontariff market barriers, and attempting to force technology transfers. In 2010 some US CEOs openly questioned whether China was still interested in creating a fair trade environment for foreign companies. The Chinese government thereupon affirmed that it would continue to make market access and competition available to and attractive for foreign firms.

In contrast, severe criticism from China was directed toward US protectionist policies in terms of Chinese shareholdings in American firms. Bids from a Chinese oil company (China National Offshore Oil Corporation [CNOOC]) to take over Unocal in 2005 and an attempt by the Chinese-owned Ralls Corporation to buy four Oregon wind parks in 2012 were politicized and, in the latter case, blocked because of national-security concerns. Chinese investors felt they were being excluded from large shareholding and takeover projects for political reasons.

An interlacing with other issues that attract a great deal of domestic political attention in the United States has further aggravated bilateral economic conflicts. Prominent economic advisers and union representatives view trade with China as the reason for decreased industrial production capacity and increased unemployment. The United States has accused

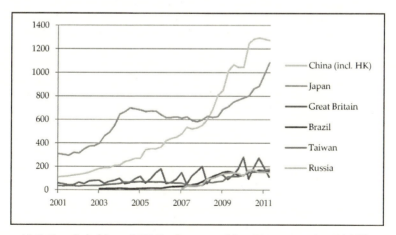

Figure 10.2. Top six holders of US Treasury securities, 2001–2011 (in US$ billions).
Source: US Department of the Treasury 2012a.

Chinese manufacturers of copyright infringements and product piracy that have caused US companies' loss of technology. Serious deficiencies in quality and safety have been found in foodstuffs and toys imported from China. These negative reports exacerbate mistrust of China in US public opinion. On the one hand, Americans perceive China to be the beneficiary of globalization at the expense of US production capacity and employment. On the other hand, American consumers can choose from a wide range of inexpensive Chinese products that, despite all the politicoeconomic frictions, are still very much in demand in the United States.

Competition between the Superpowers and International Order

Economic interconnections and interdependencies have given rise to dilemmas that will be difficult for the US government to resolve. On the one hand, the United States hails Chinese economic growth and proffers close cooperation in its official statements. On the other hand, there is an undercurrent of deep uncertainty behind official US statements regarding the best way to handle China's growing power. Will China be a "responsible superpower" following established rules and taking into consideration inveterate US prerogatives? Or will it act as an increasingly headstrong, challenging new power, primarily serving its own national interests? Due to these uncertainties, Washington's China policy tends toward hedging, forward-deployed diplomacy, and a strengthening of US alliances in the Asia-Pacific region in order to provide as little leeway as possible for unpredictable or undesirable actions by the Chinese government.[20]

Numerous Chinese analyses interpret these approaches as part of a classic containment policy. Following decades-old Maoist analyses and concept archetypes, observers define tension-laden ties to the United States as the "main contradiction" in China's international relations. From this point of view, Chinese foreign policy must adapt to changing power constellations and transitory structures, perpetually coming to terms with the current hegemony.[21] Whereas China is growing stronger, US strength is waning due to economic decline, domestic political barriers that inhibit effective actions, and loss of international credibility.[22]

The dialectics of superpower relations is thus working in China's favor, as long as China does not experience a systemic crisis or relinquish its dynamism with regard to foreign affairs. The traditional Chinese and Maoist strategies of keeping political processes in flux while (temporarily) in a weaker position, of avoiding any premature fixation of one's own position, and of undermining the (currently) stronger party and/or awaiting the outcome of its own self-destructive actions are still alive and well in this mind-set.[23]

The constantly recurring Chinese criticisms of "superpower policy," "hegemony," and "Cold War mentality" are barely disguised references to the role of the United States in the Asia-Pacific region and the world as a whole. The Chinese government, castigating unilateralism, calls for a multipolar world order in which other powers (Russia, the EU, China, India) and an upgrading of the United Nations counterbalance US dominance. The US-dollar-dominated global monetary policy is a "thing of the past," as Chinese president Hu Jintao stated at the beginning of 2011. The governor of the Chinese central bank has even suggested setting up a new global reserve currency with the International Monetary Fund (IMF) in the form of a currency basket with modified special drawing rights. Since the 2007 global financial crisis, Chinese criticism of US dominance in world politics and finance has grown fiercer.

Table 10.2 provides a brief overview of each country's interests based on the analyses in the preceding sections.

Domestic Determinants of Sino-American Relations

US policy vis-à-vis China is naturally subject to fluctuations in domestic policy.[24] Very different issues come into play here. On the one hand, the US government is confronted with energetic lobbying by US companies and trade associations (e.g., the US-China Business Council and the Club for Growth) in favor of trade with China. On the other hand, in addition to an influential pro-Taiwan lobby, other interest groups (religious groups, Free Tibet activists, and unions) lobby their congressmen, in many cases successfully, with criticisms of China.

On the Chinese side, occurrences in 1999 and 2001 that caused frictions in Sino-American relations illustrate the public pressure to which the Chinese government is subjected when it must prevail as the unrelenting defender of national interests against the United States. In both countries, latent reciprocal concepts of the enemy might at any time provide fertile breeding ground for larger crises.[25]

In all, Sino-American relations are quite complex. The introduction of new cooperative measures in 2002 and intensified political and diplomatic exchanges have not offset the fundamental causes of tensions and divergent interests. In many policy areas, the United States and China remain rivals. Mistrust, instability, and susceptibility to crises overshadow bilateral relations.[26]

This is not to say that the current state of affairs will bring about a comprehensive ideological politicoeconomic "competition between systems" (analogous to the Cold War) or automatically develop into a military conflict (analogous to historical experiences when new, aspiring powers have overthrown existing political leaders).[27] The power of economic interdependence and pragmatic foreign policy is currently sufficiently stable to maintain constructive, albeit tense, cooperation between the United States

Table 10.2. Areas of Cooperation and Conflict in Sino-American Relations

Area of Interaction	Common Ground	Divergent Positions
National sovereignty and human rights	• Maintaining stability in the PRC and the Taiwan Strait • Preventing normative conflicts from harming overall relations	• PRC: No interference in domestic affairs; inviolable integrity of national territories (including Taiwan, Tibet, and Xinjiang) • US: Compliance with universal human rights conventions; democratization; supplying defensive weapons to Taiwan
Economy	• Further developing bilateral trade relations • Preserving international economic trade • Stabilizing the global financial system	• PRC: Improved access to advanced US technologies; dismantling of political restrictions for Chinese takeovers of US firms; establishing a new global reserve currency • US: Reducing the trade deficit with China; revaluing the CNY; protection of intellectual property rights (IPR) in China; seeing Chinese investments in the US as secondary to matters of national security
Global issues	• Combating drug trade, terrorism, crime, and epidemics • Pursuing nonproliferation of weapons of mass destruction • Curtailing climate change	• PRC: Belief that the provision of global public goods is primarily the responsibility of the highly developed nations and that China's cooperation should be voluntary • US: Belief that, based on its economic achievements, China should make larger, more verifiable contributions to global public goods
Asia-Pacific region	• Maintaining stability on the Korean Peninsula • Finding peaceful solutions to territorial disputes • Ensuring maritime safety	• PRC: No US intervention with respect to Taiwan and/or other Chinese territorial issues; dissolution of the US alliance system in the region • US: Maintaining a military presence in the western Pacific; further promotion of its bilateral alliance system
Realignment of international relations	• Avoiding disruptive changes • Gradually increasing the influence of the emerging economies	• PRC: Replacing the US-dominated world order with a multipolar order; acceptance of a central role for China in contributing to this order • US: Maintaining its global position of leadership

and China. For now, the Chinese government exhibits neither the political will nor the international influence nor the military power to challenge the United States in its dominant global role. Both sides confront very different—yet equally serious—domestic political issues, as well as national and international economic and social challenges, which lay claim to the energies of their respective governments.[28]

The greatest risk for Sino-American relations in the near future lies in unrealistic expectations fomented by domestic dynamics on both sides. The United States can hardly expect China to permanently play the role of a "junior power," constantly taking the back seat to US leadership claims. Conversely, China cannot expect the United States to remain passive, making unlimited concessions to Chinese ascension. These exaggerated expectations and unavoidable disappointments will strain reciprocal willingness to cooperate and compromise, which will likely falter time and again.[29]

NOTES

1. Sutter 2010, 2012.
2. Lampton 2009; S. Lawrence and Lum 2011.
3. S. Lawrence and MacDonald 2012; Zhao Suisheng 2012.
4. Ferguson and Schularick 2009.
5. Elwell, Labonte, and Morrison 2007; Hale and Hale 2008; Li Wei 2008; W. Morrison and Labonte 2012; Prasad 2010.
6. Glaser 2013.
7. Glaser 2013.
8. S. Lawrence and Lum 2011.
9. For scholars, see Shambaugh 2013b. For practitioners, see Bader 2012.
10. Christensen 2006; Foot 2009–2010; Friedberg 2005; S. Lawrence and Lum 2011; S. Lawrence and MacDonald 2012; Shambaugh 2013a, 2013b; Sutter 2010, 2012; Twomey 2007; Yan Xuetong 2010.
11. Twomey 2013.
12. For example, Wu Xinbo 2013.
13. Clinton 2011.
14. Lampton 2009.
15. Lampton 2008.
16. C. Freeman 2013; W. Morrison 2012.
17. US Department of the Treasury 2012a.
18. Drezner 2009; W. Morrison and Labonte 2012.
19. W. Morrison and Labonte 2012.
20. Zhao Suisheng 2012.
21. Jia Qingguo 2008.
22. Wu Xinbo 2010.
23. Heilmann and Perry 2011.
24. Sutter 2013.

25. Shirk 2007; Wu Xinbo 2013.
26. Saunders 2008; Shambaugh 2013b; Sutter 2010; Yan Xuetong 2010.
27. Art 2010; Clark 2011.
28. Lampton 2009.
29. Sutter 2010.

11

China's Relations with Europe

Sino-European relations reveal a number of parallels to the Sino-American relations described in the previous chapter. Not only is great significance accorded to economic interdependence in both cases, but the potential for tensions between China and Europe over foreign trade has also increased considerably in recent years. Moreover, the US and European governments share certain fundamental objectives with respect to their China policies.[1] Both want China to play a predictable and reliable role in international relations and hope that China's political system will open up and follow a democratic rule of law. Both would also like to see economic and social modernization continue in China without any drastic setbacks.

Beyond this common ground, however, special patterns of perception and interaction, as well as special interests stemming from the unique role of the European Union (EU) in international politics, characterize Sino-European relations. It is significant that—unlike in China's relations with the United States or Japan—conflicts relating to security policy have been of little consequence in the development of Sino-European relations.

ECONOMIC INTERDEPENDENCE AND
POTENTIAL SOURCES OF TENSIONS

Sino-European economic relations have undergone a significant upturn since the 1990s. EU imports from China rose from less than €20 billion in 1990 to €292 billion in 2011. During the same period, exports to China increased from less than €6 billion to €136 billion (see figure 11.1).

In 2011 the EU was China's most important trading partner, ahead of the United States and Japan. For the EU, the People's Republic of China (PRC) was its second most important trading partner. China was the EU's most significant supplier of imports, with a share of more than 17 percent in 2011, and the second most important destination for European exports after the United States, with a share of almost 9 percent (see table 11.1).

Exports from the PRC to the EU made up 18.6 percent of China's total exports in 2011. Imports from the EU accounted for about 12 percent of all Chinese imports. Within the EU, Germany is by far the biggest exporter to China (accounting for almost half of EU exports to China over the last several years) as well as China's largest importer (with a share of more than 20 percent).

With regard to foreign direct investment (FDI) in the PRC, the EU is among the top five FDI providers, along with Hong Kong, Taiwan, the

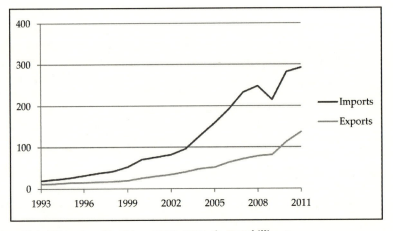

Figure 11.1. EU trade with China, 1993–2011 (in EUR billions).
Source: Eurostat.

Table 11.1.   China's and the EU's Trading Partners, 2011 (Sum of Imports and Exports)

China's Most Important Trading Partners (US$ billions)*		The EU's Most Important Trading Partners (€ billions)**	
1. EU	556	1. US	445
2. US	447	2. China	428
3. Japan	343	3. Russia	307

Note: Numbers are rounded.
Sources: *Ministry of Commerce of the PRC; **Eurostat.

United States, and Japan (see chapter 5). According to official statistics from Eurostat, the EU states invested €17.8 billion in China in 2011, considerably more than the €6 billion to €7 billion in 2009 and 2010 but only 5 percent of all EU FDI flows in 2011 and much less than FDI from the EU27 to the United States (€111 billion), Switzerland (€32 billion), and Brazil (€28 billion). The EU's FDI stock in China of €75 billion at the end of 2010 was less than 2 percent of all EU outward stock and much less than the EU's FDI stock in the United States (28 percent), Switzerland (14 percent), and Canada (5 percent). Despite China's importance to EU foreign trade, it has not been the leading BRIC (Brazil, Russia, India, and China) country in terms of receipts of European FDI (see figure 11.2).

China's outbound FDI to the EU has recently attracted much media coverage and scholarly analysis.[2] According to Eurostat, in 2011 Chinese companies invested a record €3.1 billion in the EU, but independent analysis by the Rhodium Group reports much higher figures (€7.4 billion) because it factors in third-party intermediaries.[3] However, we must place this new surge in perspective. China's share of 1.4 percent (Eurostat figures) of all FDI to the EU was just a mere fraction of that from the United States (at US$115 billion and with a share of 51 percent), Switzerland, Canada, or Brazil. Chinese FDI stock in the EU at the end of 2010 (at €6.7 billion and with a share of 0.2 percent) was dwarfed by that from the United States (at US$1,201 billion and with a share of 41 percent), Switzerland, Canada, and Japan, equaling only that from South Africa.

Tensions in Sino-European relations were increasing even prior to the post-2007 global financial crisis. European criticisms for the most part coincided with those from the United States. From the European perspective,

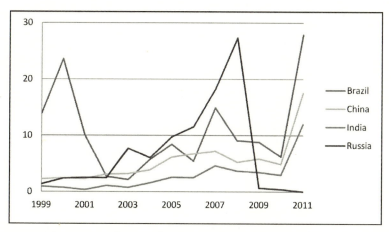

Figure 11.2. The EU's FDI flows to the BRIC countries, 1999–2011 (in EUR billions).
Source: Eurostat.

the trade deficit with China peaked in 2008 at €170 billion and amounted to €156 billion in 2011, almost the amount of the total extra-EU trade deficit. The Netherlands generally registered the largest deficit with China, followed by the United Kingdom, Italy, France, and Spain.

Many Europeans regard China as a winner in terms of globalization—as a country that uses illegal market restrictions and export subsidies to shape trade to its benefit and establishes numerous hurdles for European countries on its own ground (the lack of transparent administrative regulations, and so forth). Particular tensions have occurred in the banking and insurance sectors and in the automotive industry, as well as in energy production, information technology, medicine, and construction.

The EU Chamber of Commerce in China has repeatedly called for greater transparency and better opportunities for accessing the Chinese market, particularly through public tenders. According to the Chamber of Commerce, European companies systematically encountered discrimination in the awarding of lucrative, high-volume public tenders that went to Chinese state enterprises during the 2008–2010 economic stimulus program. The chamber also noted, as some of China's worst shortcomings, a failure to protect intellectual property rights and a lack of transparency in its certification processes. A greater opening of the Chinese market and equal opportunities for European businesses in the PRC—referred to as "positive reciprocity," "mutual balance," and a "level playing field" in the EU—are viewed as critical to the future of Sino-European relations.

Chinese manufacturers are increasingly competing with European companies in medium- to high-tech industries, such as the photovoltaics sector. Even the rail transport industry, traditionally dominated by European conglomerates, now faces competition from China in the race for lucrative markets for large-scale infrastructure projects in the emerging economies and developing nations.

As it has been with the United States, Chinese currency policy has been a virulent source of dispute with the EU. Due to the decline in the value of the US dollar against the euro, combined with the pegging of the Chinese yuan (CNY) to the dollar, the euro rose steadily against the CNY until the spring of 2008. Although the People's Bank of China (PBoC) allowed the CNY to gradually appreciate against the dollar starting in July 2005, rising a total of 15 percent (see chapter 5), it lost 7 percent against the euro during the same period. European exports to the PRC thus became more expensive than exports from US or from Asian competitors, leading to EU calls for bilateral measures or World Trade Organization (WTO) involvement. However, the euro reached a high of ¥11.1 in April 2008, after which it fell in value against the CNY, ultimately hitting a low of ¥8.2 in June 2010 in the context of the euro crisis. Despite this new constellation, Chinese currency policy remains highly controversial, and high-ranking EU representatives have repeatedly called for a significant and regulated appreciation of the CNY. Mirroring Beijing's responses to the United States, Chinese officials have called upon the EU to abandon restrictions on high-tech exports so as to decrease the trade deficit.

In 2010, when the focus in Europe turned to concerns regarding the stability of the common currency and the credit standing of several southern European countries, China at the same time openly declared its intent to acquire Irish, Spanish, Portuguese, and Greek government bonds to help settle the markets. Although it is difficult to say with certainty how much of the troubled government bonds China actually bought (there are no aggregate data on foreign purchases of public debt in the EU or in each of the member states), it is rather safe to conclude that the euro's role in China's foreign-currency portfolio has increased (perhaps up to 33 percent; see chapter 5).[4] The euro is used to diversify Chinese reserves, which are mainly held in dollars. Furthermore, China's trade policy includes support of the euro, given the position of the EU as the largest consumer goods market for Chinese exports. Finally, leveraging euro-denominated currency might generate political influence, for instance, to effect a lifting of the European weapons embargo.

SPECIAL ASPECTS OF SINO-EUROPEAN RELATIONS

One significant aspect of Sino-European relations involves how the PRC perceives the EU.[5] Although Chinese foreign policy analyses and speeches by leading politicians consistently refer to the EU as a key pole in international relations, the EU as a supranational institution nonetheless remains foreign to prevailing Chinese state-centered thinking, which is geared toward preserving national sovereignty. Chinese foreign policy only perceives the EU as a player capable of taking action as a single entity when it comes to multilateral trade policy. However, it also sees the EU and the major European nation-states as global counterbalances to US dominance. This is why the Chinese government has been placing increased priority on its political relations with the EU since the mid-1990s.[6]

This enhanced status appears to be primarily of symbolic importance, however.[7] China's foreign policy makers view the European nations as rivals, playing one country against another in matters of human rights policy as well as financing for major investment projects in China (e.g., competition for financial aid, development loans, and guarantees between individual countries). European governments often find themselves in a race for subsidies when vying for large-scale projects within China (such as nuclear power plants and high-speed rail systems). Chinese government agencies have discovered how to benefit from these rivalries by according selective priority to changing countries. Skepticism on the part of China regarding the EU political model and its effectiveness has increased in the face of the southern European debt crisis and the 2010–2012 euro crisis.

Another unique aspect of Sino-European relations is the almost complete lack of tensions regarding security policy. Unlike in Sino-US relations, the EU and China do not view each other as a military threat. The EU has few security interests in East Asia and no military presence whatsoever. Even the Taiwan question is of minor significance.[8]

The only conflict worth noting in this respect involves discussions regarding lifting European sanctions against arms suppliers to the PRC. The weapons embargo, in effect since 1989, is not legally binding, but it has been a source of ill feelings for many years. The matter came to a head in 2004–2005, resulting in differences of opinion within Europe as well as transatlantic frictions. Germany and France acted alone in favoring a lifting of the arms embargo for political reasons. After having expressed initial agreement, the United Kingdom and a number of central and eastern European countries opposed the measure. However, following massive pressure from the United States and enactment of the Chinese Anti-Secession Law in March 2005, the issue was taken off the table.[9] The subject came up again in December 2010 when the EU's high representative for foreign and security policy recommended lifting the weapons embargo in an effort to resolve a major point of contention in Sino-European relations. France and Spain voiced approval. The British government, however, attempted to attach lifting of the embargo to specific steps taken by the PRC, including on a number of issues related to human rights. Given that all EU countries would have to approve any such decision, removal of the embargo still faces high political hurdles.

Despite the intermittent flare-ups of European objection to China's handling of its ethnic minorities (for example, after the unrest in Tibet in 2008 or in Xinjiang in 2009) and repression of government critics (as evidenced by China's preventing Liu Xiaobo from accepting his Nobel Peace Prize in person in the winter of 2010 and the imprisonment of Ai Weiwei in the spring of 2011), criticism of China is accorded less weight among European politicians than among their US counterparts. In contrast to parts of the foreign policy establishment in the United States, thus far no European government has been willing to launch a foreign policy offensive to attempt to erode the ruling system in China; nor does any European government believe that such an action would necessarily be effective.

In human rights policy, for instance, the European approach that emerged in the mid-1990s differed substantially from that of the United States. The Europeans, relying on nonconfrontational measures, set up an official human rights dialogue with the PRC in 1995, due in part to the sharply opposing interests that had come to the fore within the EU regarding dealings with China. In practice, human rights policy increasingly began to rely on "capacity-building" measures (e.g., training programs for Chinese jurists, civil servants, and so forth), which the Europeans saw as a positive contribution to promoting the rule of law in China.[10]

Europe's China policy has developed in line with strategy papers and lists of measures published by the European Commission in 1995, 1998, 2001, 2003, and 2006. The EC-China Trade and Economic Cooperation Agreement of 1985 forms the legal basis for Sino-European relations. European negotiators hope that this agreement will eventually be superseded by a new regulatory framework (the Partnership and Cooperation Agreement), which is expected to cover topics such as labor law, intellectual property, bilateral investments, trade, climate change, and human rights. Negotiations on the new agreement, initiated in 2007, have been complicated and lengthy (by the end of 2012, they still had not been concluded).

The EU's strategy paper of 2006 highlights the union's interest in constructive and responsible cooperation with the PRC to overcome a variety of problems in the relationship, both bilateral and international. In addition to trade, the paper emphasizes environmental protection, employment, energy, security, and migration issues. The EU has worked to involve the PRC more closely in international issues, such as climate change and joint development work, an effort known as "effective multilateralism." In terms of its Africa policy, it has called on China to employ the good-governance principles promoted by the World Bank, the EU, and the United States in carrying out development aid. All in all, it has become clear in recent strategy papers that the EU is prepared to recognize the PRC's advancement to a superpower, but it also expects greater Chinese willingness to cooperate in solving problems in bilateral relations and at a global level.

The Chinese government published its first strategy paper on EU policy in 2003. The paper describes China's interests in Sino-European relations as well as the policy areas in which China sees potential for greater cooperation, that is, expanding economic cooperation, including reducing trade barriers and reinforcing international and regional cooperation (within the framework of the United Nations and the Asia-Europe Meeting [ASEM]). In contrast, the Chinese strategy paper accords the human rights dialogue much less attention. The specified areas of cooperation mainly relate to the protection of cultural and social rights and the rights of the handicapped. In its strategy paper, the PRC calls for significantly more EU involvement in environmental protection and poverty reduction.

The demands of the PRC vis-à-vis its European partners dominate the Chinese position on EU policy, while the assumption of international responsibility on the part of China plays a lesser role. Accordingly, Brussels and Beijing take widely varying approaches to the development of Sino-European relations in terms of perspectives, interests, and demands.

Numerous meetings have been held at different levels and in varying forms for the purpose of implementing the objectives described in the EU strategy papers. According to official EU documents, the EU-China dialogue architecture rests on three pillars: the political dialogue (including the strategic dialogue since 2005 and the human rights dialogue since 1995), the economic and sectoral dialogue (including the high-level economic and trade dialogue since 2008), and the high-level people-to-people dialogue (since 2012). The annual EU-China Summit (first held in 1998 and alternately hosted in the PRC and Europe) brings together the Chinese premier and the president of the European Council and the European Commission.

Biannual meetings on the human rights dialogue are geared above all toward supporting the development of the rule of law, protecting human rights and the rights of minorities, preserving religious freedom, protecting Tibetan autonomy, and involving China more closely in international human rights regimes. Since to date the European Commission assesses the results as unsatisfactory, plans are underway to coordinate the human rights dialogue more closely with the existing thirteen dialogues held by the individual EU member states. However, as yet European demands for "verifiable" progress in the area of human rights protection and political reform in China have not had any direct impact.

The high-level economic and trade dialogue conducted for the first time in April 2008 follows the Sino-US model and aims at helping to reduce trade tensions and barriers. For instance, following the 2009 dialogue, both sides reported that despite the challenges imposed by the global economic crisis, they would dispense with protectionist measures and take responsibility for the opening of global markets. The economic dialogue is flanked by talks between the European Central Bank (ECB) and the PBoC.

In addition to the dialogues noted above, the pragmatic working relationship between the EU and the PRC involves a number of additional medium- to long-term Sino-European cooperation initiatives. These "sectoral dialogues" occur as regular meetings at the ministerial level and also as informal collaborations, some of which involve representatives from private industry and civil society. The goal of these sectoral dialogues, which are now conducted in more than fifty different issue areas, is to lay a broad foundation for expanding political relations. The following areas are among those dealt with to date: agriculture, civil aviation, intellectual property protection, competition policy, consumer protection, employment and social security, science and technology, energy safety, environmental protection and sustainable development, space flights, and satellite technology.

However, the large number of collaborative initiatives has not as yet contributed to a better coordinated or more effective European China policy. Cooperative initiatives with China at the national or EU level generally exist alongside one another without any coordination. This reduces the effects of individual initiatives, some of which are heavily endowed financially.

Sino-European relations have expanded considerably since the mid-1990s. The relationship has suffered only short-term impacts from intermittent crises, such as those occurring annually prior to 1997 due to the European petitions submitted to the UN Human Rights Commission criticizing China, in 1993–1994 due to the French supply of weapons to Taiwan, in 1996 due to a Tibet resolution by the German Bundestag critical of China, and from 1992 to 1997 due to UK-Chinese controversies regarding the Hong Kong handover.

Recently, however, comments by politicians from both sides and the results of academic studies have indicated a certain disillusionment with respect to the substance and yield of these exchanges.[11] The "strategic partnership" promoted time and again by the EU Commission and the Chinese since 2003 has not brought about the expected results. Further expectations of a possible "axis" of close cooperation between Europe and China have proven completely exaggerated.[12] The reasons for such disillusionment on both sides are many and varied.[13] Both sides apparently expected more from the development of bilateral relations. The Europeans have been disappointed by their own inability to guide the PRC toward "effective multilateralism" and frustrated in their support of internal political change. The Chinese, for their part, have interpreted the "strategic partnership" as an opportunity not only to play Europe off against the United States but also to receive official status as a market economy from the EU Commission in order to reduce the risk of trade sanctions.

Despite such expectations, Sino-European conflicts have increased in frequency and intensity since 2006. The European Union and its member states have criticized the fundamental foreign-trade and currency imbalances as well as the fact that the PRC has not lived up to its global responsibilities, for example, in blatantly pursuing its own national interests with respect to Africa policy and climate protection. The PRC, in turn, has complained of increasing protectionism in Europe (with regard to Chinese investments, for example), unjustified retaliatory trade measures (such as punitive tariffs on imports from Chinese textile exporters), and indiscriminate European following of the United States (for example, in maintaining the weapons embargo).

All in all, Sino-European relations encompass many areas that involve complementary interests and in which communication is ensured at an institutional level. However, the relationship also has a pronounced potential for conflict that will not be resolved in the near term due to, from the European perspective, China's foreign-trade policies and the incompatible aspects of its political order. The Chinese, for their part, see most European criticism as resulting from ignorance, prejudice, or arrogance.

How Sino-European relations develop in the future will not, however, depend on the EU as a collective international player. Rather, they will depend on China's relations with the individual member states, among which Germany, as Europe's largest economy, will play a prominent role.

SINO-GERMAN RELATIONS

Since the 1990s, comprehensive Asia-related policy documents ("regional concepts") prepared by the German Foreign Ministry have stated the primary interests, objectives, and tasks of Germany's China policy. The 2002 paper, which is still applicable today, names the "integration of China, which is rapidly increasing in political and economic significance, into the community of nations" as one of Germany's prime foreign policy objectives. Beyond economic relations, the paper specifies security, human rights, and developmental policies as meriting special attention. Specialized regional concepts prepared by individual German ministries to cover their specific areas of responsibility set forth more specific initiatives to implement Germany's China policy.

The Chinese political elite more or less openly identifies the German government as the most important political actor in Europe, with Chinese leaders seeking out friendly relations with some German chancellors. In May 2004, Chancellor Gerhard Schröder and Premier Wen Jiabao declared the German-Chinese relationship a "strategic partnership in global responsibility." Initially, relations were relaxed under Chancellor Angela Merkel as well. In October 2007, however, Sino-German relations took a dramatic turn for the worse when the Dalai Lama visited the chancellor's office. Even though the visit was said to have been private, it provided an opportunity for the PRC to express strong protest and disrupt cooperation in some areas at short notice. The conflict was not officially settled until the foreign ministerial talks in June 2008. The fact that the Chinese government did not hesitate to risk its otherwise good relationship with the federal government of Germany, one of its most important trading partners, illustrates how abruptly Chinese foreign policy can take a hard line, if only symbolically, as soon as Beijing senses doubts about its territorial integrity or national sovereignty.

Diplomatic relations regained an even footing in 2010 when Chancellor Merkel and Premier Wen agreed to hold annual government consultations presided over by the two heads of government and including a large number of cabinet members. At the first of these government consultations, held in Berlin in June 2011, the parties signed twenty-two bilateral agreements to intensify cooperation in trade, technology, justice, consumer protection, transport, the environment, and education, among other areas. The

German state's main interest in China undoubtedly is to promote exports and secure an economic presence in China, as vividly demonstrated by the fact that large trade delegations that actively promote projects and interests benefiting German enterprises always accompany German chancellors and foreign ministers on their various visits to China.

One notable aspect of Sino-German relations is the prominent role played by the CEOs of major German corporations (Volkswagen, Siemens, Bayer, BASF, Daimler, and BMW are among the leading investors in China). The Asia-Pacific Committee of German Business (APA), an umbrella organization founded in 1993 that encompasses all key interest groups relating to business with China, has strongly advocated expansion of trade relations with China regardless of any political crises occurring at the time. The Chinese government treats the chairmen of the APA, usually prominent CEOs of the aforementioned corporations and preferred negotiation partners in the PRC, as key representatives of the German economy.

In recent years, Sino-German trade relations have developed at a rapid pace. In fact, Germany became by far China's most important European trading partner as early as the 1990s (see table 11.2 for official Chinese trade statistics in US dollars).

For its part, China overtook Japan as Germany's most important Asian trading partner in 2002. German trade with China increased fivefold between 2000 and 2011, rising from €28 billion to €144.3 billion according to

Table 11.2.   China's Most Important Trading Partners, 2011

Country	Trade Volume (in US$ Billions)	Share (%)
1. EU 27	556	15.3
2. US	447	12.3
3. ASEAN	363	10.0
4. Japan	343	9.4
5. Hong Kong	283	7.8
6. South Korea	246	6.8
7. Germany	169	4.6
8. Taiwan	160	4.4
9. Australia	117	3.2
10. Brazil	84	2.3

Note: Numbers are rounded.
Sources: Ministry of Commerce of the PRC; National Bureau of Statistics of the PRC.

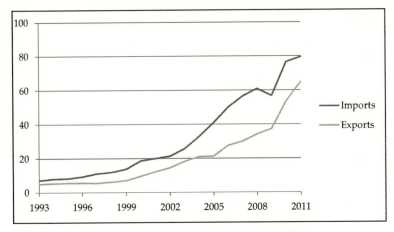

Figure 11.3. German trade with China, 1993–2011 (in EUR billions).
Source: German Federal Statistical Office.

figures from the German Federal Office of Statistics. Exports from Germany also rose fivefold during this period, increasing from €9.5 billion to €64.8 billion, and imports to Germany grew from €18.5 billion to approximately €79.5 billion. Hence Germany has built up a substantial trade deficit with China, amounting to about €14.7 billion (see figure 11.3). We should note that Chinese statistics from the Ministry of Commerce paint a different picture. According to this source, in 2011 China ran a trade deficit with Germany (US$16.3 billion). This statistical discrepancy most probably is due to the role of Hong Kong and the Netherlands as intermediaries in Sino-German trade.

China's significance for German foreign trade has been growing by leaps and bounds (see table 11.3). In 2009 and 2010, China surpassed the Netherlands as the Federal Republic of Germany's primary import partner, a position it lost narrowly in 2011. Even more impressive is China's rise in significance as a sales market for German exports.

Although exports to the traditionally important markets of France, the United States, the Netherlands, the United Kingdom, Italy, and Austria declined (some substantially) during the economic crisis, exports to the PRC continued to grow. In the ranking of Germany's key export partners, China moved up from eleventh place in 2007 to eighth place in 2009, and it reached fifth place in 2011, just behind the United Kingdom. By the end of 2011, more than 6 percent of all German exports were going to China.

China's significance as a capital goods market for German engineering, automotive, and special chemical products increased dramatically during the post-2007 global downturn. During a period when other export markets were weakening, engineering exports to China rose from €8.8 billion in

Table 11.3. Germany's Imports and Exports, 2011 (in € Billions)

Main Origins of Imports		Main Export Destinations	
1. Netherlands	82.0	1. France	101.5
2. China	79.5	2. United States	73.7
3. France	66.2	3. Netherlands	69.3
4. United States	48.3	4. United Kingdom	65.5
5. Italy	48.2	5. China	64.8
6. United Kingdom	44.8	6. Italy	62.1
7. Russia	40.6	7. Austria	57.6
8. Belgium	38.3	8. Switzerland	47.7
9. Austria	37.5	9. Belgium	46.9
10. Switzerland	36.9	10. Poland	43.5

Notes: Numbers are rounded.
Source: German Federal Statistical Office.

2007 to €18.8 billion in 2011. In 2009, the PRC overtook both the United States and France to become Germany's primary capital goods market, with one-tenth of German machine exports being shipped to China.

The German automotive industry is also becoming increasingly entwined with the Chinese market. Whereas China bought motor vehicles worth €4.9 billion in 2007, this figure climbed to €17.7 billion by 2011. In 2010, China became the third most important market for the German automotive industry (see figure 11.4).Demand from China also contributed to Germany's rapid economic recovery between 2009 and 2011. However, this led to concerned debates about the risks of German export dependency on China, which might have serious consequences for the bilateral relationship in the event of economic or political disruptions in China (see figure 11.4).

Before 1998, German direct investment in China was sluggish, but investments accelerated in the run-up to China's 2001 entry into the WTO. Germany became Europe's biggest investor in China in 2001, albeit far behind Hong Kong, Taiwan, Japan, and the United States. In 2011 the Federal Republic of Germany ranked second, behind only the United Kingdom, as the most important European investor in China. According to figures from the Chinese government, German companies invested US$1.1 billion in the PRC in 2011. This figure represents 0.9 percent of all FDI received by the PRC and 18 percent of European FDI in China.

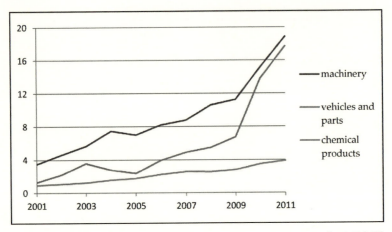

Figure 11.4. German exports to China by product group, 2001–2011 (in EUR billions).
Source: German Federal Statistical Office.

Table 11.4.   The Main Markets for German Exports by Product Group, 2011

Product	Country	Trade Volume (in € billions)	Share (%)
Machinery	1. China	18.8	11.5
	2. United States	13.3	8.2
	3. France	11.8	7.2
Motor vehicles and vehicle parts	1. United States	19.1	10.3
	2. United Kingdom	18.0	9.7
	3. China	17.7	9.5
	4. France	14.4	7.7
Chemicals	1. France	9.7	9.6
	2. Netherlands	7.7	7.6
	3. Italy	7.4	7.3
	9. China	3.9	3.9

Note: Numbers are rounded.
Source: German Federal Statistical Office.

In cumulative terms, according to Chinese statistics, German companies invested nearly US$19 billion in China between 1978 and 2011, corresponding to 1.6 percent of all FDI during that period. German statistics report a higher figure: fifty-five hundred companies reportedly invested about €21 billion in China. The majority of German investments went into the production of motor vehicles and motor vehicle parts. Conversely, eight hundred Chinese companies, most of them small and medium-size companies (SMEs), invested less than €1 billion in Germany.

After years of low-friction trade relations, toward the end of the first decade of the twenty-first century the number of lawsuits by German companies based on charges of unfair competition began to increase markedly. The CEOs of Siemens and BASF, for instance, have repeatedly voiced public criticism—even in the presence of the Chinese premier during a 2010 trip by Chancellor Merkel to China—of the deterioration in investment terms and business conditions for foreign companies in China due to a variety of market-access restrictions and the forced transfer of technological expertise. Despite such complaints, however, many large German corporations and SMEs have rapidly expanded their presence in China, building new production and service locations and making new investments in companies and partnerships, enabling them since 2011 to register revenue growth in the Chinese market that significantly exceeds that in the traditional US or European markets. For some German corporations, the Chinese market grew tremendously after 2008. In 2011, for instance—following dramatic increases in the preceding years—Daimler generated more than 10 percent, Siemens nearly 9 percent, and Bayer about 7 percent of their respective group revenue in China (see table 11.5).

A new development occurred when Chinese enterprises, both within China and abroad, began competing more actively with German companies, even in the high-tech sectors. In railways and infrastructure, for example, Chinese corporate groups have become successful competitors with German firms, particularly in the developing and emerging economies. Moreover, in the photovoltaics industry, which for many years Germany regarded as the industrial sector of the future and subsidized accordingly, Chinese producers rose to become global market leaders within only a few years, in part due to generous financing from Chinese state banks. Some German media and the public had already conjured up an "economic war" with China, claiming that China was ruthlessly using unfair trading practices, from export dumping to technology piracy.

Sino-German joint development work was also subjected to sharp criticism from Germany during the first decade of the twenty-first century. Following the first cooperation agreements in the early 1980s, over the course of the 1990s China became the biggest recipient of German development aid. Perception that China was not fulfilling key criteria to qualify for German aid due to its systematic human rights violations triggered criticism.

As China's economic and technological capacity grew, critics began questioning the basic notion that Germany should provide costly aid to the

Table 11.5. Revenue of Large German Enterprises in Key Markets, 2008–2011

Company	Sales Market	2008 (€ Billions)	2009 (€ Billions)	2010 (€ Billions)	2011 (€ Billions)	Share in 2011 (%)
Daimler	Germany	21.8	18.8	19.3	19.8	18.6
	United States	20.0	16.6	20.2	22.2	20.8
	China	3.2	4.3	9.1	11.1	10.4
Siemens	Germany	12.8	11.5	11.4	10.8	14.7
	United States	14.8	15.7	14.8	14.4	19.6
	China	4.9	5.2	5.8	6.4	8.7
Bayer	Germany	4.8	4.1	4.4	4.6	12.6
	United States	7.1	6.8	7.1	7.3	19.2
	China	n/a	1.7	2.4	2.5	6.8

Note: Numbers are rounded.
Sources: *Bayer Annual Report* 2010, 2011; *Daimler Annual Report* 2011; *Siemens Annual Report* 2010, 2011.

PRC. Just after formation of the Christian Democrat–Liberal government coalition in the fall of 2009, the minister in charge of joint development work announced that the Federal Ministry for Economic Cooperation and Development (BMZ) would phase out financial and then technical cooperation with China. Ongoing cooperative projects were completed as stipulated in the respective contracts.

The BMZ's exit from China did not signify the end of German development aid to China, however. The Federal Ministry of the Environment (BMU) has increasingly come to the fore as a provider of subsidies for environmental and resource protection and for renewable energy promotion. It has also become an increasingly important source of project funding for German joint development projects, mainly carried out by the German Organization for International Cooperation (GIZ), which posts employees to China and uses local employees. In all probability, the role of the BMU in Germany's China policy will increase further as a result of the Sino-German focus on environmental, climate, and energy cooperation. Global climate objectives and China's contribution to these aims, as well as the expertise of and market opportunities for German companies in these fields, justify this new level of commitment. Thus German development policy vis-à-vis China will remain embedded in state export promotion.

Despite Chancellor Merkel's greater emphasis on areas of political conflict in Germany's relationship with the PRC and bouts of disgruntlement, particularly over the Tibet question, German relations with the PRC thus far have been less tense than those of many other countries. One reason for this is the steady growth in trade and investment relations, which have been relatively free of conflict. This low tension level, however, basically stems from the absence of serious historical or security-related conflicts, such as those that have repeatedly burdened other powers in their relations with China (namely, the United States, Britain, Japan, India, Russia, and Vietnam). Against this backdrop of economic complementarity and an absence of historical burdens, China has identified Germany as a dominant player in Europe and its preferred partner.[14]

NOTES

1. Gill and Murphy 2008; Grant and Barysch 2008.
2. For example, Clegg and Voss 2012; Godement and Parello-Plesner 2011; Hanemann and Rosen 2012.
3. Hanemann and Rosen 2012.
4. For more on foreign debt, see Casarini 2012; Godement and Parello-Plesner 2011. On China's foreign-currency portfolio, see Casarini 2012.
5. Lisbonne de Vergeron 2007; Shambaugh 2008b; Zhu Liqun 2008.
6. Casarini 2006.
7. Holslag 2012.
8. Cabestan 2008.
9. Gill and Murphy 2008; Sandschneider 2006.
10. Grant and Barysch 2008.
11. Cabestan 2007; Holslag 2006, 2012; Men Jing 2012.
12. Scott 2007; Shambaugh 2004.
13. Berkofsky 2006; Grant and Barysch 2008; Holslag 2012; Men Jing 2012; Shambaugh, Sandschneider, and Zhou 2008b.
14. Kundnani and Parello-Plesner 2012.

12

Empire and Guerrilla

China's Multifaceted Foreign Relations

A multifaceted understanding of the primary forces that drive People's Republic of China's (PRC) external relations not only presents a challenge to Western foreign policy and commercial enterprises but also affects our overall perceptions and assessments of the world as it evolves at the outset of the twenty-first century.

In the preceding chapters, we have attempted to provide a sober and discriminating view of the facts and controversies—with all their contradictions and ambiguities—affecting major sectors of Chinese foreign policy and foreign trade. Departing from this approach, the final chapter aims to encourage discussion. We present our own assessments of the broad consequences for the West of China's rise to power with respect to foreign policy, foreign trade, and domestic and social policies.

This closing chapter outlines four basic dimensions of Chinese foreign policy and foreign trade and describes their effects on China's bilateral and multilateral relations: (1) China's "imperial" relations with other countries that focus on the PRC's expanding opportunities to exert regional and global influence as a major power, (2) the forces of interdependence that affect China, (3) China's often misunderstood unconventional foreign relations in the shadow of the empire, and (4) China's "guerrilla-like" foreign relations, in many ways an increasingly significant threat developing outside the bounds of the imperial shadow.

IMPERIAL FEATURES

Without intending to give a moralistic or ideological slant, we use the terms "empire" and "imperial" in this chapter in a descriptive historical sense to portray an autocratic and centralist empire that reigns over unusually large territories and populaces. This type of empire aims to use diplomatic, economic, and military instruments, as well as cultural and technological tools, to enhance its own influence and impact on the outside world. Such national expansionism also includes asymmetrical relations with other either dependent or subordinate countries and economies (see box 12.1).

This imperial dimension of China's relations with other countries is generally the focal point of public debate in the Western media and foreign policy circles. Examples include China's rivalry with the United States, its territorial disputes with Japan and other countries that share borders with China in Southeast Asia, military armaments programs, and disputes over trade and monetary policy with the European Union (EU). Viewed from this perspective, China seems obsessed with pursuing a foreign policy that will overcome the status quo in the global order established under American leadership to allow it to become the most powerful nation in the world in terms of trade and commerce, military and diplomacy, and technology and research by the middle of the twenty-first century at the latest. This strategy aims to establish centralist, hierarchical control mechanisms guided by planned, long-term strategic action.

This book cites numerous examples of such an approach, among which are China's heavily state-subsidized global economic expansion, diplomatic

---

BOX 12.1. THE IMPERIAL DIMENSIONS OF CHINA'S EXTERNAL RELATIONS

Objectives and characteristics:

- Establishing China as a major economic, military, and political power and, ultimately, as a superpower
- Building up a competitive relationship with Japan on a regional level and with the United States globally
- Refusing to accept the status quo (i.e., the existing order) as a product of the past

Means to the ends:

- Exercising centralist, hierarchical control, using a planned, long-term approach
- Employing conventional diplomatic, economic, and military instruments of superpower politics
- Centrally coordinating foreign trade and monetary policies in pursuit of political goals

campaigns to secure broad support for China in international disputes, and the PRC's very ambitious military modernization program. These expansionist efforts have led to growing fears in the West that a post-American globalization phase driven and led by China might emerge. There are even concerns among China's neighbors about a possible return to the hierarchical and asymmetrical principles of order stemming from the traditional Chinese tributary system.

At the same time, however, any imperial aspirations that China may hold have undeniable weaknesses and limits as evidenced, among other things, by the continued presence of the United States in the Asia-Pacific region, where it maintains a system of bilateral security treaties; the probable formation of counteralliances in Southeast Asia (potentially led by Vietnam or Indonesia); the weaknesses of Chinese soft power; China's own reservations regarding the costs and risks of possible superpower status; and the general lack of a Chinese missionary-like foreign policy agenda similar to that which was essential for US expansionism in the twentieth century.

INTERDEPENDENCE

Powerful forces of multilateral international involvement serve to counteract any unilateral development and projection of Chinese power. The economic destinies shared by the PRC and the United States, whereby neither country can cause or tolerate extensive destabilization of the other without striking at the very heart of its own stability and power, illustrate this most clearly (see box 12.2).

The forces of interdependence have drawn China into an increasingly dense network of international contractual obligations and organizations, ranging from the regulations of the World Trade Organization (WTO) to international climate-protection treaties and UN human rights conventions. Aimed at promoting cooperation and self-restraint, these obligations and organizations are having visible effects on the foreign policy practices of the Chinese government. Except in cases of open diplomatic disputes, such mechanisms focus on cultivating China's identity (self-perception) and image (public perception) as a "responsible major power."

This cooperative attitude, however, can run counter to the interests of the national expansion of power. Evidence of this surfaces repeatedly in the form of intense rivalry among various state authorities in the PRC (such as central ministries and service branches of the armed forces) as they wrestle for control over the form and substance of foreign-relations, foreign-trade, and security policy.

Contrary to what we might expect from the authoritarian character of China's one-party system, PRC foreign policy is the product of interactions between a multitude of players, interests, and initiatives. A highly structured strategy characterizes only isolated areas of policy making, such as

BOX 12.2. THE DIMENSIONS OF INTERDEPENDENCE IN CHINA'S EXTERNAL RELATIONS

Objectives and characteristics:

- Intensifying multilateral involvement in international treaties and organizations
- Working toward an identity and image as a "responsible major power"

Means to the end:

- Employing traditional instruments of diplomacy, international law, trade, and investment
- Using currency reserves to purchase American and European government bonds; pursuing foreign direct investment (FDI) through state-bank credits and sovereign wealth funds
- Funding projects in the developing and emerging countries through state banks, without linking credits to political "good governance" conditions

security policy. Even though the PRC's foreign-trade policy is crucial to its international advancement, regional governments, state-owned businesses, and even private economic actors routinely undermine the objectives and codes of conduct dictated by the central government.

IN THE IMPERIAL SHADOW

China's unconventional foreign relations in the shadow of the empire include a large number of initiatives that are not centrally coordinated, as well as many widely scattered commitments, especially in the foreign-trade sector (see box 12.3). It is true that the central government sets long-term priorities and funding programs. However, these are implemented by decentralized, nonstandardized initiatives or by experimental programs established for specific purposes that allow further enhancement of foreign policy, foreign-trade, or monetary-policy instruments.

These approaches constitute the most astonishing dimension of China's foreign relations and are frequently the object of gross misunderstandings in the West. Western discourse on the subject of China continues to show a strong tendency to project Cold War categories and experiences involving the former Soviet Union onto the PRC. However, it is impossible to comprehend China's dynamics on the basis of such a categorization. The

BOX 12.3. UNCONVENTIONAL FOREIGN RELATIONS
IN THE SHADOW OF THE EMPIRE

Objectives and characteristics:

- The central government defines the objectives and priorities of foreign relations. However, these are implemented by decentralized, nonstandardized initiatives.
- The central government intervenes in decentralized entities only if publicized and undeniable misconduct by Chinese players abroad threatens to damage the Chinese government's ambition to be perceived as a "responsible major power."

Means to the end:

- Creating long-term state programs and funding schemes
- Facilitating flexible implementation through decentralized, limited-risk, piecemeal, experimental programs that serve to enhance mechanisms and effectiveness incrementally

ability to innovate and adapt, which China has demonstrated in its foreign relations over the past three decades, is not founded in centralism. On the contrary, it is rooted in conscious toleration of, and indeed support for, decentralized initiatives.

The Chinese revolution was unusual in that the Chinese Communist Party (CCP) drove it forward from local base areas using mobilization methods that varied greatly from one area to the other. As a result, the experiences and perceptions that became deeply embedded in the minds of the CCP leadership reveal that in a rapidly changing world, many practical demands can best be dealt with on a decentralized basis. This notion is precisely the opposite of the centralist Soviet model. In the Chinese polity, political goals are dictated from above; however, political tools are developed experimentally and continuously from below.[1]

Since the 1990s there has also been a growing tendency for China to leave its foreign-trade relations to decentralized initiatives. The central leadership has restricted itself to defining strategic priorities and programs, while limiting direct intervention to undeniable instances of aberrations that draw international attention or run counter to cultivating the image of a cooperative, reliable power. One major example is China's economic, financial, and political involvement in Sudan, which Beijing has revised several times with an eye toward acquiring the reputation and status of a "responsible major power" in world politics. However, it is still possible for the central leadership to intervene with authoritative, ad hoc actions, casting the shadow of the empire, as it were, over many decentralized activities.

Many examples in this book document the importance of decentralized initiatives under the shadow of centralized direction. A prime example is the "going-global" program pursued by the central government through a series of mid- and long-term plans and supporting policies beginning in 2000. The generous support of state-owned banks and other privileges encouraged businesses run by the Chinese state to strengthen China's presence in lucrative foreign markets by investing heavily in the raw materials and energy sectors or by backing enterprises in other sunrise industries. The central leadership limited itself to setting targets specific to certain sectors and to offering stimulus programs; it left concrete decisions on investment and financing up to the businesses and banks. As a logical consequence, there was fierce competition among state-owned enterprises scrambling to secure the most profitable foreign commitments.

One prominent example of China's decentralized foreign relations in the shadow of the empire has been the creation of cooperative special economic zones (SEZs) in Africa, Asia, and Latin America. There is no standard template for these zones; instead, the investing Chinese businesses each establish their own models. Another example is the gradual internationalization of Chinese currency, promoted through decentralized pilot programs in Hong Kong and other locations or in bilateral swap agreements with select trade partners.

China's unconventional foreign-relations initiatives (i.e., those that are centrally encouraged but not centrally coordinated) may even include the buildup and testing of capabilities for cyber warfare through attacks on foreign public and private servers, typically initiated by provincial military or security units and apparently often without direct guidance and control from central headquarters. On the whole, the various decentralized activities conducted in the shadow of the empire have become major driving forces behind the continued development of China's foreign and security policies as well as its foreign-trade relations.

TRANSNATIONAL GUERRILLAS

We use the term "guerrilla foreign relations" to describe irregular and illegal activities that are no longer politically coordinated and are manifested by a rapidly growing, transnational shadow economy or even by organized crime involving Chinese and non-Chinese players both at home and abroad (see box 12.4). Constantly changing transnational networks primarily formed along ethnic Chinese lines power China's guerrilla-like foreign relations. The networks are highly mobile "niche nomads" with a largely invisible or chameleonlike presence. Their activities constitute the most alarming dimension of China's foreign relations as they are gaining ground and resources not only in Southeast Asia and Africa but also in Europe.

Even though only anecdotal evidence of such informal activities has come to light, many highly visible cases illustrate the dynamics of such guerrilla-like foreign relations in recent times:

- *Product and trademark piracy*—known as the *shanzhai* economy—organized on a transnational level and involving wholesale and foreign-trade enterprises in southern China as well as distribution centers in cities like Moscow, Budapest, and Dubai.
- *Underground factories and trading networks,* growing in number not only in China's neighboring countries but also increasingly in eastern and southern Europe (already well documented in Romania, Hungary, and northern Italy).
- *Extraction of raw materials* in Africa and Latin America not only by underground networks but also by privately owned Chinese enterprises and even by enterprises affiliated with Chinese government units. Such activities include illegal logging in Myanmar, Indonesia, and various African countries.
- *Manipulated public offerings* of Chinese businesses on Western financial markets, most of them relatively small, using complex company structures ("reverse mergers" or "backdoor listings") and counterfeit business documentation and accounting statements (some typical activities were exposed in a series of audits of the New York and Toronto stock exchanges in 2011).
- *Human trafficking and illegal gambling and betting operations* by global mafia networks.

BOX 12.4. GUERRILLA FOREIGN RELATIONS

Objectives and characteristics:

- Powered by independent, usually profit-oriented, extralegal units that operate on foreign territory
- Not subject to direct control or supervision by the Chinese government

Means to the end:

- A combination of legal, black market, and criminal activities
- Constantly changing transnational networks acting as "niche nomads"
- Specifically, hacker networks that can be quickly mobilized or sometimes even act on their own

- *Illegal trading in sensitive goods* ranging from protected animals and timber to nuclear and missile technology (as with Iran, in violation of international nonproliferation treaties). Presumably, this is often done with active participation in corrupt activities by Chinese businesses closely affiliated with the state or by the military (of its own accord).
- *Networks of hackers* that are mainly commercially motivated but are also sometimes political, making patriotic attacks on foreign governments or media websites critical of China, as well as launching assaults on Web-based financial transactions.

Many of these phenomena are signs of the development of a transnational underworld, originating in China but out of the direct reach of the Chinese government. It is impossible to assess the true magnitude of this underworld. However, its rapid growth is an obvious by-product of the global presence of Chinese economic players.

This is by far the most threatening aspect of China's foreign relations in the twenty-first century, for the rules of the game these criminals are playing have the potential to shake the very foundations of other societies, starting with their market, legal, judiciary, taxation, and administrative systems. The phenomenon depicted here as guerrilla foreign relations is not new or unique, but its global presence and its impact on the proliferation of shadow networks are unprecedented.

UNDERSTANDING CHINA'S RISE

How is it possible to grasp the complexity of Chinese foreign relations as described in the preceding chapters without lapsing into a narrow, distorted view that actually stems from a Cold War–era mentality and confirms widespread preconceptions but does nothing at all to explain the dynamics of China's current rise to power? Figure 12.1 illustrates the patterns of thought and categories grounding much of Western debate on China. The two arrows illustrate two particularly common attempts to comprehend China's changing role in the world. At the end of the Cold War, the general public in the West hoped for and expected China's transformation from a globally isolated Communist dictatorship with a planned economy into a major market-based, democratic power tightly enmeshed in the Western world on all levels, to the mutual benefit of all.

Obviously, this transformation of China under Western conditions as envisioned by the West never took place. Instead, the challenge by China has been increasingly depicted abroad as a change toward a system that is "mercantilistic" and reflects "state capitalism" but remains unremittingly authoritarian.[2] Although barely acceptable from a Western point of view,

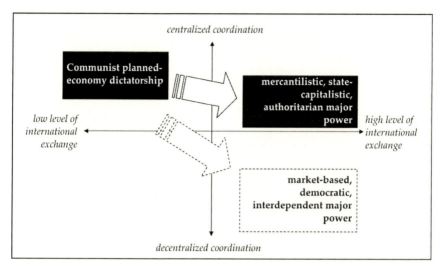

Figure 12.1. China's role in the world—patterns of Western discourse.

this system is now actively engaged in international exchanges at all levels. The PRC is not inclined to take its place in the existing global order established under Western auspices. On the contrary, it is challenging this order more strongly than ever with its own concepts of order and its own demands for coresponsibility.

In reality, the challenge China poses is far more complex than meets the eye, mainly because China's system immediately after 1978 was already far more heterogeneous than commonly assumed for a Communist system (see the left half of figure 12.2). At the beginning of its policy of reform and opening, the PRC was a highly centralized system as far as foreign policy and foreign trade were concerned. On the domestic front, however, there was the unusual variation of a decentralized and self-sufficient state-run economy. An intricate economy hidden from the public and collective sectors and—especially since the end of the 1970s—by rapidly spreading smuggling activities partly compensated for the socialist system's functional deficits and supply bottlenecks. These special components of China's political economy formed the points of departure and the preconditions for China to open up internationally, and they shaped the various dimensions of China's foreign relations today. The right-hand side of figure 12.2 lists these dimensions, which are explained above in this chapter: imperial foreign relations, multilateral integration, unconventional foreign relations in the shadow of the empire, and various types of guerrilla-like foreign relations.

In all of these dimensions, China is developing extraordinary and expansive dynamics. However, this phenomenon is only partly controlled (or

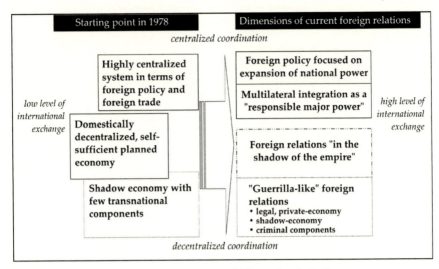

Figure 12.2. China's foreign relations as a multidimensional challenge.

controllable) politically. Despite the Chinese government's highly ambitious planning strategies, there is no omnipotent center that can coordinate all the observable activities.

The PRC is a nation of multiple identities, as reflected in the complexity of its foreign relations. It is many things at once: a developing and emerging nation, a regional power, a trading nation, a growing military power, and—in its role as a permanent member of the UN Security Council—a global leader as well. Its doctrinaire obstinacy (as reflected in its positions vis-à-vis Taiwan and Tibet) and tenacious clinging to a decades-old habit of using ideological jargon (for instance, when lashing out against "imperialistic" behavior by the Western powers) counter its innovative and flexible ideas, especially in matters of foreign trade. Resolute diplomatic advances, such as those in Africa and Latin America, and a willingness to test innovative political instruments, as in the experimental programs to internationalize Chinese currency, go hand in hand with cautious tactical maneuvering, as in matters of climate policy, and thin-skinned sensitivity to criticism from the West, especially egregious when Liu Xiaobo received the Nobel Peace Prize in 2010.

OUTLOOK

The world economy and international politics are presently experiencing a phase of great uncertainty and instability, not only regarding the role of China but also concerning the status of the United States and the European

Union. We should continue to expect disruptions in development on the part of the major global players, as well as high volatility in core areas of politics and economics.

Stabilizing and Destabilizing Factors in China's Foreign Relations

The dimensions of imperial and interdependent foreign relations will most likely have the greatest predictability with regard to China's foreign relations. China will continue to take an interest in steady interactions with the United States and Europe in foreign relations. Despite highly volatile situations in the global economy and strained relations among the major powers, the Chinese government is endeavoring to intensify its economic interdependence and multilateral commitments. These efforts are an obstacle to any unilateral development of power. At both the central and provincial levels, powerful forces within the Chinese government and economy are working to intensify international cooperation and integration.

The most seriously disruptive developments and risks might ultimately arise from dissolution of the imperial shadow. The collapse of central authority due to domestic contentions could unleash totally uncontrollable forces on a global scale, specifically innumerable guerrilla-like players and mafia networks, all acting on their own. Signs of these are already visible today, but at the moment they remain limited in scope and impact.

Anxieties and Tensions in a Belated Rising Power

Projections that China's recent stormy rise will simply continue in the future ignore many of the limitations and risks that we must take into account in assessing its role in international relations. In view of the imperial dimension of the Chinese rise to power, Western foreign policy and businesses will have to pay close attention to the fundamental risks involved in this realm. The status anxiety and behavioral patterns of modern China are analogous in several ways to those typical of the German and Japanese empires prior to 1914 and 1941, respectively, as aspiring latecomers undergoing rapid industrialization to catch up and compete with the established great powers. Major anxieties fall into two categories:

- *Entrapment from abroad*: China widely construes alliances and agreements among the old, established powers as aimed at inhibiting and holding back the new, aspiring power. These anxieties in part have resulted in the PRC's adopting an expansionist national strategy to secure raw materials, a policy laden with potential conflicts that are already having severe global repercussions. In China, as in the former German and Japanese empires, insistence on an independent "non-Western" model of development and rejection of "culturally alien" liberal concepts of order are enjoying great popularity. In essence, foreign policy discourse is still centered on rivalry with the old hegemonic power. Economic interdependence on its own will not necessarily prevent open conflict between the PRC and the United States if historical analogies with the German and Japanese empires serve as points of reference.

- *Anxieties and extreme expectations at home*: The domestic political, economic, social, and ecological challenges China faces are consuming a major amount of the political leadership's attention. Social and ethnic tensions and severe deficits in political legitimacy are not the only things that the Chinese government perceives as threatening. Extremely high expectations regarding the rapid growth of prosperity and improvements in the quality of life, expectations with little likelihood of continual fulfillment, provide a source of enormous risk and conflict. Added to this are highly emotional nationalistic trends among the population at large and on the Internet, where numerous incidents have already shown that mobilization can be the immediate response to a national "humiliation" of China and to diplomatic sellouts by the Chinese government (considered weakness or betrayal). These domestic factors contain a formula for an explosive concoction of ingredients.

Thus, the central authority sees itself as challenged in equal measure at home and abroad. Domestic destabilization could occur at any time, with consequences that vary in severity depending on the triggers and the specific context. China's foreign relations are susceptible to abrupt disruptions as well. In cases of doubt, the leadership of China will place priority on protecting its core interests—maintaining the power of the CCP, defending national sovereignty and territorial integrity, and promoting economic development—over multilateral cooperation, diplomatic considerations, and cultivation of a positive global image. At the same time, tensions are growing in international financial and trading markets, as is China's strategic rivalry with the United States and its competition with other trade and technology powers, including Japan and Germany, which until now have been in the lead. For these reasons, China's susceptibility to foreign-relations disruption will most likely increase in the years ahead.

The Limited Attraction of Western and Chinese Patterns of Order

The longer China's dynamic momentum lasts, the more the images of America, Japan, and Europe will be called into question. Thus, future interactions with China will become increasingly discomforting for the established industrial powers. Unlike during the period immediately following the end of the Cold War, the West—as represented by the United States, the European Union, and Japan—is no longer the undisputed model for the world at the outset of the twenty-first century. Former leading nations among the Group of Seven (G7) confront conspicuous shortcomings in their respective economic, political, and social orders. Political elites in many emerging and developing countries are openly questioning American and European political and economic institutions and whether they will provide viable solutions for problems arising in the twenty-first century. These voices are even raising doubts as to whether their countries can still learn anything from the established industrial nations and whether they should even attempt to do so.

China is the leading protagonist of non-Western, nonliberal concepts of order that see the state as exercising comprehensive control over and intervention in society. If the economic and military strengthening of China continues for five to ten more years, while at the same time the United States becomes weaker, as it has since the beginning of the global financial and economic turbulence in 2008, then China's rise to power will shake the international patterns of order to their very foundations, yet without China being able to replace the old order in a hegemonic way.

We should not overestimate the global magnetism of Chinese "state capitalism." In the developing and emerging countries, China's development does not meet with broad approval, since the negative side effects are all too apparent from the social, political, and ecological perspectives. In Asia, historic, military, and territorial conflicts fuel mistrust of China. Living in a climate of mutual suspicion despite extensive economic exchanges with the PRC, China's neighbors so far have chosen to place their trust in US security guarantees.

Responses to a China-Driven Globalization

Diehard American and European self-assurance—or, to put it bluntly, self-centeredness—drawn from the past will not contribute to dealing with changes associated with China's rise. In a paradoxical historical about-face, Europe and the United States might find themselves in the same position as the Qing dynasty in the face of Western expansionism in the late nineteenth century. As during the Qing, political inertia, economic weakness, and notions of moral superiority appear to shape the responses of many Western societies to the novel challenges posed by China's rise. These deficits result in a lack of agility in reaction to a new phase of globalization driven by China's international expansion.

The preconditions for actively facing Chinese economic, technological, and military competition vary widely across American and European polities and societies. In light of the pervasive political self-centeredness inside the United States, the EU, and Japan, it is very unlikely that players in the West will make a joint, concerted, and effective response to China within the foreseeable future. Current trends in the direction of international coordination in selective multistate networks and clubs made up of thematically influential states—ranging from the Group of Twenty (G20) to the regular binational or multinational government consultations—will continue to grow outside the established international organizations. Therefore, responses to China's rise will have to be based on flexible negotiating tactics, ad hoc coalition building, and intense national efforts, especially in education, research, industry, and infrastructure. With a view to the guerrilla-like business operations that are playing an increasing role in China's global expansion, vigilance is called for to defend core institutions relating to the rule of law, anticorruption, and intellectual property. In these sectors in particular, the rules of the game that presently dominate in China's domestic and foreign economies must not be allowed under any circumstances to spread to the United States or Europe since they would pose a threat to the very core of Western achievements based on the rule of law.

Overall, the appropriate responses to the challenges from China are not one-sided Sinophobia or Western arrogance, as evident in some media coverage. On the contrary, the answer lies in policy agility and economic competitiveness, combined with increased vigilance and resolute action in the face of the darker sides of China's global rise to power.

NOTES

1. Heilmann and Perry 2011.
2. Bremmer 2010.

Sources and Literature

Note: All websites have been accessed and checked as of January 2013.

GENERAL OVERVIEWS

Fairbank, John King, and Merle Goldman. 2006. *China: A New History.* Cambridge, MA: Belknap Press of Harvard University Press.

Garver, John. 1993. *Foreign Relations of the People's Republic of China.* Englewood Cliffs, NJ: Prentice Hall.

Nathan, Andrew J., and Robert S. Ross. 1997. *The Great Wall and the Empty Fortress: China's Search for Security.* New York: W. W. Norton.

Robinson, Thomas W., and David Shambaugh, eds. 1994. *Chinese Foreign Policy: Theory and Practice.* Oxford: Clarendon Press.

Sutter, Robert. 2012. *Chinese Foreign Relations: Power and Policy since the Cold War.* Lanham, MD: Rowman & Littlefield.

PRC INTERNET SOURCES

Caixin Online (news portal on finance and economics): http://www.caixin.com (Chinese); http://english.caixin.com (English)

Global Times (*Huanqiu Shibao*): http://www.huanqiu.com (Chinese); http://www.globaltimes.cn (English)

Government Organizations of the Central Government of the PRC: http://www.gov.cn (Chinese); http://english.gov.cn/index.htm (English)

Ministry of Commerce of the People's Republic of China: http://www.mofcom.gov.cn (Chinese); http://english.mofcom.gov.cn (English); http://www.mofcom.gov.cn/gzyb/gzyb.html (statistics on foreign trade)

Ministry of Finance of the People's Republic of China: http://www.mof.gov.cn (Chinese)

Ministry of Foreign Affairs of the People's Republic of China: http://www.fmprc.gov.cn/chn/gxh/tyb (Chinese); http://www.fmprc.gov.cn/eng/default.htm (English)

National Bureau of Statistics of the People's Republic of China: http://www.stats.gov.cn (Chinese); http://www.stats.gov.cn/english (English)

National Development and Reform Commission (NDRC): http://www.ndrc.gov.cn (Chinese); http://en.ndrc.gov.cn (English)

People's Bank of China (PBoC, Central Bank of the PRC): http://www.pbc.gov.cn/publish/main/index.html (Chinese); http://www.pbc.gov.cn/publish/english/963/index.html (English)

People's Daily (*Renmin Ribao*): http://peopledaily.com.cn (Chinese); http://english.peopledaily.com.cn (English)

State Administration of Foreign Exchange (SAFE): http://www.safe.gov.cn (Chinese and English)

White Papers of the Chinese Government: http://www.china.com.cn/ch-book/index.htm (Chinese); http://www.china.org.cn/e-white (English)

Xinhua (Official News Agency of the PRC): http://www.xinhuanet.com (Chinese); http://www.xinhuanet.com/english2010 (English)

INTERNET SOURCES OUTSIDE CHINA

China Digital Times: http://chinadigitaltimes.net

China Elections and Governance: http://chinaelectionsblog.net

China Media Project (Hong Kong): http://cmp.hku.hk

Sinocism: http://www.sinocism.com

Wall Street Journal, China Realtime Report: http://blogs.wsj.com/chinarealtime

William A. Joseph (Wellesley College, United States): http://chinapoliticsnews.blogspot.com

ANALYSES BY RESEARCH INSTITUTES AND POLITICAL CONSULTANCIES

Brookings Institution: http://www.brookings.edu/fp/china/china_hp.htm; http://www.brookings.edu/fp/cnaps/center_hp.htm

Brussels Institute of Contemporary China Studies: http://www.vub.ac.be/biccs/site

Carnegie Endowment for International Peace: China Program: http://www.carnegieendowment.org/programs/china

Center for Strategic and International Studies (CSIS):http://csis.org/program/comparative-connections; http://www.csis.org/china

Chatham House: The China Project: http://www.chathamhouse.org.uk/research/asia/current_projects/china

Council on Foreign Relations: http://www.cfr.org/region/china/ri271

Heritage Foundation: http://www.heritage.org/Research/AsiaandthePacific/china-taiwan.cfm
Hoover Institution: China Leadership Monitor: http://www.hoover.org/publications/clm
International Institute for Strategic Studies: China Project: http://www.iiss.org/programmes/north-east-asia/china-project
Jamestown Foundation: China Brief: http://www.jamestown.org/china_brief
National Bureau of Asian Research: http://www.nbr.org
RAND Corporation: http://www.rand.org/hot_topics/china
University of Nottingham, China Policy Institute: http://www.nottingham.ac.uk/cpi/index.aspx
Woodrow Wilson International Center: http://www.wilsoncenter.org/index.cfm?fuseaction=topics.home&topic_id=1462

ONLINE SUBJECT BIBLIOGRAPHY

China and the United States

Congressional Research Service, Reports on Foreign Policy and Regional Affairs: http://www.fas.org/sgp/crs/row/index.html
US-China Business Council: http://www.uschina.org
US-China Economic and Security Review Commission: http://www.uscc.gov

China-Germany/China-EU Relations

Directorate General for Trade of the European Commission (relations with China): http://ec.europa.eu/trade/creating-opportunities/bilateral-relations/countries/china
EU Chamber of Commerce in China: http://www.europeanchamber.com.cn/view/home
EU-China Civil Society Forum: http://www.eu-china.net/english/About-Us/About-us.html
Federal Statistical Office (Germany): http://www.destatis.de/jetspeed/portal/cms

Environmental and Climate Policy

Ministry of Environmental Protection of the PRC (reports on the state of the environment): http://english.mep.gov.cn
United States Environmental Protection Agency: China Environmental Law Initiative: http://www.epa.gov/ogc/china/initiative_home.htm
Woodrow Wilson International Center for Scholars: China Environment Forum: http://www.wilsoncenter.org/index.cfm?fuseaction=topics.home&topic_id=1421

Foreign Trade and Investment

Chinese Academy of Social Sciences, Institute of World Economics and Politics: http://www.iwep.org.cn (Chinese); http://en.iwep.org.cn (English)

Heritage Foundation, China Global Investment Tracker: http://www.heritage.org/
research/projects/china-global-investment-tracker-interactive-map
Ministry of Commerce of the PRC (IFDI and OFDI): http://www.fdi.gov.cn/pub/FDI/
default.htm (Chinese); http://www.fdi.gov.cn/pub/FDI_EN/default.htm (English)
Rhodium Group: http://rhgroup.net/interactive/china-investment-monitor

Human Rights Policy

Amnesty International: http://web.amnesty.org/library/eng-chn/index
China Society for Human Rights Studies (CSHRS): http://www.chinahumanrights.org
Human Rights in China: http://www.hrichina.org
Human Rights Watch: http://www.hrw.org

PRC and Taiwan

Mainland Affairs Council (Taiwan): http://www.mac.gov.tw/welcome02/wel-
come02.htm (Chinese); http://www.mac.gov.tw/mp.asp?mp=3 (English)
Strait Exchange Foundation (SEF) (Taiwan): http://www.sef.org.tw/mp.asp?mp=1 (Chi-
nese); http://www.sef.org.tw/ct.asp?xItem=110671&CtNode=4716&mp=300 (English)
Taiwan Affairs Office of the State Council of the PRC: http://www.gwytb.gov.cn
(Chinese); http://www.gwytb.gov.cn/en (English)

Security Policy

International Institute for Strategic Studies: China Project: http://www.iiss.org/pro-
grammes/north-east-asia/china-project
Stockholm International Peace Research Institute: http://www.sipri.org
United States Army War College, Strategic Studies Institute: http://www.strategic-
studiesinstitute.army.mil/asia-pacific/china
United States Naval War College, China Maritime Studies: http://www.usnwc.edu/
Publications/Publications.aspx

ACADEMIC JOURNALS

Asian Survey (Berkeley)
ASIEN (Hamburg)
China and World Economy (Beijing)
China Information (Leiden)
China Journal (Canberra)
China Quarterly (Cambridge, UK)
China Security (Washington, DC)
Chinese Journal of International Politics (Oxford)
Current History (Philadelphia)
Foreign Affairs (New York)
Foreign Policy (Washington, DC)

International Relations of the Asia-Pacific (Oxford)
Internationale Politik (Berlin)
Issues and Studies (Taipei)
Journal of Contemporary China (London)
Journal of Current Chinese Affairs [prior to 2009: *China Aktuell*] (Hamburg)
National Interest (Washington, DC)
Orbis (Philadelphia)
Pacific Affairs (Vancouver)
The Washington Quarterly (Washington, DC)
World Politics (Cambridge, UK)

SOURCES CITED IN THE TEXT

Alden, Chris. 2007. *China in Africa*. London: Zed Books.

Alden, Chris, and Daniel Large. 2011. "China's Exceptionalism and the Challenges of Delivering Difference in Africa." *Journal of Contemporary China* 20, no. 68: 21–38.

Alden, Chris, Daniel Large, and Ricardo Soares de Oliveira, eds. 2008. *China Returns to Africa: A Rising Power and a Continent Embrace*. New York: Columbia University Press.

Algieri, Franco. 2008. "It's the System That Matters: Institutionalization and Making of EU Policy toward China." In *China-Europe Relations*, edited by David Shambaugh, Eberhard Sandschneider, and Zhou Hong, 65–83.

Anderson, Jonathan. 2009. "China Monetary Policy Handbook." In *China's Emerging Financial Markets*, edited by James R. Barth, John A. Tatom, and Glenn Yago, 167–265.

Arora, Vivek, and Athanasios Vamvakidis. 2010. "China's Economic Growth: International Spillovers." Working Paper WP/10/165. Washington, DC: International Monetary Fund.

Art, Robert J. 2010. "The United States and the Rise of China: Implications for the Long Haul." *Political Science Quarterly* 125, no. 3: 359–91.

Ba, Alice D. 2011. "Staking Claims and Making Waves in the South China Sea: How Troubled Are the Waters?" *Contemporary Southeast Asia* 33, no. 3: 269–91.

Bader, Jeffrey A. 2012. *Obama and China's Rise: An Insider's Account of America's Asia Strategy*. Washington, DC: Brookings Institution Press.

Bajoria, Jayshree. 2010. "The China–North Korea Relationship." Backgrounder, October 7. New York: Council on Foreign Relations.

Ball, Desmond. 2011. "China's Cyber Warfare Capabilities." *Security Challenges* 7, no. 2: 81–103.

Bank for International Settlement, ed. 2012. *Currency Internationalisation: Lessons from the Global Financial Crisis and Prospects for the Future in Asia and the Pacific*. BIS Paper 61. Basel, Switzerland.

Barth, James R., John A. Tatom, and Glenn Yago, eds. 2009. *China's Emerging Financial Markets: Challenges and Opportunities*. Santa Monica, CA: Milken Institute.

Bergsten, C. Fred, Charles Freeman, Nicholas R. Lardy, and Derek Mitchell. 2008. *China's Rise: Challenges and Opportunities*. Washington, DC: Peterson Institute for International Economics and Center for Strategic and International Studies.

Bergsten, C. Fred, Bates Gill, Nicholas R. Lardy, and Derek R. Mitchell. 2006. *China: The Balance Sheet: What the World Needs to Know Now about the Emerging Super-power.* New York: Public Affairs.

Berkofsky, Axel. 2006. "The EU-China Strategic Partnership: Rhetoric versus Reality." In *Facing China's Rise,* edited by Marcin Zaborowski, 103–14.

Bertelsmann Foundation, ed. 2010. *Managing the Crisis: A Comparative Assessment of Economic Governance in 14 Economies.* Gütersloh, Germany: Bertelsmann Foundation.

Beukel, Erik. 2011. "Popular Nationalism in China and the Sino-Japanese Relationship: The Conflict in the East China Sea: An Introductory Study." DIIS Report 2011:01. Copenhagen: Danish Institute for International Studies.

Blasko, Dennis J. 2012. *The Chinese Army Today: Tradition and Transformation for the 21st Century.* London: Routledge.

Blumenthal, Dan. 2010. "Sino-U.S. Competition and U.S. Security: How Do We Assess the Military Balance?" *NBR Analysis* (December): 3–29. http://www.nbr.org/publications/nbranalysis/pdf/A10_Sino_US_Competition.pdf.

Brandt, Loren, and Thomas G. Rawski, eds. 2008. *China's Great Economic Transformation.* Cambridge: Cambridge University Press.

Brandt, Loren, Thomas G. Rawski, and Xiaodong Zhu. 2007. "International Dimensions of China's Long Boom." In *China's Rise and the Balance of Influence in Asia,* edited by William W. Keller and Thomas G. Rawski, 14–46.

Branstetter, Lee, and Nicholas R. Lardy. 2008. "China's Embrace of Globalization." In *China's Great Economic Transformation,* edited by Loren Brandt and Thomas G. Rawski, 633–82.

Brautigam, Deborah. 2009. *The Dragon's Gift: The Real Story of China in Africa.* Oxford: Oxford University Press.

Brautigam, Deborah, Thomas Farole, and Tang Xiaoyang. 2010. "China's Investment in African Special Economic Zones." World Bank Poverty Reduction and Economic Management Network, Economic Premise, Report 5.

Bremmer, Ian. 2010. *The End of the Free Market: Who Wins the War between States and Corporations?* New York: Portfolio.

Bremmer, Ian, and Nouriel Roubini. 2011. "A G-Zero World: The New Economic Club Will Produce Conflict, Not Cooperation." *Foreign Affairs* 90, no. 2: 2–7.

Breslin, Shaun. 2011. "The Soft Notion of China's 'Soft Power.'" Asia Programme Paper ASP PP 2011/03. London: Chatham House.

Brown, Kerry, and Loh Su Hsiung. 2011. "Trying to Read the New 'Assertive' China." Asia Programme Paper ASP PP 2011/02. London: Chatham House.

Burdekin, Richard C. K. 2008. *China's Monetary Challenges: Past Experiences and Future Prospects.* Cambridge: Cambridge University Press.

Burles, Mark, and Abram N. Shulsky. 2000. *Patterns in China's Use of Force: Evidence from History and Doctrinal Writings.* Santa Monica, CA: RAND Corporation.

Bush, Richard C. 2005. *Untying the Knot: Making Peace in the Taiwan Strait.* Washington, DC: Brookings Institution Press.

Bush, Richard C., and Michael E. O'Hanlon. 2007. *A War like No Other: The Truth about China's Challenge to America.* Hoboken, NJ: Wiley and Sons.

Buszynski, Leszek. 2012. "The South China Sea: Oil, Maritime Claims, and U.S.-China Strategic Rivalry." *The Washington Quarterly* 35, no. 2: 139–56.

Cabestan, Jean-Pierre. 2007. "EU and China: Heading Towards Bumpy Relations." In *Interpreting China's Development*, edited by Wang Gungwu and John Wong, 251–55.

———. 2008. "The Taiwan Issue in Europe-China Relations: An Irritant More Than Leverage." In *China-Europe Relations*, edited by David Shambaugh, Eberhard Sandschneider, and Zhou Hong, 84–101.

———. 2009. "China's Foreign- and Security-Policy Decision-Making Process under Hu Jintao." *Journal of Current Chinese Affairs* 38, no. 3: 63–97.

Carlson, Allen. 2011. "Moving beyond Sovereignty? A Brief Consideration of Recent Changes in China's Approach to International Order and the Emergence of the *Tianxia* Concept." *Journal of Contemporary China* 20, no. 68: 89–102.

Carpenter, Ted Galen. 2005. *America's Coming War with China: A Collision Course over Taiwan*. New York: Palgrave/Macmillan.

Casarini, Nicola. 2006. "The Evolution of the EU-China Relationship: From Constructive Engagement to Strategic Partnership." Occasional Paper 64. Paris: Institute for Security Studies.

———. 2012. "For China, the Euro Is a Safer Bet Than the Dollar." EUISS Analysis, June. Paris: European Union Institute for Security Studies.

Cernat, Lucian, and Kay Parplies. 2010. "Chinese Foreign Direct Investment: What's Happening behind the Headlines?" Vox, July 16. http://www.voxeu.org/article/chinese-foreign-direct-investment-whats-happening-behind-headlines.

Chaffin, Greg, and Andrew S. Erickson. 2012a. "Building an Active, Layered Defense: Chinese Naval and Air Force Advancement." Policy Q&A. National Bureau of Asian Research, September 10. http://nbr.org/research/activity.aspx?id=272#.Ueu1jxYWFEd.

———. 2012b. "China's Navy and Air Force: Advancing Capabilities and Missions." Policy Q&A. National Bureau of Asian Research, September 27. http://www.nbr.org/research/activity.aspx?id=276#.Ueu1uBYWFEc.

Chambers, Michael R. 2007. "Framing the Problem: China's Threat Environment and International Obligations." In *Right-Sizing the People's Liberation Army*, edited by Roy Kamphausen and Andrew Scobell, 19–67.

Chan, Gerald. 2006. *China's Compliance in Global Affairs: Trade, Arms Control, Environmental Protection, Human Rights*. Series on Contemporary China 3. Singapore: World Scientific.

Chao Chien-min. 2011. "Upholding the Values of Democracy and Freedom, Creating a Vision of Cross-Strait Peace." Mainland Affairs Council, November 2. http://www.mac.gov.tw/ct.asp?xItem=99038&ctNode=6338&mp=3.

Chase, Michael S. 2010. "China's Growing Naval Power." Policy Memo, December. Washington, DC: Progressive Policy Institute.

———. 2011. "Chinese Suspicion and US Intentions." *Survival* 53, no. 3: 133–50.

———. 2012. "Chinese Nuclear Force Modernization: How Much Is Enough?" *China Brief* 12, no. 8: 12–15.

Chase, Michael S., and Andrew S. Erickson. 2012. "The Conventional Missile Capabilities of China's Second Artillery Force: Cornerstone of Deterrence and War Fighting." *Asian Security* 8, no. 2: 115–37.

Chen Dingding. 2009. "China's Participation in the International Human Rights Regime: A State Identity Perspective." *Chinese Journal of International Politics* 2, no. 3: 399–419.

Chen Qimao. 2011. "The Taiwan Straits Situation since Ma Came to Office and Conditions for Cross-Straits Political Negotiations: A View from Shanghai." *Journal of Contemporary China* 20, no. 68: 153–60.

Chen, Titus C. 2010. "China's Increasing Important Role in Global Human Rights Regimes." Paper prepared for the 2010 annual meeting of the American Political Science Association, Washington, DC, September 2–5.

Cheng, Dean. 2012. "China's Military Role in Space." *Strategic Studies Quarterly* 6, no. 1: 55–77.

Cheung, Yin-Wong, and Xingwang Qian. 2009. "The Empirics of China's Outward Direct Investment." CESifo Working Paper 2621. Munich: CESifo.

Chin, Gregory, and Eric Helleiner. 2008. "China as a Creditor: A Rising Financial Power?" *Journal of International Affairs* 62, no. 1: 87–102.

China Investment Corporation (CIC). 2012. *CIC Annual Report 2011*. Beijing: CIC.

Choo, Jaewoo. 2008. "Mirroring North Korea's Economic Dependence on China." *Asian Survey* 48, no. 2: 343–72.

Christensen, Thomas J. 1996. "Chinese *Realpolitik*: Regarding Beijing's World-View." *Foreign Affairs* 75, no. 5: 37–52.

———. 2006. "Fostering Stability or Creating a Monster? The Rise of China and U.S. Policy toward East Asia." *International Security* 31, no. 1: 81–126.

———. 2007. "A Strong and Moderate Taiwan." Speech to the US-Taiwan Business Council, Defense Industry Conference, Annapolis, Maryland. USC US-China Institute, September 11. http://www.china.usc.edu/ShowArticle.aspx?articleID=803&AspxAutoDetectCookieSupport=1.

———. 2011. "The Advantages of an Assertive China: Responding to Beijing's Abrasive Diplomacy." *Foreign Affairs* 90, no. 2: 54–67.

———. 2012. "The Meaning of the Nuclear Evolution: China's Strategic Modernization and US-China Security Relations." *Journal of Strategic Studies* 35, no. 4: 447–87.

Chu, Yunhan, and Andrew J. Nathan. 2007. "Seizing the Opportunity for Change in the Taiwan Strait." *The Washington Quarterly* 31, no. 1: 77–91.

Chu Shulong. 2006. "The Cross–Taiwan Strait Relations: Hard to Start and Move." In *Sources of Conflict and Cooperation in the Taiwan Strait*, edited by Zheng Yongnian and Raymond Ray-kuo Wu, 109–26.

Chung, Jae Ho. 2005. "China's Ascendancy and the Korean Peninsula: From Interest Reevaluation to Strategic Realignment?" In *Power Shift*, edited by David Shambaugh, 151–69.

Clark, Ian. 2011. "China and the United States: A Succession of Hegemonies?" *International Affairs* 87, no. 1: 13–28.

Clegg, Jeremy, and Hinrich Voss. 2012. "Chinese Overseas Direct Investment in the European Union." ECRAN Paper. London: Europe China Research and Advice Network.

Cliff, Roger. 2010. *The Development of China's Air Force Capabilities*. CT-346. Santa Monica, CA: RAND Corporation.

Cliff, Roger, Mark Burles, Michael S. Chase, Derek Eaton, and Kevin L. Pollpeter. 2007. *Entering the Dragon's Lair: Chinese Anti-access Strategies and Their Implications for the United States*. Santa Monica, CA: RAND Project Air Force.

Cliff, Roger, John F. Fei, Jeff Hagen, Elizabeth Hague, Eric Heginbotham, and John Stillion, eds. 2011. *Shaking the Heavens and Splitting the Earth: Chinese Air Force*

Employment Concepts in the 21st Century. Santa Monica, CA: RAND Project Air Force.

Clinton, Hillary Rodham. 2011. "Inaugural Richard C. Holbrooke Lecture on a Broad Vision of U.S.-China Relations in the 21st Century." US Department of State, January 14. http://www.state.gov/secretary/rm/2011/01/154653.htm.

Cohen, Warren I. 2010. *America's Response to China: A History of Sino-American Relations.* 5th ed. New York: Columbia University Press.

Conrad, Björn. 2012. "China in Copenhagen: Reconciling the 'Beijing Climate Revolution' and the 'Copenhagen Climate Obstinacy.'" *China Quarterly* 210: 435–55.

Cordesman, Anthony H., and Martin Kleiber. 2007. *Chinese Military Modernization: Force Development and Strategic Capabilities.* Washington, DC: CSIS Press.

Craig, Susan L. 2007. *Chinese Perceptions of Traditional and Nontraditional Security Threats.* Carlisle, PA: US Army War College, Strategic Studies Institute.

Dai Bingguo. 2010. "Zhichi zou heping fazhan daolu [Support Following the Peaceful Path of Development]." *Dangdai shijie* 21: 4–8.

———. 2012. "Asia, China and International Law." *Chinese Journal of International Law* 11, no. 1: 1–3.

Das, Dilip K. 2009. "The Evolution of Renminbi Yuan and the Protracted Debate on Its Undervaluation: An Integrated View." *Journal of Asian Economics* 20, no. 5: 570–79.

Davis, Jonathan E. 2011. "From Ideology to Pragmatism: China's Position on Humanitarian Intervention in the Post–Cold War Era." *Vanderbilt Journal of Transnational Law* 44, no. 2: 217–83.

de Grauwe, Paul, Romain Houssa, and Guilia Piccillo. 2012. "African Trade Dynamics: Is China a Different Trading Partner?" *Journal of Chinese Economic and Business Studies* 10, no. 1: 15–45.

de Lisle, Jacques. 2012. "Troubled Waters: China's Claims and the South China Sea." *Orbis* 56, no. 4: 608–42.

Dent, Christopher M. 2008. *China, Japan and Regional Leadership in East Asia.* Northampton, MA: Edward Elgar.

Devadason, Evelyn. 2010. "ASEAN-China Trade Flows: Moving Forward with ACFTA." *Journal of Contemporary China* 19, no. 66: 653–74.

Ding Sheng. 2008. *The Dragon's Hidden Wings: How China Rises with Its Soft Power.* Lanham, MD: Lexington Books.

———. 2010. "Analyzing Rising Power from the Perspective of Soft Power: A New Look at China's Rise to the Status Quo Power." *Journal of Contemporary China* 19, no. 64: 255–72.

Dittmer, Lowell, and George T. Yu. 2010. *China, the Developing World, and the New Global Dynamic.* Boulder, CO: Lynne Rienner.

Dobbins, James. 2012. "War with China." *Survival* 54, no. 4: 7–24.

Drezner, Daniel W. 2009. "Bad Debts: Assessing China's Financial Influence in Great Power Politics." *International Security* 34, no. 2: 7–45.

Dumbaugh, Kerry. 2007. "U.S.-China Relations: Current Issues and Implications for U.S. Policy." CRS Report for Congress RL 33877. Washington, DC: Congressional Research Service.

———. 2008. "Taiwan: Recent Developments and U.S. Policy Choices." CRS Report for Congress RL 33510. Washington, DC: Congressional Research Service.

Dumbaugh, Kerry, and Mark P. Sullivan. 2005. "China's Growing Interest in Latin America." CRS Report for Congress RS 22119. Washington, DC: Congressional Research Service.

Economist, The. 2010. "Trading Places: The World's Largest Container Ports." *The Economist,* August 24.

Economy, Elizabeth C. 2010. "China's Green Energy and Environmental Policies." Statement made before the US-China Economic and Security Review Commission, U.S. House of Representatives. Council on Foreign Relations, April 8. http://www.cfr.org/china/chinas-green-energy-environmental-policies/p21855.

Economy, Elizabeth C., and Michel C. Oksenberg, eds. 1999. *China Joins the World: Progress and Prospects.* New York: Council on Foreign Relations Press.

Edmonds, Richard Louis. 2011. "The Evolution of Environmental Policy in the People's Republic of China." *Journal of Current Chinese Affairs* 40, no. 3: 13–35.

Eichengreen, Barry. 2011. *Exorbitant Privilege: The Rise and Fall of the Dollar and the Future of the International Monetary System.* Oxford: Oxford University Press.

Eichengreen, Barry, Charles Wyplosz, and Yung Chul Park, eds. 2008. *China, Asia, and the New World Economy.* Oxford: Oxford University Press.

Eisenman, Joshua. 2007. "China's Post–Cold War Strategy in Africa: Examining Beijing's Methods and Objectives." In *China and the Developing World,* edited by Joshua Eisenman, Eric Heginbotham, and Derek Mitchell, 29–59.

———. 2012. "China-Africa Trade Patterns: Causes and Consequences." *Journal of Contemporary China* 21, no. 77: 793–810.

Eisenman, Joshua, Eric Heginbotham, and Derek Mitchell, eds. 2007. *China and the Developing World: Beijing's Strategy for the 21st Century.* Armonk, NY: M. E. Sharpe.

Eisenman, Joshua, and Joshua Kurlantzick. 2006. "China's Africa Strategy." *Current History* 105, no. 691: 219–24.

Elwell, Craig K., Marc Labonte, and Wayne M. Morrison. 2007. "Is China a Threat to the U.S. Economy?" CRS Report for Congress RL 33604. Washington, DC: Congressional Research Service.

Emmers, Ralf. 2010. "The Prospects for Managing and Resolving Conflict in the South China Sea." *Harvard Asia Quarterly* 12, nos. 3–4: 13–17.

Erickson, Andrew S. 2012. "China's Modernization of Its Naval and Air Power Capabilities." In *Strategic Asia 2012–13,* edited by Ashley J. Tellis and Travis Tanner, 61–125.

Erickson, Andrew S., and Gabe Collins. 2012. "China's Real Blue Water Navy." *The Diplomat* (online), August 30. http://thediplomat.com/2012/08/30/chinas-not-so-scary-navy.

Erickson, Andrew S., Abraham M. Denmark, and Gabriel Collins. 2012. "Beijing's 'Starter Carrier' and Future Steps." *Naval War College Review* 65, no. 1: 15–54.

Evenett, Simon J., ed. 2010. *The US-Sino Currency Dispute: New Insights from Economics, Politics and Law.* London: Centre for Economic Policy Research.

Fell, Dafydd. 2012. *Government and Politics in Taiwan.* London: Routledge.

Ferchen, Matt. 2011. "China–Latin America Relations: Long-Term Boon or Short-Term Boom?" *Chinese Journal of International Politics* 4, no. 1: 55–86.

Ferguson, Niall, and Moritz Schularick. 2009. "The End of Chimerica." HBS Working Paper 10-037. Boston: Harvard Business School.

Finkelstein, David M. 2007. "China's National Military Strategy: An Overview of the 'Military Strategic Guidelines.'" In *Right-Sizing the People's Liberation Army*, edited by Roy Kamphausen and Andrew Scobell, 69–140.

———. 2011. "Commentary on China's External Grand Strategy." CNA, January. http://www.cna.org/sites/default/files/research/China%27s%20External%20Grand%20Strategy%20D0023641.A3.pdf.

Finkelstein, David M., and Kristen Gunness, eds. 2007. *Civil-Military Relations in Today's China: Swimming in a New Sea*. Armonk, NY: M. E. Sharpe.

Foot, Rosemary. 1998. "China in the ASEAN Regional Forum: Organizational Processes and Domestic Modes of Thought." *Asian Survey* 38, no. 5: 425–40.

———. 2006. "Chinese Strategies in a US-Hegemonic Global Order: Accommodating and Hedging." *International Affairs* 82, no. 1: 77–94.

———. 2009–2010. "China and the United States: Between Cold War and Warm Peace." *Survival* 51, no. 6: 123–46.

Foot, Rosemary, and Andrew Walter. 2011. *China, the United States, and Global Order*. Cambridge: Cambridge University Press.

Frankel, Jeffrey. 2010. "The Renminbi since 2005." In *The US-Sino Currency Dispute*, edited by Simon J. Evenett, 51–59.

Frankel, Jeffrey, and Shang-jin Wei. 2007. "Assessing China's Exchange Rate Regime." *Economic Policy* 22, no. 51: 575–627.

Fravel, M. Taylor. 2005. "Regime Insecurity and International Cooperation: Explaining China's Compromises in Territorial Disputes." *International Security* 30, no. 2: 46–83.

———. 2007–2008. "Power Shifts and Escalation: Explaining China's Use of Force in Territorial Disputes." *International Security* 32, no. 3: 44–83.

———. 2008. *Strong Borders, Secure Nation: Cooperation and Conflict in China's Territorial Disputes*. Princeton, NJ: Princeton University Press.

———. 2010. "International Relations Theory and China's Rise: Assessing China's Potential for Territorial Expansion." *International Studies Review* 12, no. 4: 505–32.

———. 2011. "China's Strategy in the South China Sea." *Contemporary Southeast Asia* 33, no. 3: 292–319.

Fravel, M. Taylor, and Alexander Liebman. 2011. "Beyond the Moat: The PLAN's Evolving Interests and Potential Influence." In *The Chinese Navy*, edited by Phillip C. Saunders, Christopher D. Yung, Michael D. Swaine, and Andrew Nien-Dzu Yang, 41–80.

Fravel, M. Taylor, and Evan S. Medeiros. 2010. "China's Search for Assured Retaliation: The Evolution of Chinese Nuclear Strategy and Force Structure." *International Security* 35, no. 2: 48–87.

Freeman, Charles W., III. 2013. "The Commercial and Economic Relationship." In *Tangled Titans*, edited by David Shambaugh, 181–209.

Freeman, Duncan, and Gustaaf Geeraerts. 2011. "Europe, China and Expectations for Human Rights." *Chinese Journal of International Politics* 4, no. 2: 179–203.

Friedberg, Aaron L. 2005. "The Future of U.S.-China Relations: Is Conflict Inevitable?" *International Security* 30, no. 2: 7–45.

———. 2006. "'Going Out': China's Pursuit of Natural Resources and Implications for the PRC's Grand Strategy." *NBR Analysis* 17, no. 3 (September): 5–34. http://www.nbr.org/publications/issue.aspx?id=66#.UevL4BYWFEc.

————. 2011. *A Contest for Supremacy: China, America, and the Struggle for Mastery in Asia*. New York: W. W. Norton.

Friedberg, Aaron L., and Robert S. Ross. 2009. "Here Be Dragons: Is China a Military Threat?" *The National Interest* 103: 19–34.

Gallagher, Kevin P., Amos Irwin, and Katherine Koleski. 2012. "The New Banks in Town: Chinese Finance in Latin America." Inter-American Dialogue, February 16. http://www.thedialogue.org/PublicationFiles/TheNewBanksinTown-FullText-newversion_1.pdf.

Gao, Haihong, and Yongding Yu. 2012. "Internationalisation of the Renminbi." In *Currency Internationalisation*, edited by Bank for International Settlement, 105–24.

Gill, Bates. 2007. *Rising Star: China's New Security Diplomacy*. Washington, DC: Brookings Institution Press.

————. 2011. "China's North Korea Policy: Assessing Interests and Influences." USIP Special Report 283. Washington, DC: United States Institute of Peace.

Gill, Bates, Chin-hao Huang, and Stephen J. Morrison. 2007. "China's Expanding Role in Africa: Implications for the United States." CSIS Report, January. Washington, DC: CSIS Press.

Gill, Bates, and Yanzhong Huang. 2006. "Sources and Limits of Chinese Soft Power." *Survival* 48, no. 2: 17–36.

Gill, Bates, and Melissa Murphy. 2008. "China-Europe Relations: Implications and Policy Responses for the United States." CSIS Report, May. Washington, DC: CSIS Press.

Gill, Bates, and James Reilly. 2007. "The Tenuous Hold of China Inc. in Africa." *The Washington Quarterly* 30, no. 3: 37–52.

Glaser, Bonny. 2007. "Ensuring the 'Go Abroad' Policy Serves the Chinese Domestic Priorities." *China Brief* 7, no. 5: 2–5.

————. 2013. "The Diplomatic Relationship: Substance and Process." In *Tangled Titans*, edited by David Shambaugh, 151–79.

Godement, François, and Jonas Parello-Plesner. 2011. "The Scramble for Europe." London: European Council on Foreign Relations.

Goh, Evelyn. 2011. "Rising Power . . . to Do What? Evaluating China's Power in Southeast Asia." RSIS Working Paper 226. Singapore: S. Rajaratnam School of International Studies.

Goldstein, Morris, and Nicholas Lardy. 2009. *The Future of China's Exchange Rate Policy*. Washington, DC: Peterson Institute for International Economics.

Gompert, David C., and Phillip C. Saunders. 2011. *The Paradox of Power: Sino-American Strategic Restraint in an Age of Vulnerability*. Washington, DC: National Defense University Press.

————. 2012. "Sino-American Strategic Restraint in an Age of Vulnerability." Strategic Forum 273. Washington, DC: National Defense University, Institute for National Strategic Studies.

Gonzalez-Vicente, Ruben. 2011. "China's Engagement in South America and Africa's Extractive Sectors: New Perspectives for Resource Curse Theories." *The Pacific Review* 24, no. 1: 65–87.

Grant, Charles, and Katinka Barysch. 2008. "Can Europe and China Shape a New World Order?" London: Centre for European Reform.

Grunow, Dieter. 2011. "Structures and Logic of EP Implementation and Administration in China." *Journal of Current Chinese Affairs* 40, no. 3: 37–75.

Gu Jing. 2009. "China's Private Enterprises in Africa and the Implications for African Development." *European Journal of Development Research* 21, no. 4: 570–87.

Guo, Sujian, and Shiping Hua, eds. 2007. *New Dimensions of Chinese Foreign Policy.* Lanham, MD: Lexington Books.

Haggard, Stephan, Jennifer Lee, and Marcus Noland. 2012. "Integration in the Absence of Institutions: China–North Korea Cross-Border Exchange." *Journal of Asian Economics* 23, no. 2: 130–45.

Hagström, Linus. 2012. "'Power Shift' in East Asia? A Critical Reappraisal of Narratives on the Diaoyu/Senkaku Islands Incident in 2010." *Chinese Journal of International Politics* 5, no. 3: 267–97.

Hale, David D., and Lyric Hughes Hale. 2008. "Reconsidering Revaluation: The Wrong Approach to the U.S.-Chinese Trade Imbalance." *Foreign Affairs* 87, no. 1: 57–66.

Halloran, Richard. 2012. "A Revolution for China's Air Force." *Air Force Magazine* 95, no. 2: 44–48.

Hanemann, Thilo, and Daniel H. Rosen. 2012. *China Invests in Europe: Patterns, Impacts and Policy Implications.* New York: Rhodium Group.

Hao, Yufan. 2009. "The Korean Peninsula: A Chinese View on the North Korean Nuclear Issue." In *Challenges to Chinese Foreign Policy: Diplomacy, Globalization, and the Next World Power,* edited by Yufan Hao, C. X. George Wei, and Lowell Dittmer, 155–71.

———. 2013. "Domestic Chinese Influences on U.S.-China Relations." In *Tangled Titans,* edited by David Shambaugh, 125–48.

Hao, Yufan, and Lin Su, eds. 2005. *China's Foreign Policy Making: Societal Force and Chinese American Policy.* Aldershot, UK: Ashgate.

Hao, Yufan, C. X. George Wei, and Lowell Dittmer, eds. 2009. *Challenges to Chinese Foreign Policy: Diplomacy, Globalization, and the Next World Power.* Lexington: University Press of Kentucky.

He Wenping. 2007. "The Balancing Act of China's Africa Policy." *China Security* 3, no. 3: 23–40.

Heath, Timothy R. 2012. "What Does China Want? Discerning the PRC's National Strategy." *Asian Security* 8, no. 1: 54–72.

Heilmann, Sebastian, and Elizabeth J. Perry, eds. 2011. *Mao's Invisible Hand: The Political Foundations of Adaptive Governance in China.* Cambridge, MA: Harvard University Press.

Heilmann, Sebastian, and Dirk Schmidt. 2010. "China Country Report." In *Managing the Crisis,* edited by the Bertelsmann Foundation.

Hickey, Dennis Van Vranken. 2011. "Rapprochement between Taiwan and the Chinese Mainland: Implications for American Foreign Policy." *Journal of Contemporary China* 20, no. 69: 231–47.

Hofmann, Katharina, Jürgen Kretz, Michael Roll, and Sebastian Sperling. 2007. "Contrasting Perceptions: Chinese, African, and European Perspectives on the China-Africa Summit." *Internationale Politik und Gesellschaft* 2: 75–90.

Holmes, James. 2012. "The Sino-Japanese Naval War of 2012: OK, It's Probably Not Going to Happen. But If It Did, Who Would Win?" *Foreign Policy* (online), August 20. http://www.foreignpolicy.com/articles/2012/08/20/the_sino_japanese_naval_war_of_2012.

Holslag, Jonathan. 2006. "The EU and China: The Great Disillusion." *European Foreign Affairs Review* 11, no. 4: 555–80.

———. 2012. "The Elusive Axis: Assessing the EU-China Strategic Partnership." *Journal of Common Market Studies* 49, no. 2: 293–313.

Hong Junhao. 2005. "The Internet and China's Foreign Policy Making: The Impact of Online Public Opinions as a New Societal Form." In *China's Foreign Policy Making*, edited by Yufan Hao and Lin Su, 93–109.

Houser, Trevor. 2008. "The Roots of Chinese Oil Investment Abroad." *Asia Policy* 5: 141–66.

Hu Jintao. 2005a. "Build towards a Harmonious World of Lasting Peace and Common Prosperity." Speech by President Hu Jintao of the People's Republic of China at the United Nations Summit, New York. Permanent Mission of the People's Republic of China to the UN, September 15. http://www.fmprc.gov.cn/ce/ceun/eng/zt/shnh60/t212915.htm.

———. 2005b. "Four-Point Guidelines on Cross-Straits Relations Set Forth by President Hu." China.org.cn, March 5. http://www.china.org.cn/english/2005lh/121825.htm.

———. 2007. "Tuijin 'yiguo liangzhi' shixian he zuguo heping tongyi daye [Pushing Ahead with the Great Task of Achieving 'One Country, Two Systems' and Reuniting Our Country Peacefully]." Report to the 17th Congress of the Chinese Communist Party. Xinhua, October 15. http://news.xinhuanet.com/tai_gang_ao/2007-10/15/content_6981908.htm.

———. 2008. "Jian 'Gao Taiwan tongbao shu' 30 zhounian: Hu Jintao fabiao zhongyao jianghua [Important Speech by Hu Jintao on the Occasion of the 30th Anniversary of the 'Message to Our Fellow Countrymen on Taiwan']." Taiwan Affairs Office of the State Council PRC, December 31. http://www.gwytb.gov.cn/speech/speech/201101/t20110123_1723962.htm.

———. 2009. "Zhongda chuangxin: 'Liaowang' zaiwen chanshu Hu Jintao shidai guan de wu da zhuzhang" ['Liaowang' Text Explains 5 Major Points Made by Hu Jintao with Respect to Views on the Present Day]." Xinhua, November 24. http://news.xinhuanet.com/politics/2009-11/24/content_12530093.htm.

———. 2011. "China's Hu Jintao Answers Questions with Washington Post." *Washington Post*, January 16. http://www.washingtonpost.com/wp-dyn/content/article/2011/01/16/AR2011011601921.html.

———. 2012. "Full Text of Hu Jintao's Work Report to the 18th Party Congress of the Chinese Communist Party." Xinhua, November 8. http://news.xinhuanet.com/english/special/18CCPnc/2012-11/17/c_131981259.htm.

Hu Shaohua. 2006. "Why the Chinese Are So Anti-Japanese." *JPRI Critique* 13, no. 1. http://www.jpri.org/publications/critiques/critique_XIII_1.html.

Ikenberry, G. John. 2013. "The Rise of China, the United States, and the Future of the Liberal International Order." In *Tangled Titans*, edited by David Shambaugh, 53–73.

International Crisis Group. 2009. "Shades of Red: China's Debate over North Korea." Asia Report 179. International Crisis Group, November 2. http://www.crisisgroup.org/~/media/Files/asia/north-east-asia/179_shades_of_red___chinas_debate_over_north_korea.pdf.

———. 2011. "China and Inter-Korean Clashes in the Yellow Sea." Asia Report 200. International Crisis Group, January 27. http://www.crisisgroup.org/~/media/Files/asia/north-east-asia/200%20--%20China%20and%20Inter-Korean%20 Clashes%20in%20the%20Yellow%20Sea.pdf.

———. 2012. "Stirring Up the South China Sea (I)." Asia Report 223. International Crisis Group, April 23. http://www.crisisgroup.org/~/media/Files/asia/north-east-asia/223-stirring-up-the-south-china-sea-i.pdf.

International Institute for Strategic Studies (IISS), ed. 2012. *The Military Balance 2012*. London: Routledge.

Irvine, Roger. 2010. "Primacy and Responsibility: China's Perception of Its International Role." *China Security* 6, no. 3: 77–96.

Jackson, James K. 2012. "U.S. Direct Investment Abroad: Trends and Current Issues." CRS Report for Congress RS21118. Washington, DC: Congressional Research Service.

Jakobson, Linda, and Dean Knox. 2010. "New Foreign Policy Actors in China." SIPRI Policy Paper 26. Stockholm: Stockholm International Peace Research Institute.

Jia Qingguo. 2008. "Learning to Live with the Hegemon: China's Policy towards the United States since the End of the Cold War." In *China-U.S. Relations Transformed*, edited by Zhao Suisheng, 45–57.

Joffe, Josef. 2009. "The Default Power: The False Prophecy of America's Decline." *Foreign Affairs* 88, no. 5: 21–35.

Johnston, Alastair Iain. 1998. "China's Militarized Interstate Dispute Behaviour, 1949–1992: A First Cut at the Data." *China Quarterly* 153: 1–30.

Kamphausen, Roy. 2012. "China's Land Forces: New Priorities and Capabilities." In *Strategic Asia 2012–13*, edited by Ashley J. Tellis and Travis Tanner, 27–58.

Kamphausen, Roy, and Andrew Scobell, eds. 2007. *Right-Sizing the People's Liberation Army: Exploring the Contours of China's Military*. Carlisle, PA: US Army War College, Strategic Studies Institute.

Kan, Shirley. 2011. "China/Taiwan: Evolution of the 'One China' Policy—Key Statements from Washington, Beijing, and Taipei." CRS Report for Congress RL 30341. Washington, DC: Congressional Research Service.

Kaplan, Robert D. 2005. "How We Would Fight China." *Atlantic Monthly*, June 1. http://www.theatlantic.com/magazine/archive/2005/06/how-we-would-fight-china/303959/#.

———. 2011. "Why John J. Mearsheimer Is Right (about Some Things)." *The Atlantic Monthly*, December 20. http://www.theatlantic.com/magazine/archive/2012/01/why-john-j-mearsheimer-is-right-about-some-things/308839.

Keller, William W., and Thomas G. Rawski, eds. 2007. *China's Rise and the Balance of Influence in Asia*. Pittsburgh, PA: University of Pittsburgh Press.

Kelly, James A. 2004. "Overview of U.S. Policy toward Taiwan." Testimony at a Hearing on Taiwan, US House of Representatives, International Relations Committee, Washington, DC. US Department of State Archive, April 21. http://2001-2009.state.gov/p/eap/rls/rm/2004/31649.htm.

Kennedy, Scott. 2012. "China in Global Governance: What Kind of Status Quo Power?" In *From Rule Takers to Rule Makers*, edited by Scott Kennedy and Shuaihua Cheng, 9–21.

Kennedy, Scott, and Shuaihua Cheng, eds. 2012. *From Rule Takers to Rule Makers: The Growing Role of Chinese in Global Governance*. Bloomington: Indiana University, Research Center for Chinese Politics and Business; Geneva: International Centre for Trade and Sustainable Development.

Kim, Samuel S. 1994. "China's International Organizational Behaviour." In *Chinese Foreign Policy*, edited by Thomas W. Robinson and David Shambaugh, 401–34.

———. 1999. "China and the United Nations." In *China Joins the World*, edited by Elizabeth C. Economy and Michel C. Oksenberg, 42–89.

Kinzelbach, Katrin, and Hatla Thelle. 2011. "Taking Human Rights to China: An Assessment of the EU's Approach." *China Quarterly* 205: 60–79.

Kiselycznyk, Michael, and Phillip C. Saunders. 2010a. "Assessing Chinese Military Transparency." China Strategic Perspectives 1. Washington, DC: National Defense University, Institute for National Strategic Studies.

———. 2010b. "Civil-Military Relations in China: Assessing the PLA's Role in Elite Politics." China Strategic Perspectives 2. Washington, DC: National Defense University, Institute for National Strategic Studies.

Kitchen, Nicholas, ed. 2012. *China's Geoeconomic Strategy*. Special Report SR012. London: LSE IDEAS.

Kleine-Ahlbrandt, Stephanie, and Andrew Small. 2008. "China's New Dictatorship Diplomacy: Is Beijing Parting with Pariahs?" *Foreign Affairs* 87, no. 1: 38–56.

Kong Bo. 2006. "Institutional Insecurity." *China Security* 3: 64–88.

Krekel, Bryan, Patton Adams, and George Bakos. 2012. "Occupying the Information High Ground: Chinese Capabilities for Computer Network Operations and Cyber Espionage." Paper prepared for the US-China Economic and Security Review Commission by Northrop Grumman Corp., March 7.

Kristensen, Hans M., and Robert S. Norris. 2011. "Chinese Nuclear Forces, 2011." *Bulletin of the Atomic Scientists* 67, no. 6: 81–87.

Kulacki, Gregory. 2011. "China's Nuclear Arsenal: Status and Evolution." Union of Concerned Scientists. http://www.ucsusa.org/assets/documents/nwgs/UCS-Chinese-nuclear-modernization.pdf.

Kundnani, Hans, and Jonas Parello-Plesner. 2012. "China and Germany: Why the Emerging Special Relationship Matters for Europe." Policy Brief. London: European Council on Foreign Relations.

Kurlantzick, Joshua. 2007. *Charm Offensive: How China's Soft Power Is Transforming the World*. New Haven, CT: Yale University Press.

Lai Hongyi. 2010. *The Domestic Sources of China's Foreign Policy: Regimes, Leadership, Priorities and Processes*. China Policy Series. London: Routledge.

Lai Hongyi and Liang Fook Lye. 2007. "Featuring 'Harmonious World' for 'Peaceful Rise.'" In *Interpreting China's Development*, edited by Wang Gungwu and John Wong, 209–17.

Lai Shin-Yuan. 2010a. "Defending the Core Interests of Taiwan's People while Advancing Cross-Strait Relations." Speech at the International Symposium on Cross-Strait Interactions and Power Relations in East Asia. Mainland Affairs Council, December 6. http://www.mac.gov.tw/ct.asp?xItem=90879&ctNode=5908&mp=3.

———. 2010b. "Taiwan's Mainland Policy: Borrowing the Opponent's Force and Using It as One's Own—Turning the Threat of War into Peace and Prosperity." American Enterprise Institute Speech. Mainland Affairs Council, August 5. http://www.mac.gov.tw/ct.asp?xItem=86792&ctNode=5908&mp=3.

———. 2011. "Facing the Challenges of Cross-Strait Relations in 2012." Carnegie Endowment for International Peace, July 7. http://carnegieendowment.org/files/070711_transcript_CrossStrait_Lai.pdf.

Lampton, David M., ed. 2001. *The Making of Chinese Foreign and Security Policy in the Era of Reform, 1978–2000*. Stanford, CA: Stanford University Press.

———. 2008. *The Three Faces of Chinese Power: Might, Money, and Minds*. Berkeley: University of California Press.

———. 2009. "The United States and China in the Age of Obama: Looking Each Other Straight in the Eyes." *Journal of Contemporary China* 18, no. 62: 703–27.

Lanteigne, Marc. 2009. *Chinese Foreign Policy: An Introduction*. London: Routledge.

Lardy, Nicolas R. 2006. "China in the World Economy: Opportunity or Threat?" In *China*, edited by C. Fred Bergsten, Bates Gill, Nicholas R. Lardy, and Derek R. Mitchell, 73–117.

Lawrence, Robert Z. 2008. "China and the Multilateral Trading System." In *China, Asia, and the New World Economy*, edited by Barry Eichengreen, Charles Wyplosz, and Yung Chul Park, 145–67.

Lawrence, Susan V., and Thomas Lum. 2011. "U.S.-China Relations: Policy Issues." CRS Report for Congress R41108. Washington, DC: Congressional Research Service.

Lawrence, Susan V., and David MacDonald. 2012. "U.S.-China Relations: Policy Issues." CRS Report for Congress R41108. Washington, DC: Congressional Research Service.

Lee Chun-yi. 2010. "Between Dependency and Autonomy: Taiwanese Entrepreneurs and Local Chinese Governments." *Journal of Current Chinese Affairs* 39, no. 1: 37–71.

Lee, John. 2012. "China's Geostrategic Search for Oil." *The Washington Quarterly* 35, no. 3: 75–92.

Lemoine, Françoise. 2010. "Past Successes and New Challenges: China's Foreign Trade at a Turning Point." *China and World Economy* 18, no. 3: 1–23.

Lewis, John, and Xue Litai. 2012. "Making China's Nuclear War Plan." *Bulletin of the Atomic Scientists* 68, no. 5: 45–65.

Lewis, Nicole E. 2010. "Reassessing China's Role in North Korea." Expert Brief, June 22. New York: Council on Foreign Relations.

Li Anshan. 2007. "China and Africa: Policy and Challenges." *China Security* 3, no. 3: 69–93.

Li Cheng. 2001. *China's Leaders: The New Generation*. Lanham, MD: Rowman & Littlefield.

———. 2011. "China's Midterm Jockeying: Gearing Up for 2012" (Part 4: Top Leaders of Major State-Owned Enterprises). *China Leadership Monitor* 34. http://www.brookings.edu/~/media/research/files/papers/2011/2/china%20leadership%20li/02_china_leadership_li.pdf.

Li Mingjiang. 2009a. "Introduction: 'Soft Power': Nurture Not Nature." In *Soft Power*, edited by Li Mingjiang, 1–18.

———, ed. 2009b. *Soft Power: China's Emerging Strategy in International Politics*. Lanham, MD: Lexington Books.

Li Nan. 2010. "Chinese Civil-Military Relations in the Post-Deng Era: Implications for Crisis Management and Naval Modernization." China Maritime Studies 4. Newport, RI: US Naval War College.

————. 2011. "The Evolution of China's Naval Strategy and Capabilities: From 'Near Coast' and 'Near Seas' to 'Far Seas.'" In *The Chinese Navy*, edited by Phillip C. Saunders, Christopher D. Yung, Michael D. Swaine, and Andrew Nien-Dzu Yang, 109–40.

Li Wei. 2008. "China-U.S. Economic Relations and the Trade Imbalance Issue." In *China-U.S. Relations Transformed*, edited by Zhao Suisheng, 103–15.

Liao Xuanli. 2006. *Chinese Foreign Policy Think Tanks and China's Policy towards Japan*. Hong Kong: Chinese University Press.

Lieberthal, Kenneth, and Mikkal Herberg. 2006. "China's Search for Energy Security: Implications for U.S. Policy." *NBR Analysis* 17, no. 1 (April): 5–42. http://nbr.org/publications/nbranalysis/pdf/vol17no1.pdf.

Lin Chong-Pin. 2008. "More Carrot Than Stick: Beijing's Emerging Taiwan Policy." *China Security* 4: 1–27.

Linden, Greg, Kenneth L. Kraemer, and Jason Dedrick. 2009. "Who Captures Value in a Global Innovation Network? The Case of Apple's iPod." *Communications of the ACM* 52, no. 3: 140–44.

Lisbonne de Vergeron, Karine. 2007. *Contemporary Chinese Views of Europe*. London: Royal Institute of International Affairs.

Lu Ning. 1997. *The Dynamics of Foreign Policy Decisionmaking in China*. Boulder, CO: Westview Press.

————. 2001. "The Central Leadership, Supraministry Coordinating Bodies, State Council Ministries, Party Departments." In *The Making of Chinese Foreign and Security Policy in the Era of Reform, 1978–2000*, edited by David M. Lampton, 39–60.

Luo, Yadong, Qiuzhe Xue, and Binjie Han. 2010. "How Emerging Market Governments Promote Outward FDI: Experience from China." *Journal of World Business* 45, no. 1: 68–79.

Ma Jun, Linan Liu, and Hui Miao. 2012. "Roadmap for RMB Internationalization." *Asia Economics Special* (Deutsche Bank, Hong Kong), June 25. http://tx3.cdn.caijing.com.cn/upload/ppic551/Roadmap%20for%20RMB%20internationalization%20June%202012.pdf.

Ma Mung. 2008. "Chinese Migration and China's Foreign Policy." *Journal of Chinese Overseas* 4, no. 1: 91–109.

Ma Yingjeou. 2008. "Full Text of President Ma's Inaugural Address." *China Post*, May 20. http://www.chinapost.com.tw/taiwan/national/national-news/2008/05/21/157332/Full-text.htm.

————. 2010. "Gaige, kaichuang, zhuiqiu gongyi [Reform, Innovation, and Striving for Justice]." Speech by President Ma Yingjeou on the occasion of the National Holiday of the Republic of China on October 10, 2010. Tianwan.com. http://www.tianwan.com/news_content.asp?articleid=2039.

————. 2011. "Ma zongtong zhuchi Zhonghua Minguo 100 nian kaiguo jinian dianli ji yuandan tuanbai [President Ma on the Centenary of the Founding of the Republic of China and New Year's Day]." Office of the President, Republic of China (Taiwan), January 1. http://www.president.gov.tw/Default.aspx?tabid=131&itemid=23185.

————. 2012. "Zhonghua Minguo di 13 ren zongtong Ma Yingjiu jiu zhiyan shuo [Inaugural Speech by Ma Yingjeou on the Occasion of His Appointment as 13th President of the Republic of China]." Office of the President, Republic of China

(Taiwan), May 20. http://www.president.gov.tw/Default.aspx?tabid=1103&itemi d=27201&rmid=2780.

Manyin, Mark E. 2013. "Senkaku (Diaoyu/Diaoyutai) Island Dispute: U.S. Treaty Obligations." CRS Report for Congress R42761. Washington, DC: Congressional Research Service.

Mazarr, Michael J. 2012. "Rivalry's New Face." *Survival* 54, no. 4: 83–106.

Mazza, Michael, and Dan Blumenthal. 2012. "China's Strategic Forces in the 21st Century: The People's Liberation Army's Changing Nuclear Doctrine and Force Posture." In *The Next Arms Race*, edited by Henry D. Sokolski, 83–109.

Mearsheimer, John J. 2001. *The Tragedy of Great Power Politics*. New York: W. W. Norton.

———. 2006. "China's Unpeaceful Rise." *Current History* 105, no. 690: 160–62.

Medeiros, Evan S. 2009. *China's International Behavior: Activism, Opportunism, and Diversification*. Santa Monica, CA: RAND Project Air Force.

Medeiros, Evan S., and M. Taylor Fravel. 2003. "China's New Diplomacy." *Foreign Affairs* 82, no. 6: 22–35.

Men Jing. 2007. "Changing Ideology in China and Its Impact on Chinese Foreign Policy." In *New Dimensions of Chinese Foreign Policy*, edited by Sujian Guo and Shiping Hua, 7–39.

———. 2012. "The EU and China: Mismatched Partners?" *Journal of Contemporary China* 21, no. 74: 333–49.

Michel, Serge, and Michel Beuret. 2009. *China Safari: On the Trail of Beijing's Expansion in Africa*. New York: Nation Books.

Miller, Frank, and Andrew J. Scobell. 2005. "'Decisionmaking under Stress' or 'Crisis Management'? In Lieu of a Conclusion." In *Chinese National Security*, edited by Andrew J. Scobell and Larry M. Wortzel, 229–47.

Miller, Ken. 2010. "Coping with China's Financial Power: Beijing's Financial Foreign Policy." *Foreign Affairs* 89, no. 4: 96–109.

Mitchell, Derek. 2006. "China's Foreign and Security Policy: Partner or Rival?" In *China*, edited by C. Fred Bergsten, Bates Gill, Nicholas R. Lardy, and Derek R. Mitchell, 118–54.

Mochizuki, Mike M. 2005. "China-Japan Relations: Downward Spiral or New Equilibrium?" In *Power Shift*, edited by David Shambaugh, 135–50.

Mohr, Mark, ed. 2006. "The Chinese People's Liberation Army: Should the United States Be Worried?" Asia Program Special Report 135. Washington, DC: Woodrow Wilson International Center for Scholars.

Moore, Thomas G., and Dixia Yang. 2001. "Empowered and Restrained: Chinese Foreign Policy in the Age of Economic Interdependence." In *The Making of Chinese Foreign and Security Policy in the Era of Reform, 1978–2000*, edited by David M. Lampton, 191–229.

Morrison, J. Stephen. 2008. "Will Darfur Steal the Olympic Spotlight?" *The Washington Quarterly* 31, no. 3: 181–90.

Morrison, Wayne. 2012. "China-U.S. Trade Issues." CRS Report for Congress RL 33536. Washington, DC: Congressional Research Service.

Morrison, Wayne, and Marc Labonte. 2012. "China's Holdings of U.S. Securities: Implications for the U.S. Economy." CRS Report for Congress RL 34314. Washington, DC: Congressional Research Service.

Mosher, Steven. 2000. *Hegemon: China's Plan to Dominate Asia and the World.* San Francisco: Encounter Books.

Mulvenon, James. 2009. "Chairman Hu and the PLA's 'New Historic Missions.'" *China Leadership Monitor* 27. http://media.hoover.org/sites/default/files/documents/CLM27JM.pdf.

———. 2012. "The Bo Xilai Affair and the PLA." *China Leadership Monitor* 38. http://media.hoover.org/sites/default/files/documents/CLM38JM.pdf.

Mulvenon, James C., and Andrew N. D. Yang, eds. 2002. *The People's Liberation Army as Organization: Reference Volume v1.0.* Santa Monica, CA: RAND Corporation.

Murphy, Melissa. 2008. *Decoding Chinese Politics: Intellectual Debates and Why They Matter.* Washington, DC: CSIS Press.

Murphy, Melissa, and Wen Jin Yuan. 2009. "Is China Ready to Challenge the Dollar? Internationalization of the Renminbi and Its Implications for the United States." CSIS Report, October. Washington, DC: CSIS Press.

Nathan, Andrew J., and Andrew Scobell. 2012. *China's Search for Security.* New York: Columbia University Press.

National Air and Space Intelligence Center. 2010. *China's People's Liberation Army Air Force 2010.* Wright-Patterson Air Force Base, OH: National Air and Space Intelligence Center.

Naughton, Barry. 2007. *The Chinese Economy: Transitions and Growth.* Cambridge, MA: MIT Press.

Nodskov, Kim. 2009. "The Long March to Power: The New Historic Mission of the People's Liberation Army." Copenhagen: Royal Danish Defence College.

Nye, Joseph S., and Wang Jisi. 2009. "The Rise of China's 'Soft Power' and Its Implications for the United States." In *Power and Restraint,* edited by Richard Rosecrance and Gu Guoliang, 23–34.

Nye, Joseph S., Jr. 2004. *Soft Power: The Means to Success in World Politics.* New York: Public Affairs.

———. 2010. "American and Chinese Power after the Financial Crisis." *The Washington Quarterly* 33, no. 4: 143–53.

O'Rourke, Ronald. 2012. "China's Naval Modernization: Implications for U.S. Navy Capabilities—Background and Issues for Congress." CRS Report for Congress RL 33153. Washington, DC: Congressional Research Service.

Office of Naval Intelligence. 2009. *The People's Liberation Army Navy: A Modern Navy with Chinese Characteristics.* Suitland, MD: Office of Naval Intelligence.

Ohashi, Hideo. 2005. "China's Regional Trade and Investment Profile." In *Power Shift,* edited by David Shambaugh, 71–95.

Pan Chengxin. 2009. "What Is Chinese about Chinese Businesses? Locating the 'Rise of China' in Global Production Networks." *Journal of Contemporary China* 18, no. 58: 7–25.

Park, Donghyun, and Kwanho Shin. 2010. "Can Trade with the People's Republic of China Be an Engine of Growth for Developing Asia?" *Asian Development Review* 27, no. 1: 160–81.

Park, Yoon Jung. 2009. "Chinese Migration in Africa." Occasional Paper 24. Braamfontein: South Africa Institute of International Affairs.

Payette, Alex, and Guillaume Mascotto. 2012. "'Crafting' China's Energy Policy: Toward an Inclusive Approach to Policymaking." *Issues and Studies* 47, no. 3: 141–75.

Pearson, Margaret M. 2010. "Domestic Institutional Constraints on China's Leadership in East Asian Economic Cooperation Mechanisms." *Journal of Contemporary China* 19, no. 66: 621–33.

Pollpeter, Kevin. 2012. "Controlling the Information Domai: Space, Cyber, and Electronic Warfare." In *Strategic Asia 2012–13*, edited by Ashley J. Tellis and Travis Tanner, 163–94.

Prasad, Eswar. 2010. "The U.S.-China Economic Relationship: Shifts and Twists in the Balance of Power." Testimony. Brookings, February 25. http://www.brookings.edu/research/testimony/2010/02/25-us-china-debt-prasad.

Prasad, Eswar, and Lei (Sandy) Ye. 2012. "The Renminbi's Role in the Global Monetary System." Report. Brookings, February. http://www.brookings.edu/research/reports/2012/02/renminbi-monetary-system-prasad.

Przystup, James J. 2012. "Japan-China Relations: Happy 40th Anniversary . . . ? Part 2." *Comparative Connections* 14, no. 2: 105–18.

Ramo, Joshua Cooper. 2004. *The Beijing Consensus*. London: Foreign Policy Centre.

Ratner, Ely. 2011. "The Emergent Security Threats Reshaping China's Rise." *The Washington Quarterly* 34, no. 1: 29–44.

Reilly, James. 2009. "The Rebirth of *Minjian Waijiao*: China's Popular Diplomacy toward Japan." Working Paper 115. Oakland, CA: Japan Policy Research Institute.

Rid, Thomas. 2012. "Cyber War Will Not Take Place." *Journal of Strategic Studies* 35, no. 1: 5–32.

Rigger, Shelley. 2011. *Why Taiwan Matters: Small Island, Global Powerhouse*. Lanham, MD: Rowman & Littlefield.

———. 2013. "Taiwan in U.S.-China Relations." In *Tangled Titans*, edited by David Shambaugh, 293–311.

Robinson, Thomas W., and David Shambaugh, eds. 1994. *Chinese Foreign Policy: Theory and Practice*. Oxford: Clarendon Press.

Rose, Caroline. 2008. "Sino-Japanese Relations after Koizumi and the Limits of 'New Era' Diplomacy." In *China, Japan and Regional Leadership in East Asia*, edited by Christopher M. Dent, 52–64.

Rosecrance, Richard, and Gu Guoliang, eds. 2009. *Power and Restraint: A Shared Vision for the U.S.-China Relationship*. New York: Public Affairs.

Rosenberg, David. 2010. "Governing the South China Sea: From Freedom of the Seas to Ocean Enclosure Movements." *Harvard Asia Quarterly* 12, no. 3–4: 4–12.

Ross, Robert S. 2012. "The Problem with the Pivot: Obama's New Asia Policy Is Unnecessary and Counterproductive." *Foreign Affairs* 91, no. 6: 70–82.

Roy, Denny. 2005. "The Sources and Limits of Sino-Japanese Tensions." *Survival* 47, no. 2: 191–214.

Sandschneider, Eberhard. 2006. "Is China's Military Modernization a Concern for the EU?" In *Facing China's Rise*, edited by Marcin Zaborowski, 27–47.

Saunders, Phillip C. 2006. "China's Global Activism: Strategy, Drivers, and Tools." Occasional Paper 4. Washington, DC: National Defense University, Institute for National Strategic Studies.

———. 2008. "Managing a Multifaceted Relationship between the USA and China." In *China-U.S. Relations Transformed*, edited by Zhao Suisheng, 119–40.

Saunders, Phillip C., and Joshua K. Wiseman. 2011. "Buy, Build, or Steal: China's Quest for Advanced Military Aviation Technologies." China Strategic Perspectives

4. Washington, DC: National Defense University, Institute for National Strategic Studies.

Saunders, Phillip C., Christopher D. Yung, Michael D. Swaine, and Andrew Nien-Dzu Yang, eds. 2011. *The Chinese Navy: Expanding Capabilities, Evolving Roles.* Washington, DC: National Defense University Press.

Schubert, Gunter. 2010. "The Political Thinking of the Mainland Taishang: Some Preliminary Observations from the Field." *Journal of Current Chinese Affairs* 39, no. 1: 73–110.

Schucher, Günther. 2007. "Dashed Hopes: EU-China Relations after the EU's 2006 Communication on China." *China Aktuell* 36, no. 6: 83–98.

Scissors, Derek. 2009. "Chinese Foreign Investment: Insist on Transparency." Backgrounder 2237. Washington, DC: Heritage Foundation.

———. 2010. "Tracking Chinese Investment: Western Hemisphere Now Top Target." Web Memo 2952. Washington, DC: Heritage Foundation.

Scobell, Andrew. 2003. *China's Use of Military Force: Beyond the Great Wall and the Long March.* Cambridge: Cambridge University Press.

Scobell, Andrew, and Andrew J. Nathan. 2012. "China's Overstretched Military." *The Washington Quarterly* 35, no. 4: 135–48.

Scobell, Andrew, and Larry M. Wortzel, eds. 2005. *Chinese National Security: Decision-making under Stress.* Carlisle, PA: US Army War College, Strategic Studies Institute.

———. 2006. *Shaping China's Security Environment: The Role of the People's Liberation Army.* Carlisle, PA: US Army War College, Strategic Studies Institute.

Scott, David. 2007. "China and the EU: A Strategic Axis for the Twenty-First Century?" *International Relations* 21, no. 1: 23–45.

Segal, Adam. 2012. "Chinese Computer Games: Keeping Safe in Cyberspace." *Foreign Affairs* 91, no. 2: 14–20.

Segal, Gerald. 1995. "Tying China into the International System." *Survival* 37, no. 2: 60–73.

Setser, Brad. 2008. "China: Creditor to the Rich." *China Security* 4, no. 4: 17–23.

Setser, Brad, and Arpana Pandey. 2009. "China's $1.5 Trillion Bet: Understanding China's External Portfolio." Center for Geoeconomic Studies Working Paper, May update. New York: Council on Foreign Relations.

Shambaugh, David. 2002. *Modernizing China's Military: Progress, Problems, and Prospects.* Berkeley: University of California Press.

———. 2004. "China and Europe: The Emerging Axis." *Current History* 103, no. 674: 243–48.

———, ed. 2005a. *Power Shift: China and Asia's New Dynamics.* Berkeley: University of California Press.

———. 2005b. "Return to the Middle Kingdom? China and Asia in the Early Twenty-First Century." In *Power Shift*, edited by David Shambaugh, 23–47.

———. 2008a. "China Eyes Europe in the World: Real Convergence or Cognitive Dissonance?" In *China-Europe Relations*, edited by David Shambaugh, Eberhard Sandschneider, and Zhou Hong, 127–47.

———. 2008b. "Understanding the Jabberwock." *The National Interest* 94 (March–April): 55–57.

———. 2011. "Coping with a Conflicted China." *The Washington Quarterly* 34, no. 1: 7–27.

————, ed. 2013a. "Tangled Titans: Conceptualizing the U.S.-China Relationship." In *Tangled Titans*, edited by David Shambaugh, 3–26.

————. 2013b. *Tangled Titans: The United States and China*. Lanham, MD: Rowman & Littlefield.

Shambaugh, David, Eberhard Sandschneider, and Zhou Hong, eds. 2008a. *China-Europe Relations: Perceptions, Policies and Prospects*. London: Routledge.

————. 2008b. "From Honeymoon to Marriage: Prospects for the China-Europe Relationship." In *China-Europe Relations*, edited by David Shambaugh, Eberhard Sandschneider, and Zhou Hong, 303–37.

Shen Dingli. 2006. "North Korea's Strategic Significance to China." *China Security* 2, no. 4: 19–34.

Shi, Tianjin, and Diqing Lou. 2010. "Subjective Evaluation of Changes in Civil Liberties and Political Rights in China." *Journal of Contemporary China* 19, no. 63: 175–99.

Shirk, Susan L. 2007. *China: Fragile Superpower: How China's Internal Politics Could Derail Its Peaceful Rise*. Oxford: Oxford University Press.

Smith, Sheila A. 2012. "Japan and the East China Sea Dispute." *Orbis* (summer): 370–90.

Snyder, Scott. 2009. *China's Rise and the Two Koreas: Politics, Economics, Security*. Boulder, CO: Lynne Rienner.

Sohn, Injoo. 2011. "After Renaissance: China's Multilateral Offensive in the Developing World." *European Journal of International Relations* 18, no. 1: 77–101.

Sokolski, Henry D., ed. 2012. *The Next Arms Race*. Carlisle, PA: US Army War College, Strategic Studies Institute.

Solomon, Richard. 1999. *Chinese Negotiating Behavior: Pursuing Interests through "Old Friends."* Washington, DC: United States Institute of Peace.

Song, Guoyou, and Wen Jin Yuan. 2012. "China's Free Trade Agreement Strategies." *The Washington Quarterly* 35, no. 4: 107–19.

Stockholm International Peace Research Institute (SIPRI), ed. 2012. *SIPRI Yearbook 2012*. Stockholm: SIPRI.

Stokes, Mark A. 2012. "The Second Artillery Force and the Future of Long-Range Precision Strike." In *The Chinese Navy*, edited by Phillip C. Saunders, Christopher D. Yung, Michael D. Swaine, and Andrew Nien-Dzu Yang, 127–60.

Stokes, Mark A., and Dean Cheng. 2012. "China's Evolving Space Capabilities: Implications for U.S. Interests." Paper prepared for the US-China Economic and Security Review Commission by Northrop Grumman Corp., April 26.

Sutter, Robert. 2010. "Assessing China's Rise and US Leadership in Asia: Growing Maturity and Balance." *Journal of Contemporary China* 19, no. 65: 591–604.

————. 2012. *Chinese Foreign Relations: Power and Policy since the Cold War*. 3rd ed. Lanham, MD: Rowman & Littlefield.

————. 2013. "Domestic American Influences on U.S.-China Relations." In *Tangled Titans*, edited by David Shambaugh, 103–24.

Swaine, Michael D. 2010. "Perceptions of an Assertive China." *China Leadership Monitor* 32. http://media.hoover.org/sites/default/files/documents/CLM32MS.pdf.

————. 2011. "China's Assertive Behavior Part One: On 'Core Interests.'" *China Leadership Monitor* 34. http://media.hoover.org/sites/default/files/documents/CLM34MS.pdf.

————. 2012a. "China's Assertive Behavior Part Four: The Role of the Military in Foreign Crises." *China Leadership Monitor* 37. http://media.hoover.org/sites/default/files/documents/CLM37MS.pdf.

————. 2012b. "China's Assertive Behavior Part Three: The Role of the Military in Foreign Policy." *China Leadership Monitor* 36. http://media.hoover.org/sites/default/files/documents/CLM36MS.pdf.

————. 2012c. "Chinese Leadership and Elite Responses to the U.S. Pacific Pivot." *China Leadership Monitor* 38. http://media.hoover.org/sites/default/files/documents/CLM38MS.pdf.

Swaine, Michael D., Andrew N. D. Yang, and Evan S. Medeiros, eds. 2007. *Assessing the Threat: The Chinese Military and Taiwan's Security*. Washington, DC: Carnegie Endowment for International Peace.

Tanner, Murray Scott. 2007. *Chinese Economic Coercion against Taiwan: A Tricky Weapon to Use*. Santa Monica, CA: RAND Corporation.

Tao Xie. 2009. *U.S.-China Relations: China Policy on Capitol Hill*. London: Routledge.

Taylor, Ian. 2008. "The Future of China's Overseas Peacekeeping Operations." *China Brief* 8, no. 6: 7–9.

————. 2009. *China's New Role in Africa*. Boulder, CO: Lynne Rienner.

Tellis, Ashley J. 2012. "Uphill Challenges: China's Military Modernization and Asian Security." In *Strategic Asia 2012–13*, edited by Ashley J. Tellis and Travis Tanner, 3–24.

Tellis, Ashley J., and Travis Tanner, eds. 2012. *Strategic Asia 2012–13: China's Military Challenges*. Washington, DC: National Bureau of Asian Research.

Thompson, Drew. 2005. "China's Soft Power in Africa: From the 'Beijing Consensus' to Health Diplomacy." *China Brief* 5, no. 21: 1–4.

Thornton, John L. 2008. "Long Time Coming: The Prospects for Democracy in China." *Foreign Affairs* 87, no. 1: 2–22.

Tkacik, John J. 2007. "China's Quest for a Superpower Military." Backgrounder 2036. Washington, DC: Heritage Foundation.

Tonnesson, Stein. 2010. "China's Changing Role in the South China Sea: Reflections on a Scholar's Workshop." *Harvard Asia Quarterly* 12, nos. 3–4: 18–29.

Transatlantic Academy. 2011. *Global Shift: How the West Should Respond to the Rise of China*. Washington, DC: Transatlantic Academy.

Tucker, Nancy Bernkopf, and Bonnie Glaser. 2011. "Should the United States Abandon Taiwan?" *The Washington Quarterly* 34, no. 4: 23–37.

Tung Chen-Yuan. 2007. *Cross-Strait Economic Relations in the Era of Globalization: China's Leverage and Taiwan's Vulnerability*. Morrisville, NC: Lulu Enterprises.

Twomey, Christopher P. 2007. "Missing Strategic Opportunity in U.S. China Policy since 9/11: Grasping Tactical Success." *Asian Survey* 47, no. 4: 536–59.

————. 2008. "Explaining Chinese Foreign Policy toward North Korea: Navigating between the Scylla and Charybdis of Proliferation and Instability." *Journal of Contemporary China* 17, no. 56: 401–23.

————. 2013. "The Military-Security Relationship." In *Tangled Titans*, edited by David Shambaugh, 235–59.

United Nations Conference on Trade and Development (UNCTAD). 2010. *World Investment Report 2010: Investing in a Low-Carbon Economy*. Geneva: UNCTAD.

————. 2012. *World Investment Report 2011: Non-equity Modes of International Production and Development*. Geneva: UNCTAD.

United Nations Framework Convention on Climate Change (UNFCCC). 1997. "Clean Development Mechanism (CDM)." UNFCCC. http://unfccc.int/kyoto_ protocol/mechanisms/clean_development_mechanism/items/2718.php.

———. 1998. "Kyoto Protocol to the United Nations Framework Convention on Climate Change." UNFCCC. http://unfccc.int/resource/docs/convkp/kpeng.pdf.

———. 2009. "Copenhagen Accord (Decision 2/CP.15)." UNFCCC, December 18. http://unfccc.int/resource/docs/2009/cop15/eng/11a01.pdf#page=4.

———. 2010. "Appendix II: Nationally Appropriate Mitigation Actions of Developing Country Parties (China)." UNFCCC. http://unfccc.int/meetings/cop_15/ copenhagen_accord/items/5265.php.

———. 2012. "CDM Insights: Intelligence about the CDM at the End of Each Month." UNFCCC. https://cdm.unfccc.int/Statistics/Public/CDMinsights/index.html.

US-China Economic and Security Review Commission (USCC), ed. 2012. *2012 Annual Report to Congress.* USCC. http://www.uscc.gov/Annual_Reports/2012-annual-report-congress.

US Department of Defense, Office of the Secretary of Defense. 2010. *Annual Report to Congress: Military and Security Developments Involving the People's Republic of China 2010.* Washington, DC: DOD. http://www.defense.gov/pubs/pdfs/2010_ CMPR_Final.pdf.

———. 2012. *Annual Report to Congress: Military and Security Developments Involving the People's Republic of China 2012.* Washington, DC: DOD.

US Department of the Treasury. 2011. *Report to Congress on International Economic and Exchange Rate Policies.* Washington, DC: DOT.

———. 2012a. *Report on Foreign Portfolio Holdings of U.S. Securities as of June 30, 2011.* Washington DC: DOT.

———. 2012b. *Report to Congress on International Economic and Exchange Rate Policies.* Washington, DC: DOT.

US Trade Representative. 2011. *2011 Report to Congress on China's WTO Compliance.* Washington, DC: US Trade Representative.

Valencia, Mark. 1997. "Asia, the New Law of the Sea and International Relations." *International Affairs* 73, no. 2: 263–82.

Wachman, Alan M. 2007. *Why Taiwan? Geostrategic Rationales for China's Territorial Integrity.* Stanford, CA: Stanford University Press.

Walter, Andrew. 2011. "Global Economic Governance after the Crisis: The G2, the G20, and Global Imbalances." Working Paper 452. Seoul: Institute for Monetary and Economic Research/Bank of Korea.

Wan Ming. 2006. *Sino-Japanese Relations: Interaction, Logic, and Transformation.* Washington, DC: Woodrow Wilson Center Press; Stanford, CA: Stanford University Press.

Wang Chen. 2011. "Nation Makes Impressive Advances in Human Rights." Speech by the Minister of the State Council Government Information Office Made at the Opening Ceremony of the Fourth Beijing Forum on Human Rights. China Human Rights, September 22. http://www.chinahumanrights.org/Exchanges/ Conference/t20110923_811342.htm.

Wang, Dong. 2010. "China's Trade Relations with the United States in Perspective." *Journal of Current Chinese Affairs* 39, no. 3: 165–210.

Wang, Gungwu, and John Wong, eds. 2007. *Interpreting China's Development.* Singapore: World Scientific.

Wang, Hongying. 2001. *Weak State, Strong Networks: The Institutional Dynamics of Foreign Direct Investment in China.* Oxford: Oxford University Press.

Wang, Hongying, and Yeh-chung Lu. 2008. "The Conception of Soft Power and Its Policy Implications: A Comparative Study of China and Taiwan." *Journal of Contemporary China* 17, no. 56: 425–47.

Wang, Hongying, and James N. Rosenau. 2009. "China and Global Governance." *Asian Perspective* 33, no. 3: 5–39.

Wang Jisi. 2011. "China's Search for a Grand Strategy: A Rising Great Power Finds Its Way." *Foreign Affairs* 90, no. 2: 68–79.

Wang Yi. 2012. "Gonggu shenhua liang'an guanxi, kaichuang heping fazhan xin jumian [Strengthening and Deepening Cross-Strait Relations, Opening a New Phase of Peaceful Development]." *Qiushi*, April 16. http://www.qstheory.cn/zxdk/2012/201208/201204/t20120412_150797.htm.

Wei Da. 2010. "Has China Become 'Tough'?" *China Security* 6, no. 3: 97–104.

Whiting, Allen S. 2001. "China's Use of Force, 1950–96, and Taiwan." *International Security* 26, no. 2: 103–31.

Wu, Friedrich. 2005a. "China Inc. International." *International Economy* 19, no. 4: 26–31.

———. 2005b. "The Globalization of Corporate China." *NBR Analysis* 16, no. 3 (December): 5–29. http://www.nbr.org/publications/nbranalysis/pdf/vol16no3.pdf.

Wu Xinbo. 2010. "Understanding the Geopolitical Implications of the Global Financial Crisis." *The Washington Quarterly* 33, no. 4: 155–63.

———. 2012 "Forging Sino-US Partnership in the Twenty-First Century: Opportunities and Challenges." *Journal of Contemporary China* 21, no. 75: 391–407.

———. 2013. "Chinese Visions of the Future of U.S.-China Relations." In *Tangled Titans*, edited by David Shambaugh, 371–88.

Xi Jinping. 2010. "Full Text of Chinese Vice President Xi Jinping's Speech at World Investment Forum." Government Organizations of the Central Government of the PRC, September 7. http://english.gov.cn/2010-09/07/content_1697902.htm.

Xiang Lanxin. 2012. "China and the 'Pivot.'" *Survival* 54, no. 5: 113–28.

Xin Qiang. 2010. "Beyond Power Politics: Institution-Building and Mainland China's Taiwan Policy Transition." *Journal of Contemporary China* 19, no. 65: 525–39.

Xing, Yuqing, and Neal Detert. 2010. "How the iPhone Widens the U.S. Trade Deficit with PRC." ADBI Working Papers Series 257. Tokyo: Asian Development Bank.

Xinhuashe. 2006. "Zhongguo dui Feizhou zhengce wenjian [China's Africa Policy]." Xinhua, January 12. http://news.xinhuanet.com/world/2006-01/12/content_4042333.htm.

Yan Xuetong. 2010. "The Instability of China-U.S. Relations." *Chinese Journal of International Politics* 3, no. 3: 263–92.

Yan Xuetong and Qi Haixia. 2012. "Football Game Rather Than Boxing Match: China-US Intensifying Rivalry Does Not Amount to Cold War." *Chinese Journal of International Politics* 5, no. 2: 105–27.

Yao, Shujie, and Jing Zhang. 2011. "Chinese Economy 2010: Post-Crisis Development." Briefing Series 67. Nottingham, UK: University of Nottingham, China Policy Institute.

———. 2012. "Goodbye to Double-Digit Growth." Policy Paper 3. Nottingham, UK: University of Nottingham, China Policy Institute.

Yi Jingtao. 2007. "China's Exchange Rate Policymaking in the Hu-Wen Era." Briefing Series 29. Nottingham, UK: University of Nottingham, China Policy Institute.
———. 2008. "Policy Options for China's Exchange Rate Regime in the Post-reform Era." Discussion Paper 26. Nottingham, UK: University of Nottingham, China Policy Institute.
Yu Jie. 2012. "Firms with Chinese Characteristics: The Role of Companies in Chinese Foreign Policy." In *China's Geoeconomic Strategy*, edited by Nicholas Kitchen, 32–37.
Yu Yongding. 2012. "Revisiting the Internationalization of the Yuan." ADBI Working Paper Series 366. Tokyo: Asian Development Bank Institute.
Yuan Jing-dong. 2010. "China's Role in Establishing and Building the Shanghai Cooperation Organization (SCO)." *Journal of Contemporary China* 19, no. 67: 855–69.
Zaborowski, Marcin, ed. 2006. *Facing China's Rise: Guidelines for an EU Strategy.* Chaillot Paper 94. Paris: Institute for Security Studies.
Zeng Ka. 2010. "Multilateral versus Bilateral and Regional Trade Liberalization: Explaining China's Pursuit of Free Trade Agreements (FTAs)." *Journal of Contemporary China* 19, no. 66: 635–52.
Zhang Wanfa. 2007. "Tapping Soft Power: Managing China's 'Peaceful Rise' and the Implications for the World." In *New Dimensions of Chinese Foreign Policy*, edited by Sujian Guo and Shiping Hua, 109–31.
Zhang Yunling. 2010. *China and Asian Regionalism.* Singapore: World Scientific.
Zhang Yunling and Tang Shiping. 2005. "China's Regional Strategy." In *Power Shift*, edited by David Shambaugh, 48–68.
Zhao Suisheng. 2008. *China-U.S. Relations Transformed: Perspectives and Strategic Interactions.* New York: Routledge.
———. 2009. "The Prospect of China's Soft Power: How Sustainable?" In *Soft Power*, edited by Li Mingjiang, 247–66.
———. 2011. "China's Approaches toward Regional Cooperation in East Asia: Motivations and Calculations." *Journal of Contemporary China* 20, no. 68: 53–67.
———. 2012. "Shaping the Regional Context of China's Rise: How the Obama Administration Brought Back Hedge in Its Engagement with China." *Journal of Contemporary China* 21, no. 75: 369–89.
Zheng Yongnian and Sow Keat Tok. 2005. "China's 'Peaceful Rise': Concept and Practice." Discussion Paper 1. Nottingham, UK: University of Nottingham, China Policy Institute.
———. 2007. "'Harmonious Society' and 'Harmonious World': China's Policy Discourse under Hu Jintao." Briefing Series 26. Nottingham, UK: University of Nottingham, China Policy Institute.
Zheng Yongnian and Raymond Ray-kuo Wu, eds. 2006. *Sources of Conflict and Cooperation in the Taiwan Strait.* Singapore: World Scientific.
Zheng Yongnian, Jingtao Yi, and Minjia Chen. 2007. "Revaluation of the Chinese Currency and Its Impact on China." Discussion Paper 24. Nottingham, UK: University of Nottingham, China Policy Institute.
Zhonghua Renmin Gongheguo [People's Republic of China]. 2005. *Fan fenlie guojiafa* [Anti-secession Law]. Passed at the Third Plenary Session of the Tenth NPC, March 14. http://news.xinhuanet.com/newscenter/2005-03/14/content_2694168.htm.

Zhonghua Renmin Gongheguo Guojia Tongjiju [National Bureau of Statistics of the PRC]. Annual. *Zhongguo tongji nianjian* [Statistical Yearbook of the People's Republic of China]. Beijing: China Statistical Publishing House.

Zhonghua Renmin Gongheguo Guowuyuan Xinwen Bangongshi [State Council Government Information Office]. 2000. "The One-China Principle and the Taiwan Issue." Taiwan Documents Project, February 21. http://www.taiwandocuments.org/white.htm.

———. 2005. "Zhongguo de heping fazhan daolu [China's Path to Peaceful Development]." Beijing: State Council Government Information Office.

———. 2008. "China's Policy on Latin America and the Caribbean." Xinhua, November 5. http://news.xinhuanet.com/english/2008-11/05/content_10308117.htm.

———. 2010. "Full Text: Progress in China's Human Rights in 2009." China Human Rights, September 26. http://www.chinahumanrights.org/Messages/Focus/73/11/t20100926_935218.htm.

———. 2011a. "2010 nian Zhongguo de guofang [China's Defense in 2010]." Beijing: State Council Government Information Office.

———. 2011b. "Zhongguo de heping fazhan [China's Peaceful Development (White Paper)]." White Papers of the Chinese Government, September 6. http://www.china.com.cn/ch-book/node_7126563.htm.

———. 2012a. "Full Text: Diaoyu Dao, an Inherent Territory of China." People Daily News, December 23. http://www.peopledailynews.com/index.php?option=com_content&view=article&id=112:full-text-diaoyu-dao-an-inherent-territory-of-china&catid=93:cultureartsnews&Itemid=60.

———. 2012b. "Full Text: National Human Rights Action Plan of China (2012–2015)." China Human Rights, June 11. http://www.chinahumanrights.org/Messages/China/t20110612_901423.htm.

Zhonghua Renmin Gongheguo Guowuyuan Xinwen Bangongshi/Guowuyuan Taiwan Bangongshi [State Council Government Information Office and the Taiwan Affairs Office]. 2000. "Baipishu: Yige Zhongguo de yuanze yu Taiwan wenti [White Paper: The One-China Principle and the Taiwan Problem]." Beijing: State Council Information Office.

Zhonghua Renmin Gongheguo Shangwubu, Guojia Tongjiju, and Waihui Guanliju [Ministry of Commerce of the PRC, National Bureau of Statistics, State Administration of Foreign Exchange], eds. Annual. *Niandu Zhongguo duiwai zhijie touzi tongji gongbao* [Statistical Bulletin of China's Outward Foreign Direct Investment]. Beijing: China Statistical Publishing House.

Zhu Liqun. 2008. "Chinese Perceptions of the EU and the China-Europe Relationship." In *China-Europe Relations*, edited by David Shambaugh, Eberhard Sandschneider, and Zhou Hong, 148–73.

———. 2010. "China's Foreign Policy Debates." Chaillot Paper 121. Paris: EU Institute for Security Studies.

Zweig, David. 2010. "The Rise of a New 'Trading Nation.'" In *China, the Developing World, and the New Global Dynamic*, edited by Lowell Dittmer and George T. Yu, 37–59.

Zweig, David, and Zhimin Chen, eds. 2007. *China's Reforms and International Political Economy*. London: Routledge.

Appendix

Chinese-English Glossary

Chapter 1

baquan (霸权)	hegemony
beiqiang nanruo xiqiang dongruo (北强南弱西强东弱)	North-South and West-East development gap
bu ke pohuai de (不可破坏的)	indestructible
bu ke qinfan de (不可侵犯的)	inviolable
chijiu heping (持久和平)	lasting peace
duojihua (多极化)	multipolarity
fuzeren de daguo (负责任的大国)	responsible major power
gongdan zeren (共担责任)	shared responsibility
gongtong fanrong (共同繁荣)	prosperity for all
heping fazhan (和平发展)	peaceful development
heping jueqi (和平崛起)	peaceful rise
hexin liyi (核心利益)	core interests
huli gongying (互利共赢)	win-win situation
liyi gongtongti (利益共同体)	community of interests
liyi jiaorong (利益交融)	convergence of interests
minzhuhua (民主化)	democratization
pingdeng xieshang (平等协商)	negotiate on an equal footing

qiangquan zhengzhi (强权政治)	power politics
wenming duoyangxing (文明多样性)	diversity of cultures
yichao duoqiang (一超多强)	one superpower and several major powers
zizhu xuanze shehui zhidu (自主选择社会制度)	to independently choose one's own social system
zonghe guoli (综合国力)	comprehensive national strength

Chapter 2

guowu weiyuan (国务委员)	State councilor
lingdao xiaozu bangongshi (领导小组办公室)	Staff Office of Leading Small Group (LSG)
waishi gongzuo lingdao xiaozu (外事工作领导小组)	Foreign Affairs Leading Small Group

Chapter 3

duobianzhuyi (多边主义)	multilateralism
duojihua (多极化)	multipolarization
heping yanbian (和平演变)	peaceful evolution
minzhuhua (民主化)	democratization
waixuan gongzuo (外宣工作)	overseas propaganda work ("public diplomacy")
wenhua zhiminhua (文化殖民化)	cultural colonization

Chapter 4

anquan he fazhan liyi (安全和发展利益)	security and development interests
Di'er paobing (第二炮兵)	Second Artillery
diqu redian (地区热点)	hot spots
fan ganshe (反干涉)	counterinterventionism
fangyuxingde guofang zhengce (防御性的国防政策)	national defense that is defensive in nature
ganrao (干扰)	meddling in domestic affairs
guomin jundui (国民军队)	national army
haijun (海军)	navy

heli shidu de (合理适度的)	appropriate and moderate
jiji fangyu (积极防御)	active defense
jixiehua (机械化)	mechanization
jubu (youxian) zhanzheng (局部 [有限] 战争)	local (limited) wars
jundui feizhengzhihua (军队非政治化)	depoliticization of armed forces
jundui feidanghua (军队非党化)	de-party-ification of armed forces
kongjun (空军)	air force
lishi biran de xuanze (历史必然的选择)	choice necessitated by history
lujun (陆军)	ground forces
qiangda jundui (强大军队)	powerful armed forces
qianzhi (牵制)	contain, restrict room for maneuver
re'ai heping de minzu bingxing (热爱和平的民族禀性)	peace-loving national disposition
ren bufan wo, wo bufan ren (人不犯我我不犯人)	we will not attack unless we are attacked
weihu shijie heping de jianding liliang (维护世界和平的坚定力量)	staunch force upholding world peace
xinxi duikang (信息对抗)	information warfare
xinxihua tiaojian xia de jubu zhanzheng (信息化条件下的局部战争)	localized war under conditions of informatization
yilü (疑虑)	mistrust
yu woguo guoji diwei xiangcheng (与我国国际地位相称)	commensurate with China's international standing
yufang (预防)	prevention
Zhongyang junshi weiyuanhui (中央军事委员会)	Central Military Commission

Chapter 5

longtou qiye (龙头企业)	leading enterprises ("national champions")
yinjinlai (引进来)	"bring in" (attract foreign investments)

zouchuqu (走出去)	"go out"/"go global" (pursue overseas investments)

Chapter 7

yi ren wei ben (以人为本)	prioritizing the people (and people's livelihood)

Chapter 8

Jingji hezuo jiagou xieyi (经济合作架构协议)	Economic Cooperation Framework Agreement
liang'an guanxi heping fazhan (两岸关系和平发展)	peaceful development across the Taiwan Strait
Taishang (台商)	Taiwanese businesspeople
yi zhong, gebiao (一中各表)	different interpretations of the notion of one China
yige Zhongguo jiagou (一个中国架构)	one-China framework
zhiduhua hezuo (制度化合作)	institutionalized cooperation
Zhonghua minzu weida fuxing (中华民族伟大复兴)	great revival of the Chinese nation
Zhonghua Taibei (中华台北)	Chinese Taipei

Chapter 9

fankang qinlüe de zhengyi zhi zhan (反抗侵略的正义之战)	a just war to defend an invasion
Zhongyang duiwai lianluo bu (中央对外联络部)	Central Committee International Liaison Department

Chapter 10

qianzhi (牵制)	containment
zhuyao maodun (主要矛盾)	main contradiction

Chapter 12

shanzhai jingji (山寨经济)	"village economy" (product and trademark piracy)

Index

160; FDI from and to the EU, 174–75; FDI to and from China, *98*; Japan as a source of, 150; origins of Chinese FDI, *100*; role of FDI in China's opening up, 97; Sino-German FDI flows, 185–86. *See also* inward foreign direct investment; outward foreign direct investment
foreign exchange, 19, 88–91, 95–96, 103. *See also* Chinese yuan; US dollar
foreign investment, 20, 36, 98, 105, 155. *See also* foreign direct investment; inward foreign direct investment; outward foreign direct investment
Forum on China-Africa Cooperation (FOCAC), 34
France, 25, 34, 102, 176, 178, 184–86
free trade, 28, 93, 95, 135, 136

G20. *See* Group of Twenty
G7. *See* Group of Seven
G8. *See* Group of Eight
GAD. *See* General Armaments Department
GATT. *See* General Agreement on Tariffs and Trade
GDP. *See* gross domestic product
General Agreement on Tariffs and Trade (GATT), 7
General Armaments Department (GAD), 51–52
General Logistics Department (GLD), 51
General Political Department (GPD), 51
General Staff Department (GSD), 51, 69, 71
German Organization for International Cooperation (GIZ), 188
Germany, 7, 83–84, 103, 114, 146, 178, 202; benefits from Chinese demand, 106; Chinese human rights dialogues with, 123; Chinese OFDI in, 102; Chinese trade with, 86, 105–6, 174, 183–85; development aid from, 188; experience after the Plaza Accord, *95*; FDI share of, 99; interests,

objectives, and tasks of Germany's China policy, 182; as a preferred partner, 189; trade frictions between China and, 187
GHG. *See* greenhouse gas
GIZ. *See* German Organization for International Cooperation
GLD. *See* General Logistics Department
global financial crisis, 3, 25, 84, 107, 175; China's involvement in the, 27, 88, 91, 94–95, 105, 169
globalization, 24, 40, 168, 176, 193, 203
GPD. *See* General Political Department
grand strategy, 1, 8, 10
greenhouse gas (GHG), 107, 111, 114–16, 118, 161, 164
gross domestic product (GDP), 3, 105, 112, *124*; carbon dioxide emissions per unit of, 115; China's military budget in percent of, 58; China's official reserves as a percentage of, 90, *95*; China's trade as a percentage of, 83–85; Chinese domestic savings as a share of, 101; FDI to and from China as a share of, *98*
Group of Eight (G8), 27
Group of Seven (G7), 149, 203
Group of Twenty (G20), 1, *8*, 25–27, 105, 107, 162, 204
GSD. *See* General Staff Department
Gulf War, 7, 24, 55, 57, 63

hegemonism, 4, 33, 52
HIV, 39
Hong Kong, 50, 74, *106*, 130, 150, 174, *183*, 185; CNY-denominated bonds in, 91; FDI to China from, 99; as an important export destination, 86; as intermediary in Sino-German trade, 184; OFDI flows towards, 101, 104; one country, two systems, *131–32*; ranking among the world's top container ports, 83–84; UK-Chinese controversies regarding, 181; US aircraft carrier in, 21
Hu Jintao, 16, 18, 23, 136; civilian military leadership of, 49, 53;

SIPRI. *See* Stockholm International Peace Research Institute
Six-Party Talks, *8*, 153–54, 161
small and medium-size enterprise (SME), 187
SME. *See* small and medium-size enterprise
soft power, 24, 40–43, 193
South Africa, 27, 33–34, 39–40, 102, 105, 114, 175
South Korea. *See* Republic of Korea (ROK)
Soviet Union, *7*, 57, 62, 145, 152, 156, 159, 194; fear in China of an attack by the, 52, 54; lesson of the failure of the, 72, 76; power triangle with the United States, China and the, 33, 56
Spain, 176, 178
special administrative region (SAR), 132
special economic zone (SEZ), 39, 97, 196
Spratly Islands, 74
SSBN. *See* nuclear-powered ballistic missile submarine
Standing Committee of the National People's Congress, 48
State Administration of Foreign Exchange (SAFE), 91, 96, 103
State Administration of Science, Technology and Industry for National Defense, 50
State Council: "863 program" and the, 52; army under the, 50; deciding on large projects, 103; direction of FDI, 98; exchange rate policy of the, 97; human rights policy of the, 123; ministerial-level agencies under the, 19; Ministry of National Defense and the, 49; security institutions report to the, 48; weapons purchase, 58
State Environmental Protection Administration (SEPA), 113
State-Owned Assets Supervision and Administration Commission (SASAC), 19, 103
state-owned enterprises/companies, 15, 59, 107; competition among, 103, 196; OFDI of, 101–3, 105;

permission to swap foreign exchange for, 88; role in policy making, 19–20, 97, 102–3, 194
Stockholm International Peace Research Institute (SIPRI), 58
Strait Exchange Foundation (SEF), 130, 134–37, 141
Strategic and Economic Dialogue (S&ED), 161–62
strategic partnership, 164, 181–82
submarine, 62, 64, 67–68, 71, 73, 140
Sudan, 16, 34, 126; China's attitude toward, 36; Chinese aid for, 163, 195; Chinese citizens in, 38, 40; oil reserves in, 37

Taiwan, *7–8*, 15, 32, 42, 50, 53, 146–47, 150, 185; China's economic relations with, *84*, 86–87, 98–99, 103, 105–6, 133–37, 160, 174, *183*; Chinese government policy toward, 4–5, *11*, 16, 18, 21, 24, 33, 57, 64, 66, 73–76 129–33, 137–39, 149, 153, 162, *170*, 200; U.S. relations with, 56, 61, 66, 141–42, 162–64, 169. *See also* Strait Exchange Foundation; Taiwan issue; Taiwan Strait, Taiwan Relations Act
Taiwan issue, 18, 53, 129–43, 149, 178, 181. *See also* Strait Exchange Foundation; Taiwan Relations Act; Taiwan Strait
Taiwan Relations Act (TRA), 142
Taiwan Strait, 6, 9, 69, 129–43, *170*; China's armed forces focus on, 61, 63–64, 76, 67, 153, 164; crisis in, 7, 56–57, 72, 76; military strength in the, *140*; *See also* Strait Exchange Foundation; Taiwan issue
Tajikistan, 30
Taliban, *8*, 161
territorial disputes, 32, 66, 70, 72–74, 78, 170, 192; East China Sea, 147–51; South China Sea, 29–30, 164
terrorism, *8*, 24, 30, 53, 60, *170*; America's fight against, 24, 31. *See also* counterterrorism

About the Authors

Sebastian Heilmann is director of the Mercator Institute for China Studies (MERICS) in Berlin and professor for comparative government at the University of Trier.

Dirk H. Schmidt is senior lecturer for political science and the political economy of China at the University of Trier.